THE TENDER CARNIVORE
AND THE SACRED GAME

CHARLES SCRIBNER'S SONS

NEW YORK

THE TENDER CARNIVORE
AND THE SACRED GAME

PAUL SHEPARD

Drawings by

FONS VAN WOERKOM

The author acknowledges with gratitude the grant of a
fellowship from the John Simon Guggenheim Memorial
Foundation for the preparation of a manuscript on the implications of man's primate heritage and hunting forebears.

1 3 5 7 9 11 13 15 17 19 V/C 20 18 16 14 12 10 8 6 4 2

Printed in the United States of America
Library of Congress Catalog Card Number 73-37218
SBN 684-12772-5 (cloth)

To the memory of Paul Howe Shepard,
a good hunter,

and to June,
who makes life a good gathering

CONTENTS

[vii]

Introduction

Anyone who enjoys identifying stars in the night sky has learned that the way to see the dimmest points is to look slightly to one side of them. They vanish when focused on directly and reappear when the line of vision is shifted away. This is because the more light-sensitive cells of the retina are found outside the region of the greatest acuity where we normally bring objects into focus.

Looking obliquely carries with it slightly disturbing feelings, as much psychological as visual. We often say, "Let's bring the subject up and have a look at it." But we look past a dim star to see it, as though looking at something else. It is a little like Kant's observation that "ultimate things can only be discussed indirectly."

Man's place in the world of plant and animal life, especially the evolution of his culture and mind in the context of the whole biosphere, has that same vanishing quality. The present threat to the planet from industrialization or overpopulation requires that we know our world and ourselves well. In the widespread reaction to that danger there has been a vast focusing of energy and thought, public discussion and planning. At times cause and cure seem obvious. It appeared, early in the decade of the 1970s, that an outpouring of information and political action might solve the problems. A wave of recognition passed across the world of thought, linking ecology and society.

Solution through techniques and action was an illusion. Sufficient ecological data to guide the redirection of society toward environmental harmony has existed for more than thirty years, and surely there has been no lack of social change. It seems that in staring at the environmental crisis we have missed the central spark of ecology itself, its unexpected connections to the whole of life. Putting the environment "out there" external to us has made it invisible. The failure of ecological action is not in our understanding of the cycles of elements or readiness to change, but something that can be seen only by turning slightly away from it.

It is this train of thought that has brought me, as a naturalist, to the examination of the behavior of my own species. Clearly, to study man because one's subject is ecology is full of pitfalls. I do not have the luxurious assurance, which my friends in the social sciences are blessed with, that there are only man-centered values and that he is, indeed, the most worthy, interesting, and beautiful of all creatures.

It will be difficult enough in the coming decades to reorganize the priorities in the use of resources; it will be infinitely more difficult to reassess our concept of nature to include man in it and to broaden a philosophy of life hammered into our habits of mind over many centuries. Beyond that, in the end, what we are asked to do is to reshape our image of man. The physical alteration of a worldwide economy according to steady-state, no-growth principles is formidable enough, but at its heart is the task of recognition, of a new perception of who we are.

Even if we admit that a malignant self-identity is somehow the seed of major breakdowns in the modern world, that does not get us very far. On what basis and from what standpoint can we make a new beginning? What is implied in reassessing the role of man in nature? Some very fundamental assumptions must be questioned. Our civilized world takes it as given that men of the modern world have created order from raw and elemental sources, producing both meaning and wealth where none existed before. Fear of chaos and helplessness is a spur to this idea. If ecosystems have suffered we may feel regret, but our reflection is also, "Heaven forbid that we go back to the cruder past—and, heaven knows, it is impossible anyway." We accept "the good with the bad" and seem trapped in ways of doing that impose ways of being, uniting good and evil inextricably. The sinister side-effects of industrialized development loom over a world whose course is set. It is widely believed that not to progress is unacceptable, that the other choices are catastrophe or a kind of sinking into the past, the more of which we know the less we want to be overtaken by.

In the view of ourselves as refugees from nature, those choices seem logical. But are they true alternatives? Is the duality of man and nature real? Have men's achievements come from his thrust against dehumanizing and disabling forces of nature and past time? In the image of struggle we think of the light of human rationality and imagination rising painfully over quagmires of an inchoate universe, an uncouth cacaphony. Few are the modern men who do not subscribe to a Rise of Man, as proved by recorded history.

Written history takes the moving arrow of time as its insignia. Change is the ground upon which it sees the human figure move and aspire, and events seem to stream behind into oblivion. It is the endlessly escaping moment flashing through a lens following a march of print. In a similar vein one might consider the strings of DNA that make up our chromosomes as linear records of the past to be read forward to those genes that create our human features, neglecting the rest of the genes shared with fishes or apes. Or, there is still another octave in this temporal play of attention: the time-span of one life. Charting individual growth in the mind's eye, we can imagine hundreds of different curves representing every change of the individual's physical and mental development. Traditional history is the narrowed attention following along those lines, not the whole page; not the time of one life but the time of one's life, the moment, the now as all.

Oddly enough, history is supposed to be that instrument for keeping the significance of the past, viewing the whole page or genealogy or growth pattern without losing sight of the present. Clearly there is something lacking in a tradition of history that fails to unify, to bring the past alive into the present. It is not only a matter of historians and their work, but of a cultural mode of perceiving that lacks a unifying sensibility for uniting these three octaves of the fourth dimension—the life cycle, group record, and deep evolution.

History as we know it has declared that what was not written was of little importance. It has compared primitives unfavorably with ourselves or patronized them. It has discovered heroes only in terms of the state. And it has subordinated its essential functions, invading life and being by ideology and ecological apartheid.

A different experience of self—of history—truly explores the bonds among men and between them and other life and non-life, even to the rocks and seas, recognizing that the genesis of these connections belongs in time and that they function only in continuity. The perspective of time is the only clue to our identity and, in its transforming realization, the hope of our ecological maturity.

This is not the same as saying that we learn from the lessons of history. Events in the Machiavellian sense are said to be good teachers, but that is merely the idea of a past connected to us by parallels. In that view there are ways in which contemporary problems are unique and therefore impervious to the lessons of history. In reality, the self could never be impervious to the ontogenetic, social, and ecological unity, conceived as living history, which comes together in every being.

That there is a sense in which the present and the future cannot possibly differ from the past is certainly, on the face of it, an outrageous idea. It will be looked upon here, I hope, as an effort to help crack the circle of thought and behavior by which we have, in the course of a few thousand years, alienated ourselves from our only home, planet Earth, our only time, the Pleistocene, and our only companions, our fellow creatures.

If we look upon the subjugation and annihilation of life as a failure of human behavior, a kind of pathology in the horizons of a perfectly good species, then our contemporary problems are unique only as combinations of symptoms. We know little about what is normal, and when it comes to behavior there are sharp disagreements. The problem is worsened by the inability of conventional history to see beyond the written word and modern humanism's disdain of all that preceded the works of civilization.

Our social and environmental problems have a way of producing fictitious explanations, like those personal squabbles that are only intensified by introspection. The very nature of explanation becomes so internalized that attention is held from the more discursive view in which may be found the only possibility of solution. If man's environmental crisis signifies a crippled state of consciousness as much as it does damaged habitat, then that is perhaps where we should begin. The secret lies in the darkness of the human cerebrum. But to see it we must turn our eyes toward the sidelong glimmer of a distant paradise that seems light-years away.

1

TEN THOUSAND YEARS
OF CRISIS

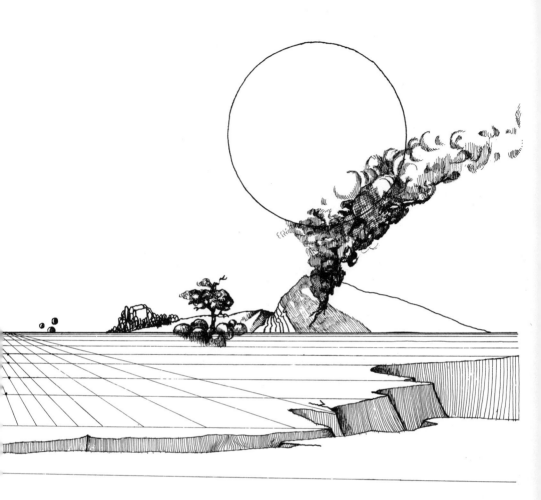

Making Wild Sheep Tame

The dawn of civilization, associated with the first agriculture, is generally seen as a great sunrise before which men lived in a mental and social twilight, waiting, straining to become fully human. We see those vague predecessors as incomplete, with a few crude tools, living days of fear and monotony, nights of terror and discomfort, with a short, brutish existence as the only reward for the struggle to survive.

Today's myth of progress and gospel of radical change, orientation to tomorrow and frantic exchange of old things for new are modern only in terms of the whole human span that

preceded them. Though we may picture ourselves as very unlike old world peasants, it is in the agrarian mind that modern
life begins.

Nobody knows for certain how or why agriculture began.
How man began the earliest tending of plants and animals may
remain a secret forever, but the epidemic of acquisitive pro-
prietorship and territorial aggrandizement that resulted from
this development is all too apparent. From what evidence there
is, it was neither a worldwide event nor a single event, but a
shifting mixture of hunting, fishing, and planting, at first in
a rather limited geographical area from Turkey to the Caspian
basin and south to the Red Sea and Palestine and, later, parallel
expansions from centers in equatorial Asia and America.

Despite many specific domestications and forms of early
agriculture in other parts of the world, particularly Southeast
Asia and Central America, the set of techniques and the set of
mind seem first to have taken form at the eastern end of the
Mediterranean Sea and to have spread from there by cultural
contact. In time, Asia and America became "centers of domestication" as agriculture spread around the globe.

The hunting and gathering peoples who preceded the
planters did not live in an unchanging world, nor were they
themselves alike everywhere or at different times. Diversity
existed because of human adaptations to local environmental
differences. The climate, species of plants and animals, types of
available food, and the manmade combinations of tools and
ideas had been changing for a million years. Men had expanded
their range, shifted with the slow tides of glacial ice, learned the
ways of other living creatures, and achieved a rich humanity
long before metals, pots, wheels, kings, and theocracies appeared.

Because of the limited archaeological evidence, it was still
thought until recently that domestication appeared abruptly, as
an inexplicable breakthrough that transformed human life
about ten thousand years ago. Now it is clear that its sudden
appearance in archaeological diggings was a local accident.
Between outright gathering and full food production there

were stages of food-collecting and incipient domestication, life ways mixing hunting and gathering in different proportions, and finally the culling or artificial hunting of animals and collecting from an extended garden plants that were more or less constantly protected and probably genetically altered by men.

The story of some cave-man genius bringing home a baby wild sheep to raise or capturing a cub-wolf from its den, or realizing in some bold flash of intuition how to grow tomatoes, thus inventing in one mighty stroke a new way of life that was thereafter imitated by the genius's friends and descendants, is nonsense; it is part of the same civilized myth that would have us believe that in some miraculous way the farmer discovered agriculture and thus raised himself above his predecessors.

A sequence of events east of the Mediterranean Sea some twenty thousand years ago may have led by uncertain steps toward agriculture. Whether these stresses and deformations of human society were the consequence of the climate and the glaciers of the last ice age has been argued inconclusively for half a century. The great wetness of the time has suggested to some that men who had previously chased big game were impeded by the waterways and swamps, that hunting faltered as large mammals became locally extinct, that fishing may have seduced men into a sedentary life, which made for a different kind of attention to the plants and earth around them. It has been suggested that after the wet came the dry; that the principal wild herd animals remaining were aurochs (the wild cattle) and the ancestors of domestic goats and sheep; and that grasses flourished on the slopes so abundantly that their seeds became an increasingly available food for people. If the use of cereals was the crux of man's pre-history, then it was inseparable from the use of fire for cooking, making them edible in large amounts.

During this stage of deteriorating cynegetics (that is, hunting and its culture) local tribes apparently tried a great variety of foods that earlier had been rejected by the reindeer hunters who preceded them. Archaeological records have shown signs of crisis during the four thousand years preceding the first farming communities. It was a time of intense food experimentation in which acorns, nuts, seeds, snails, clams, fish and other aquatic animals were gathered. The mastery of stone toolmaking faded, but there were new utensils of wood, leather, and bone, evidence of swimming and the use of boats, flint sickles, the pestle and mortar, and the bow and arrow. These innovations by seed-gleaners, shore-scavengers, and sheep-followers in the Tigris-Euphrates watershed and on the slopes of the Zagros and Palestinian mountains preceded the earliest concrete signs of domestication—the bones of livestock and seed types found only in association with man.

This was a time of trial and difficulty for the societies and cultures that had created an art and religion that had endured for twenty thousand years over much of Europe and Asia, yet it favored experiment and goaded men into versatility. By the time the climate warmed around the Mediterranean, some twelve thousand years ago, sedentary, seed-conscious people were munching local mutton in villages. For them the bison, the woolly mammoth and the rhino, the wild horse, cave bear, and reindeer, had all but passed from memory.

The lands they occupied may have looked very different from the more northerly tundras and steppes or the more southerly savannas where hunters still flourished. The rolling, open, upland terrain was flecked with patches of woodland and streams separated by grassy swards. Roaming herds of wild sheep and goats gradually became habituated to people, tolerating human presence even within the "flight-distance" at which wild animals normally flee. They were an increasingly easy kill for men whose durability, strength, and cunning had been honed through generations by their hunting forebears. But compared to their ancestors' grand chases and spearing of wild horses, plugging goats with arrows must have been a profound though perhaps unconscious disappointment.

The virtual collapse of hunting and gathering, the central activity of the ancient culture, would surely have affected the very heart of human existence. The great mystery of domestication is therefore not so much how men achieved control of plants and animals, but how human consciousness was reorganized when the cynegetic life was shattered—that is, the mental, social, and ecological complex based on hunting. All major human characteristics—size, metabolism, sexual and reproductive behavior, intuition, intelligence—had come into existence and were oriented to the hunting life. How, for example, did the male prerogative shift from the chase to the harvest of plants? Even though men at all times have continued to hunt with great élan and pride, just as women have continued to gather and to be the center of the household, it is astonishing that such a shift in vocation took place.

In the course of a few thousand years men assumed control over the harvest, however much it was ritualized in female symbols. Throughout history agriculture has been represented in feminine terms and images. Even so, men generally dominate the political order in such societies—as among Biblical peoples. Perhaps this is because, from the earliest times of farming, a major purpose of man's pastures and fields was the production of meat from grazing animals and the harvest of meat was the ancient domain of the male as a hunter. Or did control of surplus grain in some way acquire the prestige and potential power traditionally associated with the hunt and the hunter's honor in distributing the parts of the kill?

Driving the bezoar goat and urial sheep, however it may have been compensated in social status, must have seemed, as the animals became more and more tame, less worthy of a man's life. Cut off from hunting reindeer, horse, and elephant, men lost both the models and the means by which personal integrity was achieved and measured within the group by peaceful means. They found a substitute in the biggest and most dangerous potential prey remaining—men themselves.

The collapse of an ecology that kept men scarce and attuned to the mystery and diversity of all life led as though by some devilish Fall to the hunting and herding of man by man, to the hoarding of grain and the secularizing of all space. To defend his fields a farmer needed many kinsmen: sons, and co-defenders, and co-fighters, and ultimately brother ideologists.

There are many physical and environmental aspects of domestication that are still unknown. Why in more than two million years of hunting, during which climates and animals had waxed and waned, had it not happened before? What was the true order of such interrelated events as preparing grain foods by cooking, monitoring of herds, driving and butchering based on the calendar, planting and tending seeds, stockading and breeding captive animals? Even the function or purpose of the control of different species of plants and animals is imperfectly known. Were animals first kept in corrals for religious reasons or did the religious and food motives develop simultaneously?

It now appears that what had been so long thought to be the "beginning" is the climax of events that took place over a span of time three times as great as the Christian era. The great moments in the origin of agriculture were, instead, a blend or mix of activities, during which men increased their reliance on seed foods, set fires that modified the vegetation, and hunted an ever-narrowing range of medium-sized mammals, which they protected from other predators. The seeds of the ancestral wheat and barley plants were simply gathered long before they were deliberately sown.

It was once thought that men first became sedentary and then noticed luscious pods and fruits that sprouted from his own dung and garbage heaps; or that men already sedentary captured animals because there was at last a place to keep them. It is now known that men built and used efficient shelters, developed language and complex cultures, made beautiful tools, and kept fires in what are now Turkey, Czechoslovakia, France, Russia, Hungary, and probably elsewhere hundreds of centuries before agriculture.

Other first steps in the development of agriculture have been postulated, but none can explain the events between fourteen thousand and twelve thousand years ago. Even pot-making, the celebrated art of the food-production revolution, had long been anticipated insofar as containers were needed and made by people who collected but did not plant, store, or barter food.

It has been said in half-seriousness that as man tamed the dog the dog tamed man, but the dog may not even have been among the first domesticated organisms: the evidence is inconclusive because of the similarity of wild and tame canid bones at archaeological sites. A reliable chronology of the earliest presence of each of the hundreds of domestic plants and animals is slowly emerging from carbon-14 and other dating methods. Rather than explaining the beginnings of agriculture, these are after the fact and do not reveal the crucial turn at agriculture's beginnings.

What must surely have preceded farming was a shift in style and in man's sense of his place in the world; a shift whereby man would presume to own the world and wild organisms would be screened for those having a certain infantile, trusting placidity that could be nurtured and increased in captivity. Long before some degenerate auroch or wild cow was hitched to a set of stone wheels in Egypt, the destiny of the planet was altered. A group of deprived hunters, caught in a geographic and biological crisis, took up crayfish-stomping and seed-gleaning—activities that had not occupied the full attention of their ancestors for millions of years, since the earliest genus of man, *Ramapithecus,* ambled about pond and prairie edges and the father of modern men, *Australopithecus,* scavenged, sought small game, and snatched crustaceans in the shallows of ancient African lakes.

Husbandry, a Failure of Biological Style

It is hard to speak of domestic animals as failures because we are so fond of them. To us they are fellow beings, whereas we regard wild creatures as curiosities or shadows whose wills oppose our own. To denounce farming and rural life, so relatively serene at a time of urban crisis, seems to flout the last landscape of solace and respite. But in my view the urban crisis is a direct consequence of the food-producing revolution. In a sense, although farmers domesticated particular varieties of plants and animals, the farm domesticated the habitat. For whom was food mass-produced and food surpluses stored if not for the town?

"Domestication" means much more than the dictionary definition, "to become a member of the household." Individual wild creatures brought into the house, no matter how much they are loved or how long they are kept, do not become domesticated. If they live they may not thrive so well as in the wild; if they thrive they still may not reproduce or generate a lineage; and if they breed, the offspring may still prefer to go free if they can escape. There is an inborn difference between domesticates and all other animals.

"To domesticate" means to change genetically, to alter a group of organisms so that their behavior and appearance are quite different from their wild relatives, and these changes are transmitted to their offspring. By selecting parents, culling undesirables, inbreeding and crossbreeding, man uses the same processes that operate in nature.

Each gene in an individual organism acts in the context of many other genes. Hence the genetic changes resulting from domestication may affect the whole creature, its appearance, behavior, and physiology. The temperament and personality of domestic animals are not only more placid than their wild counterparts, but also more flaccid—that is, there is somehow less definition. Of course there is nothing placid about an angry bull or a mean watchdog, but their mothers were tractable, and once an organism has been stripped of its wildness it can be freaked in any direction the breeder wishes. It may be made fierce without being truly wild. The latter implies an ecological niche from which the domesticated animal has been removed. Niches are hard taskmasters. Escape from them is not freedom but loss of direction. Man substitutes controlled breeding for natural selection; animals are selected for special traits like milk production or passivity, at the expense of over-all fitness and naturewide relationships.

All populations are composed of individuals who differ from one another. Among wild animals, the diversity is constantly pared at its fringes. Reproductive success and survival are best for individuals of a certain type. In this way, natural selection is a stabilizing pressure, shaping populations into distinctly different and recognizable species. This pressure does not exclude genetic variation. Indeed, the appearance and behavior of a wild species hold true to type in spite of genetic variation. Apparent uniformity masks genetic difference. When natural selection is removed much of that hidden variation emerges and the population is flooded with external diversity.

Our subjective experience of this is in terms of individuality, and the concept of individuality in our society carries such a strong emotional force as well as political overtones that individualizing as a by-product of domestication may not easily be seen as undesirable. Though domestication broadens the diversity of forms—that is, increases visible polymorphism—it undermines the crisp demarcations that separate wild species and cripples our recognition of the species as a group. Knowing only domestic animals dulls our understanding of the way in which unity and discontinuity occur as patterns in nature, and substitutes an attention to individuals and breeds. The wide variety of size, color, form, and use of domestic horses, for example, blurs the distinctions among different species of *Equus* that once were constant and meaningful.

It is important to know, when any two organisms are compared, how they are related. However trivial that distinction may seem at first, its triviality simply signifies the poverty of biology in modern philosophy. With domestication, arbitrary re-establishment of inconsequential groupings and relationships damaged the perceptual powers of mankind. If evolutionary human ecology had only one lesson it would be that the development of human intelligence is linked to man's conscious exploration of the species system in nature. But this lost-sensibility aspect carries us away from the biological consequences of domestication.

The glandular and anatomical alterations of animal domestication are fairly well known. Consider the white rat, whose history has been comparatively well documented since it was created from the wild brown rat in the middle of the nineteenth century. In breeding for ease of keeping and uniformity, a variety of related and inadvertent changes have occurred. The tamer, more tractable, less aggressive, more fecund white rat, with its early gonadal development, less active thyroid, and smaller adrenals, is cursed with greater susceptibility to stress, fatigue, disease, and has less intelligence than its wild relative. Many of the deleterious changes have been unavoidable side effects, because of the interplay of gene action, or because genes favored by the breeder are closely linked to undesirable genes on the chromosomes.

The strong, firm style of the wild animal is due to a mix of genes that work well together—in other words, it has a stable epigenetic system. The similarity of individuals is shielded by this system against disruption by mutation. In addition, certain chromosomal aberrations may serve to keep blocks of genes together in the wild form; that is, they tend to reduce mixing or recombination in later generations. In domestication the breeder breaks up these blocks, allowing new combinations to appear in the offspring, which would render most of them unfit in nature. Some of these will be especially desirable to him, others simply monsters. Once a cluster is broken up by man-controlled breeding, producing genetic "goofies" that are protected from the rigors of the wild, new sets of captivity types can then be winnowed from them on the farm or in the laboratory. Even in zoos, where the majority of wild animals soon die, the captives that survive are those which, because of their genetic difference, are least exacting about territory, least subtle about social signals and cues, least precise in behavioral discrimination, the loss of mates and companions, and fear about human ubiquity. All domestic animals are highly social, but their social relations are degraded and generalized, just as their physiology is radically altered. They have been bred for readiness to accept human control. "Releasers"—those signals from others of their kind which trigger complex behavior sequences—are lost, along with genetically regulated responses. For them the world grows simpler.

Ritual behavior becomes abbreviated. Symbolic fighting to

settle conflicts peacefully is less frequent among domestics than among wild species. Mating patterns lose their elaborate timing as segments are lost. Hormonal changes, such as a decrease in adreno-cortical steroids, lead to submissiveness. The reproductive systems of the kept-animals lose their fine tuning to the season and to display postures, which in nature are a tightly woven sequence of steps from courtship through parental behavior. Differences between male and female—the secondary sexual characteristics—are diluted. The animals become crude pawns in the farmer's breeding game, shorn of finesse and the exquisite detail so characteristic of wild forms. The animal departs from the hard-won species type. For man the animal ceases to be an adequate representation of a natural life form. Its debased behavior and appearance mislead us and miseducate us in fundamental perceptions of the rhythms of continuity and discontinuity, and of the specific patterns of the multiplicity of nature.

Interpretations of this debauched ecology were formulated for civilization by its "educated" members. Effete dabblers from the city looked over the barnyard fence at the broken creatures wallowing and copulating in their own dung, and the concept of the bestial brute with untrammeled appetites was born. This was the model for "the animal" in philosophy, "the natural" from which men, understandably, yearned for transcendent release.

Among animals, suitable candidates for domestication are social, herd-oriented, leader- or dominance-recognizing forms. Their response to their own species (possible sex partners) and their own habitat is more a matter of learning and less of fixed responses to fixed signals. Husbandry seeks out and exploits three characteristics of these animals: the tendency of the young to follow whoever is caring for it by imprinting—the process of irreversible attachment; the gradualness of the transition from nursing to eating; and the way in which different social relations may be mediated by different senses. For example, mother-daughter nurture relationships may be based on an imprinted taste. A Scottish milkmaid lets the cow lick her bloodied hands (as well as the calf) at birth, and thereafter the cow will "let down"—give milk—for the milkmaid and the calf, but only for them.

Inborn metabolic errors condemn wild animals to swift destruction. In captivity such cripples are sometimes not only protected but prized. These flaws ("hypertrophies") in growth result in the production of extra meat, wool, silk, eggs, and milk. All such freaks carry a burden of genetic weakness. The nurture of these weaklings is a large part of modern animal science, which may be defined as the systematic creation of animal deformities, anomalies, and monsters, and the practice of keeping them alive.

Another mutant trait common to domestics is excessively delayed maturity and sexual precocity combined with rapid growth. In culling out the irascible and stubborn individuals, the hard, mature, lean line is sacrificed for animals with submissive and infantile responses. Individuals maturing at slower rates are favored. Cows and horses have long-enduring mother-child relationships just as primates do. By exploiting this relationship, new social interdependencies can be created. Infantile animals are less attached to their own kind and readily join other barnyard animals or the human household. Children are eager to adopt them as "people," and adult humans are attracted by their helpless appeal and immature faces—for juvenile qualities are as apparent in face and body as in behavior. The effect of all this is that domestic breeds are creatures who never grow up in spite of their sexual precocity.

The protected environment of domestic animals cushions them from the sculpturing forces of nature and cuts them off from many physical resources. Only when their place-preferences are removed by breeding is this loss tolerable for them. Instead of being more flexible than his wild ancestor, the domestic is specialized to accept human judgment concerning habitation and food. The capacity for living with deficiency is not a true liberation of behavior but the weakening of the choice-making faculty. Wild cattle range widely over diverse types of soils and vegetation in search of plants for which they have a special need at certain times or for trace elements and other minerals that they lick directly from the earth. They seek mud or sand, shade or bright sun, humidities and winds—the conditions that are right for them. Their deliberate instinctive exposure to rain and snow is precisely regulated to their requirements. Many have special relationships with birds, who feed near or on them, and with other animal and plant parasites, internal and external, beneficial to their health. Each step in their life cycle is carried out in the right surroundings, which may be different for feeding, giving birth, courting, resting, hiding, playing, or socializing. In zoos, mental and physical breakdowns are common because the animals lack the extensive range of choices necessary to a healthy physical or social existence. Some species simply cannot be kept alive, necessitating a constant flow of "living material" to replace the dead or dying.

Domestic animals, who also live in restricted environments, are not stir-crazy and malnourished because they are the survivors of hundreds of generations of captives. They are the well-padded drudges, insulated by blunted minds and coarsened bodies against the uniformity of the barnyard, having achieved independence from the demands of style by having no style, coming to terms with the grey world of captivity by arriving at the lowest common denominator of survival.

If this seems to slander some favorite dog or horse or pig, remember that artificial selection of juvenile qualities also favors immaturity, flexibility, and adaptability. The qualities that are admired—responsiveness to men in dogs and trainability in horses—are achieved through breeding at the expense of the traits of maturity. No one can judge the pathos of the domestic animal who has not watched its wild cousin in its natural habitat over a period of months. As long as civilized mythology ranks wild animals as poor relations to barnyard forms it will be almost impossible for most people to make unbiased comparisons.

Occasionally man himself is included in lists of domestic animals. But man is civilized, not domesticated. Domestication is the process by which the genetic make-up of organisms is modified by man to make breed lines and by which civilized man controls organisms that constitute part of his own habitat and through which he perceives all of nature. These lines are disengaged from the niche of the wild stock, stripped of biological integrity, simplified in behavior and requirements.

Among domestic animals social relationships are reduced to the crudest essentials. Pre-reproductive parts of the life cycle are minimized, courtship is reduced, and the animal's capacity to recognize its own species is impaired. Since these changes have not taken place in man, man is not properly a domestic animal, although civilization has disrupted his epigenetic stability and loosed a horde of "goofies."

The Invention of Drudgery and Catastrophe

The first cultivation was south and west of the Caspian Sea on uplands covered then with sparse woods and grass, much of it steppe and oak-pistachio savanna. The climate was warm, though glacial ice still occupied high mountain valleys. The soil on these open-forest flanks of the Zagros, Lebanese, and Palestinian mountains was light and could be worked easily. The routine was no worse than the gathering of wild grain and the digging of wild roots.

The eminent American geographer Carl Sauer has suggested that casual planting in the form of seed-waste disposal may have preceded cultivation: However, there is no evidence of early vegetable growing, and grain-producing grasses require at least a modicum of soil-breaking. By 9000 B.C. there were at least two groups of early Near East farmers, the Natufian and the Karim Shahirian. These people lived in caves and small clusters of mud huts and had domestic sheep, goats, and two grains. In archaeological digs a preponderance of immature animal bones have been found, along with flint sickle blades, grinding stones, and celts (stone axes). Living in the same region were other men subsisting entirely by hunting and gathering, some in the open, others in caves or huts. "Pure hunters" continued to persist for another two thousand years in the Near East, though as the climate grew steadily warmer, game animals like the red deer diminished. As cool habitats migrated up the mountain slopes, human population increased. When hunters finally gave way entirely to farmers in that area about 7000 B.C., the towns of Jericho in the Jordan Valley and Jarmo in the Zagros Mountains each contained as many as a hundred and twenty-five people living in houses. Subsistence farming was under way.

During this time the early techniques of agriculture were spreading from the Near East, evoking other domestications in Asia and America, which then returned new varieties of crop plants and breeds of farm animals to the Near East.

Production of storable cereals that could feed large numbers of non-farmers marked the transition from subsistence farming to institutional agriculture. By 5000 B.C. there were farmers in alluvial valleys of the Tigris and Euphrates who were using slaves to cope with the weeds and heavy soils and to cultivate vast fields planted to a single crop of hybrid grain. Agricultural surpluses and new distribution and storage systems made craft and class specializations possible and necessary.

Pigs, pottery, and weaving were developed, and the first temples signified the rise of cosmologies based on a model of the universe as a barnyard, and on hierarchical theocracies, political states, tyranny, war, and work. The coincidence of the first domestic cattle with the temples and signs of sacred bulls indicates that cows were first kept for religious rather than economic reasons.

A thousand years later there were towns of ten thousand people; farmers had occupied the flood-plains of the Nile and Danube; and nomads with herds of cattle were munching their way across the Sahara, Persia, Arabia, Morocco, Ethiopia—expanding the traditions, arrogance, and destructiveness of pastoral nomadism. In Europe, in time, the use of tree-cutting axes combined with the teeth and hooves of livestock to destroy the great forests that had closed in on ground vacated by glacial ice. Mankind stood at the gate of the modern world.

There are many kinds of farmers and herders in the world, but they differ mainly in the mixture of certain common qualities, and the qualities derive from the basic nature of tilling and tending. The early agriculturists varied widely among different peoples in the mix of hunting, gathering, and planting. The qualities derived from planting are most clearly seen in the later peasant-farmers of the civilized or historical agricultural state. They adhere to the native soil, revere their ancestors, are sober-minded, and have strong codes of conduct. They are simple, industrious, tenacious, and predictable. But simplicity can mean dull wits, and industry can be a kind word for toil, the price and token of security, respect, and piety. The other virtues are euphemisms for the simplified, repetitive life of people whose bulldog grip on their humanity is misinterpreted as contentment and wise serenity.

The peasant has wedded domesticity to agriculture. His household is like field work: banal and monotonous. Like the mating of ram and ewe, the partnership of marriage is usually arranged—at most a choice of convenience. Procreation is the household extension of production, the means of ensuring children for field hands. Prudence and practicality rule family relationships. An economy of normal abundance, combined with the fear of scarcity and famine years, creates the authoritarian family based on dogged partnerships, dominance, and submission. Children grow up holding a grudge against their elders. Where the father is a tyrant, meals are eaten in silence. The desperate, unhuman plight of the serf in an agricultural society forces him to repress his family frustrations in order to survive, to convert them into a bitter conformity, and to redirect hatred outward—toward competitors, aliens, and wild nature. Fierce unity and loyalty become the core of class struggle and ideological exploitation, expressing the fellowship of slaves.

Peasants face the outside world with coarse sullenness, emotions concealed or deadened except for scorn for the soft-hearted. Decorum and sobriety substitute for manners and gaiety. Resentment and suspicion run deep. A stoic numbness and lack of imagination are inseparable from religious faith.

Ask the peasant what he enjoys and you get no answer. Depth interviews reveal an intense dislike of his situation and a strong desire to leave the bleak rural environment. It is likely that many of us see some of these traits in our urban contemporaries and in ourselves, far from the pigsty and plow. The peasant is in us all and his warp and values are part of modern culture.

It was early farmers who, recognizing the connection between sex and reproduction, degraded sexuality by tying it to pride and productivity. Once deprived of its mystery and employed as a tool instead of as a rite of bonding and commitment, it was perverted into lasciviousness by chieftains and urban cousins.

With his anthropomorphic view of the world, as expressed in the invention of humanist gods—matriarchy and patriarchy forever contending—the peasant and villager see all misfortune as caused by someone, to be countered by magic or vengeance.

Men obtain images of themselves from the natural world. Planters and tillers see themselves as domestic animals or as plants—crops in a cosmic garden. Reserving part of the harvest for the gods is part of the custom of renewal ceremonies. Hence sacrifice came into existence; the murder of the first-born is a logical myth of men as numerous as weeds. Herders see themselves as sheep who follow "a great shepherd." Living amidst collapsing ecosystems, agrarians accept a religion of arbitrary gods, catastrophic punishments by flood, pestilence, famine, and drought in an apocalyptic theology.

It is common in sociological studies to distinguish between the planters or tribal herdsmen of the earliest agriculture and later peasants and farmers. The first do not live in so highly a structured and complex society of rulers and workers as do, say, the traditional peasants of Central Europe. The latter—the modern farmer—is an entrepreneur, a peasant businessman, who, though often puritanical and conservative, lives in a non-religious relationship to the soil and regards the land as a commodity in a modern industrial economy. However useful these distinctions are for social comparisons, they are ecologically inconsequential. All agrarian societies share symptoms of homocentricity, illusions of omnipotence, hatred of predatory wild animals, blunted body or blunted sensitivity, lack of interest in non-economic plants and animals, and the willingness to drudge, with its deep, latent resentments, crude mixtures of rectitude and heaviness, and absence of humor.

In official history 3000 B.C. marks the beginning of civilization, corresponding to the rise of equatorial valley irrigation monocultures, the city-rural complex of specialized, single-crop farms and ruling bureaucracies of the great river valleys. In the archaeological residue of the Mesopotamian states there is evidence of ox-drawn carts, trade, writing, slaves, wars, and theocratic kingships. During this same period there was debilitation of the total natural complex, pillaged ecosystems that never recovered. The signs of this were the local extinction of large wild mammals, deserts replacing forests, the degradation of grasslands and disappearance of soil, the instability of streams and drying up of springs, and the depletion of land fertility— all of which affected water supply, climate, and economy. The creeping dereliction was largely invisible then, as it seems extraneous now. Individuals were born into harsh, stony surroundings where floods and drought seemed to be eternal, a world given to rather than made by man.

The connection between the rise and fall of great alluvial valley civilizations and the ecological doom brought about by manmade machinery was clearly traced by Dr. W. C. Lowdermilk, an American soils expert. First Lowdermilk noticed that the bottomlands along the great rivers were as fertile as ever, though they now supported only one-fifth as many people as they had three thousand years before. The debacle that overtook Babylon, Kish, Ezion Geber, Timgad, Petra, Carthage, and other cities of the Near East was not simply exhaustion of the land.

Two kinds of clues helped Lowdermilk to puzzle out the role of ancient hydraulic agriculture in the ruin of these now buried cities. One was the silted-in waterways, buried irrigation channels and hydraulic works. Even the cities themselves were buried, as any spade-wielding archaeologist will testify. Jerash, once a city of two hundred and fifty thousand, now lies under thirteen feet of earth, on which exists a village of three thousand.

The other was the barren rocky slopes beyond the city walls, so characteristic of the Mediterranean world from Portugal to Palestine, and of most of the Near East and North Africa, much of India, China, and Mexico. The evidence is incontrovertible that the land was once covered with soil, grasses, and woody plants; paleontological studies—the analysis of pollen grains from ancient lake beds, by which the types of previous plant life can be determined—agree with geological, archaeological, and historical sources. In the Judean hills and on the slopes of Shansi province, Lowdermilk found ancient upland temples whose walls kept out livestock and whose sacredness repulsed the woodcutter. Within the walls forest groves survived on good soils, oases in thousands of square miles of manmade desert. On Cyprus, where lowlands temple walls held off mudflows, the plain is now eight feet above the churchyard. The church has a new floor laid over a massive silt flow thirteen feet deep. Twenty-three feet of silt had therefore come down from the slopes since the church was built, the result of clearing, burning, and grazing.

The eroded slopes and buried cities were only part of the story. Intensive land use was not primarily the cause of urban collapse. Lowdermilk reasoned that a great burst of population had followed the mastery of irrigation agriculture, which incorporated the use of the plow and the strategy of crop rotation. Faster than famine and wars could cut them down, the human hordes increased. Density in the city and flood plain sent people farther upstream, up the tributaries, and up the slopes of the watershed itself. Clearing and cultivating the lower slopes drove the shepherds and their four-legged locusts higher. Timber for ship and other construction was logged from the highlands—which were occupied in turn by charcoal-makers, subsistence farmers, and stock-keepers. The silt that began to crawl down the slopes became a perpetual revenge, so that the vast terrace systems and valley flumes required constant maintenance, not only by farmers but by armies of laborers—slaves and others. The city that preceded the present Beirut was an example of this sequence: expansion of the population of Phoenician Semites through hydraulic monocultures; increased manufacture and trade; the export of migrants; the clearing and cultivation of an upstream watershed once covered for two thousand square miles by the cedar of Lebanon tree; followed by an unremitting struggle to secure the waterworks against siltation. When some social upheaval interfered with the routines of control, the state fell.

As increasing population and demands on the land led to further subdivision and fragmentation, either the farmer relapsed into a bare subsistence economy or agriculture was reorganized on an estate or feudal basis. In the latter case some formerly "free" men became serfs and slaves. In time a growing landless, underemployed proletariat came to be a menace to the ruling classes and was placated by the state with bread and circuses.

This is a brief description of the Roman empire, which started with free farmers. Relatively speaking, Rome is a later-day example of a process that began when the ancient theocratic state reached the limits of production and, in the desert, of water. The growing population could do one of three things: starve, emigrate to the hinterland and farm the slopes, or enter urban roles of begging, brigandage, or some other more official form of raiding for tribute. This last required increased taxation and regimentation, to implement as well as to resist it, which generated revolt or evoked invasion from without, eventually followed by bureaucratic collapse—and the flumes, ditches, pipelines, conduits, terraces, reservoirs, and dikes disappeared under an avalanche of mud. War, invasion, insurrection, epidemic, and famine could each break the temporary balance maintained by infinite drudgery against the consequences of the agrarian revolution.

The destructive combination of hydraulic agriculture and theocratic state has been the major force in the creation of our over-dense society and apocalyptic culture. Outside the great valleys other combinations have been chewing at the earth's skin just as effectively though less dramatically. In Morocco, pastoral nomadism and other grazing, charcoal-making, wood-burning, and land-clearing by fire have combined to deforest a once verdant and shady country. It is difficult to overestimate the extent of the damage by that arch destroyer, the goat.

Historians have blamed the Moroccan demise on Arab nomads who hated trees, just as the Mongols were blamed for the collapse of the Mesopotamian irrigation systems. Ideology has been used to explain ecological situations. It is as though there were some cultural block against recognizing the fatal mishandling of the natural environment by the agricultural society and its urban overlords.

In China men struggled to control the Yellow River for four thousand years, while at the same time other men ravaged the upper watershed, creating gullies 600 feet deep. The mud that came down settled in the river bed, gradually lifting it high above the surrounding flood plain, and the river was contained entirely by manmade dikes. Flooding runoff from the denuded slopes occasionally overtopped the dikes. The great flood of 1852 shifted the mouth of the river 400 miles and drowned hundreds of thousands of people. The Biblical Flood of the Old Testament, about fifty-five hundred years ago, which was probably the Tigris River, had the same basic cause. There is evidence that the early Sumerian civilizations did not know floods of the Tigris, and that flooding began with upper-watershed destruction. The soils that fathered the first domestic plants and animals were ripped off the earth by hooves and teeth and sent down the Tigris and Euphrates, forming a delta that advanced 180 miles into the Persian Gulf, as though the skin had been peeled from the whole land and heaped into the sea, making 35,000 square miles of salt marsh from the top-soil.

The destruction was not necessarily the result of poor agricultural practices. It was rather the nature of husbandry itself. The record of agriculture everywhere on the planet is that of a blind force extending sand dunes and other wind damage by excavation and burial, lowering water-tables, increasing flooding, altering the composition of plant and animal communities, and diminishing the nutritive quality and stability of ecosystems. The loss of certain substances from the soil reservoir —especially phosphates, nitrates, and calcium—decreases crop food value. Change in floral composition affects a complex, stable species by replacing it with a simpler, shifting association. A forest may remain a forest, or grassland remain grassland, yet be drastically altered in richness, productivity, resistance, and soil-building ability. Changes in composition are brought about directly by overgrazing and indirectly by the cultivation of surrounding lands; they are invisible to most people, even cattlemen and other pastoralists.

No other organisms are more intricately associated with civilization than the cereals—wheat, barley, rye, corn, rice: modified annual grasses on whom the masses of mankind depend. Ecologically, the cereals are takers, not makers of soil. By contrast, perennial wild grasses work as pumps; their deep roots bring fresh nutrient minerals to the surface and structure the soil. They live in conjunction with a wide variety of flowering legumes and composites, two groups of plants essential for good soil formation, which are dependent on insect pollinators for their continued existence and in turn support a rich animal life.

As men undertook the cultivation of vast fields of cereals, they turned away from an ancient relationship with the wild nectar- and pollen-seeking bees, flies, butterflies, and beetles. Such insects had made possible the arboreal life of early primates in flowering and fruit-making tropical forests. Then they were instrumental in the evolution of prairies and savannas, which supported the first pre-human ground apes. Finally, pollinating insects supervised the evolution of the steppe and tundra flora, where the great herds of Pleistocene mammals fostered the final hunting phases of mankind.

The earliest subsistence agriculture did not abandon its dependence on flowering plants and their pollinators, but when men moved into the great river valleys and planted vast fields of grain they in part repudiated ancient connections with a host of tiny animals who compose the richest and most diverse fauna on our planet. The cereals are wind-pollinated annuals, shallow-rooted, ephemeral, without soil-forming virtues, and their association with flowering forms or pollinator insects is minimal. By supporting large, minimally nourished human populations and by their destructive effects in the environment when grown in cultivated uniformity, the cereals are truly the symbol and agent of agriculture's war against the planet.

It may seem quaint to write fervently of "land-use prac-tices" at a time when pollution is the fashionable topic of en-vironmental concern and the space and solitude of the sheep-herding life seem idyllic. With such a small fraction of society in the industrial state "living by the soil," soil erosion, forest destruction, and desert-making hardly seem to be hallmarks of our historical ecological situation. But the soil was the source of complex life long before men or agriculture first appeared. It is as fundamental to our well-being now as ever, though most of us never put our hands into it.

The ancient catastrophes no longer seem so ghastly as they did when Lowdermilk made his report. Those immense tides of people and cities seem, in the light of our atomic era, to have fallen in a peaceful ebb. In view of their modest technology it seems almost academic to recall them now. Yet we share with them a world view generated by monocultures. Current tech-nology has become more efficient and complicated without changing the direction established by ancient irrigation states. However noble the spirit and grand the human aspirations since the earliest Egyptian dynasties may be, the written record and the fortunes of the state have usurped the human record. Its vision of a man-centered universe and impoverished ecology bedecked as destiny is a heritage too uncritically accepted. In view of the enormous scope of human time and experience, perhaps mankind has unwittingly embraced a diseased era as the model of human life.

The crippling of the natural realm by hooved animals and

the replacement of the rich and varied flora of evolution with domestic varieties set precedents for the machine age. Scalping with the bulldozer succeeds gleaning with the goat; disinfecting the forest with pesticides is an extension of cleaning kitchen pots and pans with soap; polluting the air with fumes is not much different from the Sumerians polluting the water with silt. But the most damaging blows of all are the extinctions of the "useless" forms of life, those wild things that seem outside our economy and inimical to agriculture. The success of that practical philosophy is measured in human numbers. The great increase in human population began in earnest ten thousand years ago; there are now 3,500,000,000 and there will be about 6,500,000,000 in thirty more years. We have loosed a population epidemic since men ceased to hunt and gather that is the most terrifying phenomenon of the million years of human experience.

The Lower Savagery

The majority of the world's people today still live in the Neolithic period—the pre-industrial phase of agricultural civilization. Modern humanitarian movements to liberate this "third world" see only poverty, ignorance, and disease as its way of life. Their idea of help is to make tribal planters into peasants and peasants into agri-businessmen. Unfortunately, bringing the third world into the twentieth century means, in effect, intensifying ecological malpractice. The pernicious effects of our charity are then invisibly passed on by each group to neighbors, not in the form of charity, but as enslavement, annihilation, and displacement of adjacent hunters.

This ten-thousand-year-old persecution of non-farmers is not a matter of incidental border disputes or occasional arguments over killing stock; it is not a cultural clash of the kind in which differences in language and customs create misunderstanding. It is a war on hunter-gatherers. The propaganda nourishing this one-sided war is so pervasive and so much a part of our civilized view that it has entered psychological and religious theories about the nature of man and is translated into the idiom of every kind of human activity.

There are many examples of this in the written record of civilization, even in recent literature. In *From Savagery to Civilization,* the English anthropologist Graham Clark (who has since produced a more temperate and informed book) said in 1953: "Beneath the veneer of civilization there lurks the barbarian, and beneath the barbarian the savage, and beneath the lowermost trace of culture there lies exposed a solid core of animal appetite." He asserted that the hunters of "the lower savagery" have a "desperately limited" stock of ideas because they are denied "the stimulus of fresh contacts." When these woesomely lonely people meet they "glory amidst plenty in the unaccustomed feelings of solidarity." The central feature of "the primeval condition of man was his incessant quest for food," and, suffering from this "disadvantage of dependence on wild sources of food supply," men lived "the wretched existence of strand loopers" with their "low average vitality . . . general lack of resistance to infection . . . low average output of energy," which intensified their "ever present fear of starvation." "This dependent, parasitic mode of life" produced no progress and no cultural development, only a "cultural poverty" wherein men failed "to discriminate between the inner life of the soul and the external environment." Paleolithic art was "childish drawing," and its sculpture was "not cult objects but characteristic products of unregenerate male imagination." Hunters living in such a delicate balance with their environment were very vulnerable, he added, and "incapable of long-sustained labor."

These assertions are wrong. They read more like a projection backward of our own worst traits. Yet many educated people believe those puffed-up words and imagine their cave-man ancestors as instinctual animals, bashing each other with clubs, greedily gnawing bones, coupling promiscuously, unable to communicate beyond grunts.

Among the most eminent contributors to a false picture of

prehistoric life was V. Gordon Childe, the English historian whose books *Before History* and *Man Makes Himself* were widely read. He wrote: "The inherent advantages of a food-producing economy are self-evident. . . . The community of food-gatherers had been restricted in size by the food supplies available—the actual number of game animals, fish, edible roots, and berries growing in its territory. No human effort could augment these supplies, whatever magicians might say." Children, he noted, were greatly prized by farmers, while they were "liable to be a burden" to hunters, and he erroneously concluded that therefore the first loved their offspring more than the second.

The assumption that hunters were limited in numbers by food supply is perhaps due to abundant historical evidence of famine among farmers, but observations of living hunters have shown that the theory is not applicable to them. As the distinguished American ecologist Paul Sears, geographer Carl Sauer, and many others have observed, agriculture did not develop as a result of food shortage. Of course children were prized by cultivators, who had much work to do, but they were also sold by them. That children were a burden to hunters may be a mistaken generalization from observations of certain Eskimos. But the Eskimos are a recent people on the fringes of the habitable earth.

Childe enumerates the "inherent advantages of the food-producing economy" as freedom from fluctuations in food resources, freedom from the seasons, more leisure, more crafts, and permanent settlements. Curiously enough, these are not what agriculture gained but what it lost. The dense farming societies with their dependent towns were subject to crop failure and loss of stored food from rodents, fungus, and human raiders; any one cultivator's tools were cruder and fewer than those of a good late Paleolithic tool kit; and agriculturalists simply inherited built dwellings from mammoth and reindeer hunters.

The whole notion of "self-evident" advantages in the Neolithic "food-producing revolution" needs to be re-examined, including such claims that it (like modern industry later) was "freeing man even further from dependence on his immediate environment," or that "cultural creativity" required irrigation field geometry, market economy, or the calendar. There is no evidence that the irrigation city-state made men more intelligent or culturally refined. When American historians Nathaniel Weyl and Stefan Possony wrote, in *The Geography of Intellect,* that "The importance of irrigation civilizations to the geography of intellect is that they create the preconditions for the development of reasoning power, and for the selection of a bureaucratic or sacerdotal class with reference to knowledge and intellectual ability," they speak against the evidence. Transition to agriculture has even been justified biologically. Addison Gulick wrote in "A Biological Prologue for Human Values": "The change from hunting to subsisting on field crops has to be appraised as a positive evolutionary adaptation since it enabled many more people than previously to support themselves in each square mile." This is true only if it is assumed that it is better to have more people per square mile, and there is no evidence that the evolution of any species is favored by its increasing density.

The cultural hatred of hunters, with its sweeping assumptions of farming's "inherent advantages," its imagery of the barbarism and brutality of cave men, is a malicious conspiracy of slander similar to wartime propaganda invented to justify killing. The enemy must always be shown to be subhuman in order to motivate and vindicate cruelty and aggression against him. Such a misrepresentation of non-agricultural people is as old as written history and as current as the "reasons" given for the Bantu encroachment into Bushman lands in Botswana, for the Dyak farmers' and foresters' displacement of Punan hunters in Borneo, for enclosure of the Varohio Indians by mestizo ranchers in Mexico, and for the murder of various tribes of Indians by Brazilians in the northern tributaries of the Amazon. Aggrandizement is always preceded by lies that inflame social or religious antagonism. The view held by agricultural civilization—which in many ways our modern world still is—that hunting people have far more land than they need and fail to use the land properly, and therefore their land may be usurped, has clouded man's perception for ten thousand years. It is no surprise that Renaissance disciplines—archaeology, anthropology, history, philosophy, and natural science—have amplified the stereotypes of wastrel and brute: ideas sustained by the classical narcissism and religious dogma of modern culture and justifying the genocide of hunting peoples.

By 1970 some twenty-odd tribes in the world's remotest places were all that remained of hunters and gatherers. The persecutions of ethnic groups, races, and nations in the records of written history are all copies of the great prototype of genocide: the ten thousand years of eradication of hunters by farmers.

The idyll of agrarian life has no basis in reality, yet how tenacious is the illusion that there is something gracious about a life of manure-shoveling, sluice-reaming, and goat-tending. As William Allen has said of primitive farmers: "Subsistence is their reward for unremitting labour, an almost continuous burden of toil." The beginning point is boredom. Their respite is drunkenness, public trials, festivals, violence, and the sadistic and sexual use of domestic animals.

The myth that the practice of agriculture engenders respect for the soil does not stand careful examination. By the time of Babylonian King Hammurabi thirty-eight hundred years ago, men of the soil had made land alienable: it could be sold, leased, share-cropped, and profit-shared. Even during the era of pastoral poetry, at its apogee in the eighteenth century, the soils of New England and of the southern seaboard states were being permanently ruined. The mind-dulled, dog-tired peasants, victims of chronic fear of scarcity, ravaged by their own fantastic images of a cosmic battleground between fecundity and barrenness, trapped in cycles of degraded social instincts with domestic animals, have not been the authors—or readers—of romantic agrarian literature. The weaknesses of agriculture have been projected upon hunters.

Speaking to a group of colleagues several years ago, University of Michigan anthropologist Marshall Sahlins said:

Almost totally committed to the argument that life was hard in the Paleolithic, our textbooks convey a sense of impending doom, leaving the student to wonder not only how hunters managed to make a living, but whether this was living. The specter of starvation stalks the stalker in these pages. His technical incompetence is said to enjoin continuous work just to survive, leaving him without respite from the food quest and without the leisure to "build culture." Even so, for his efforts he pulls the lowest grades in thermodynamics—less energy harnessed per capita per year than any other mode of production. He is condemned to play the role of bad example, the so-called subsistence economy.

By common understanding an affluent society is one in which all the people's wants are easily satisfied; and though we are pleased to consider this happy condition the unique achievement of industrial civilization, a better case can be made for hunters and gatherers. For wants are "easily satisfied" either by producing much or desiring little. The Galbraithean course to affluence makes assumptions appropriate to market economics, that man's wants are great whereas his means are limited. The gap between means and ends can be narrowed by industrial productivity. But there is also a Zen solution to scarcity and affluence, beginning from premises opposite from our own, that human material ends are few and technical means unchanging but adequate.

The traditional dismal view of the hunter's fix goes back to Adam Smith and before. Scholars extolled a Neolithic Great Leap Forward. Some spoke of a changeover from human effort to domesticated energy sources, as if people had been liberated by a new labor-saving device. Scarcity is the peculiar obsession of a business economy, the condition of all who participate in it. The market makes available a dazzling array of "good things" within a man's reach—but never within his grasp, for one never has enough to buy everything. Life in a market economy is a double tragedy, beginning in inadequacy and ending in deprivation. Whether producer, consumer, or seller of labor, one's resources are insufficient to the possible uses and satisfactions. "You pays your money and you takes your choice." Every acquisition is a deprivation, every purchase a denial of something else that could have been had instead. We stand sentenced to life at hard labor. From this anxious vantage we look back on the hunter. If modern man, with all his technical advantages, still hasn't got the wherewithal, what chance has this naked savage with his puny bow and arrow? Having equipped the hunter with bourgeois impulses and Paleolithic tools, we judge his situation hopeless in advance.

Scarcity is not an intrinsic property of technical means. It is a relation between means and ends. We might entertain the empirical possibility that hunters are in business for their health. A fair case can be made that they often work much less than we do, and rather than a grind the food quest is intermittent, leisure is abundant, and there is more sleep in the daytime per capita than in any other society. Moreover, hunters seem neither harassed nor anxious. A few people are happy to consider few things their good fortune. It is consistent with their mobility that among hunters needs are limited, avarice inhibited, and portability is a main value in the economic scheme of things. (Reprinted in *Stone Age Economics* by Marshall Sahlins.)

The agri-culture propaganda is now fused with official fantasies of the industrial state, which decrees itself inexorable. In an extremely interesting book, *On Becoming Civilized,* Yale professor Leonard Doob shows the inevitability of the civilizing process—taking civilization, as he says, to mean a literate and technological society. Doob gives many examples of the progressive alteration of groups along parallel or converging lines toward something like the modern Western world. But his examples all start with agricultural people, who the world over live in destitute or deteriorating environments and who are socially and economically undermined by the impact of industrial economies. They have no choice because they are already the creators and creations of the centralized state or its crude form in the system of tribal villages. In effect, his book is a study of change and stress in a system which itself creates discontent and its reinforcement by the minions of industrial forces, exaggerating the desire for things and belief in ideological solutions. Doob fails to acknowledge or perhaps to realize that the real alternative to civilization is not the economy of tribal cultivators but hunting and gathering. In contrast to the people in his examples, hunter-gatherers resist the blandishments and threats of their farmer and rancher neighbors, missionaries, do-gooders, hucksters, and soldiers. They have to be run down, caught, tricked, and broken before they will leave their "lower savagery" for the gift-wrapped, sweet-scented package of civilization.

Farming, an Ecological Disease

It is rather flattering to think that the various dooms now available to us are all modern inventions, but this is true only in minor and unimportant ways—in the efficiency of the tools and particulars of the machines, the magnitude and rate of increase of the problems. Life systems in the lands, seas, and air of the earth are endangered. Poisons intended to protect crops from pests and toxic by-products of industrial civilization have encircled the globe, infiltrating the tissues of every living creature. Erosion of soil, the loss of forests, marshes, open spaces, and grasslands, the extinctions of plants and animals, are quickened by the doubling of humanity every two generations. The contemporary problems are nonetheless new only in scale. The arrogance and apathy (*hybris* and *akēdia*) behind them are as old as civilization.

It is common to observe that men thought they could plunder the soil because they could always migrate to new lands. But the amount of migration in world history by those people who *themselves* had broken the back of the environment is small: the migrants have almost always been a landless surplus. While many people now realize that we live in a finite planet that has a limited capacity to absorb our insults, we have always consciously lived in a finite world, a known space, the center of the cosmos.

Reality is seen largely in terms of immediate and personal experience. The mountain of detergent foam and dead fish in a nearby stream is a matter of concern only to local residents. The scores who died in the London smog of 1948 probably did not care whether or not all of England was smoggy, nor did Siberians care about them. For the hundreds of thousands who perished in the great floods of the Yellow River in 1852 the whole continent might as well have been sinking into the sea.

Although the scale of potential disaster has become planetary in the twentieth century, ecological calamity that kills people is not new. What were in the past isolated areas of deterioration have expanded until they merged. The purifying margins, the reservoirs of air, the uncultivated odd corners and fence rows that allow native species to survive for replacement and renewal are decreasing. But the failure of local systems of soil and water, the floods and landslides following denudation, the malnutrition brought on by failure of fertility, the poisoning by wastes, the plagues and pestilence and famine due to overcrowding, the depletion of quality in all life, and the personal insanity and social madness consequent upon all these things have struck down millions of people in the past. The disaster facing us now is a continuation of an earth trauma that began about ten thousand years ago. There was a shift to a new way of life at that time, a shift still taking place across the earth, a civilizing, progressive commitment to conflict with the natural world and with ourselves.

Those who share a language use it to define and reconfirm their cultural identity. By a parallel process behavioral differences among geographically separated groups of the same species help maintain the demarcations by which groups splinter and evolution advances. Prejudice against "others" may even have served a valuable adaptive, genetic function for man before the emergence of the political state made possible ideology—an inertial body of ideas, historically justified, by which society rationalizes organized aggression.

With the rise of the first armed cities and mercantile civilizations, men began the process of ideologizing their ecological relationships. Genocide began on earth with the extermination of hunter-gatherers and extended as biocide to the selective destruction of wild plants and animals on the new basis of politically structured values, a psychological extension of the tribal wars of civilization.

The polarity of city and country, fancied as the symbols of the artificial and natural, proves not to be an opposition at all but only a set of counterparts, the two sides of a whole. When farming freed part of an enlarged population from the drab necessity of food-producing, it was necessary to bind the food producer to the city rather than isolate him. Food was transported to the city and the products of the city to the farmer— a connection that has always been more than just economic. It has necessitated a bureaucratic political web, and, more important, a basic agreement on values and objectives. The country mouse, by telling himself that he prefers his own way of life, pretends that the differences are real. But the contrast only excites by magnifying what is relatively minor. His visit to the city is, after all, the reward of provincial time-serving with its rude, monotonous routines. The city is traditionally the bumpkin's dream of glory—he wouldn't want to live there but he couldn't do without it.

The forces working toward the destruction of our world are not merely the results of an industrial technology. Some have blamed an insufficient technology, where engines gorge, incompletely digest raw materials, and spew out waste. Others hold industry to be too efficient—as when an astounding yield of corn is achieved by overfertilizing with chemicals, which then leak through the soil and pollute streams and lakes by feeding the algae in them. Both are true and neither explains the present situation. As the biosphere fails in dozens of small ways, increasing to a hundred ways tomorrow, it is clear that these failures are extensions of events set in motion long ago, more complex because of the overloads of our electronic fossil-fuel age, greater in magnitude because of the size of the world's human population, but not a necessary and inevitable part of the human drama.

Ecologically, the industrial world is not at opposition with the underdeveloped countries. The most primitive cultivator and the most advanced industrialist fall on a single line of progression and philosophy. A body of belief not only links all members of the planet's modern cities, it links them with peasant society over the world, guiding and directing their progress through mutually shared conceptions of the stages of man's relation to nature. It also links us to the past. Our life styles and chosen goals are similar to those of the people of Sumeria six thousand years ago, but extremely unlike those of their hunter predecessors of fourteen thousand years ago. In other ways, we remain creatures of the older time. Fundamentally we are people of the Pleistocene, and in this lies our hope for tomorrow.

Can we face the possibility that hunters were more fully human than their descendants? Can we embrace the hunter as part of ourselves as a step toward repairing the injury to our planet and improving the quality of life? I do not mean by backtracking through the barnyard; perhaps that is the error of all past efforts at reclaiming a fuller humanity by "returning to nature."

2

ON THE RESPONSIBILITY
OF BEING AN APE

KNUCKLE WALKING
AFRICAN APES

GROUND MONKEYS

ARBOREAL
MONKEYS

OVERHAND
JUMPERS
&
SWINGERS

QUADRUPEDAL
RUNNERS &
JUMPERS

DIURNAL
SITTERS

WHISKERED
SMELLER

SOCIAL
GRASPER

TREE
SHREWS

SOLITARY
CLAW CLIMBER

SHREW

ANCESTRAL   INSECTIVORES

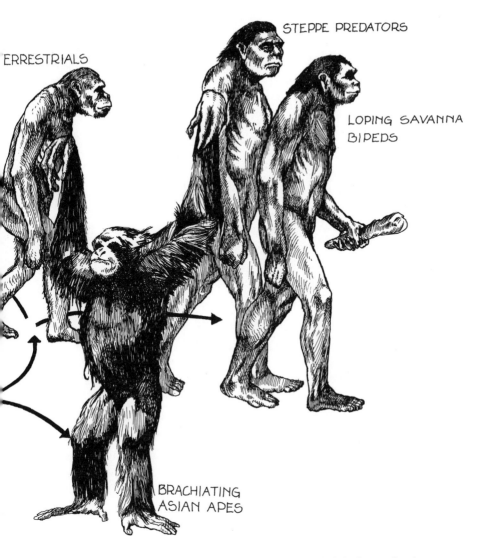

From the standpoint of evolution the more trivial the trait the more recent its origin. All essential parts evolve first, the frills come later. So ancient are the main outlines and concerns of human life that, by comparison, recorded history is short.

Civilization itself is in part a creation of historical concepts. The two—history and civilization—form a set of self-defining connections. They are related through the myth of progress, which is the sum of changes in themselves and their environment brought about by men with an acute consciousness of the forces of nature, social loneliness, and cosmic isolation.

The historical perspective creates an illusion of discovering human nature as tragically disengaged, as though existential alienation were a sign of the deeper reality of human life. In truth, history has created the alien spirit by defining man's past so as to separate him from his antiquity and his nature. Because of this, many of our concerns, such as the survival of culture, justice, and the relation of freedom and authority, seem to have arisen since recorded history began and, indeed, to exist largely as a written record.

What history has documented are occasions, not origins. Its ethical, spiritual, and practical concerns are new only in particular content, firsts only because written history is an idiom with a short memory and because it is preoccupied with the exceptional individual and ideology, neither of which is very important in the greater part of human experience or in the evolution of man.

Judging from their universality, the main features of the ten-thousand-year span of civilization are war and environmental crisis. Technology, as such, can hardly be held accountable for this. Man was already technological—a toolmaker—when he emerged as a species, and was so for two million years before the disasters of history began. The agricultural and industrial revolutions brought little change to the basic dimensions of human life, only new arrangements of its conditions.

What was man's life like before history, as he emerged as a species? If one follows the principle of looking slightly to one side, the evolution of monkeys, apes and men leads to a very different view of man than that of written records. Indeed, it is the gist of official history that the "argument from animal to man" is spurious, that man's unique ability to know separates absolutely his trials and achievements from those of his ancestors and relatives. Books in the genre of Desmond Morris's *The Naked Ape,* Robert Ardrey's *The Territorial Imperative,* and Konrad Lorenz's *On Aggression* have been challenged on that account. Our need to know the primates involves far more than the discovery of the origins of our behavior; it is to affirm them as kin and companions, as beings whose otherness is as valuable as their likeness to us, as sentient beings inseparable from their environment, who may help relate us once again to the natural world.

What problems and characteristics are in fact uniquely human cannot be clear until we know more about what is not human, and, in discovering what we are not, gain a fresh appreciation of the rich and diverse otherness of the natural world in its own right.

It is necessary, then, to know not only the hunter-gatherer peoples who were our splendid predecessors, but to go even beyond them to an older brotherhood, and to follow discovery with acknowledgment and friendship. For these reasons, studying primates is an essential prelude to studying ourselves. Many primatologists, who make such study their work, and paleontologists, who chip fossils from rock and read bones, share a growing belief that what matters most to us mattered also to our distant progenitors and also preoccupies our living non-human cousins.

The Evolution of Immaturity and Innocence

In thinking and teaching about primates as both kin and ancestors, I have attempted to pick some basic primate traits and qualities. It is a useful approach only if it is recognized that every living species, however primitive, is also a contemporary, specialized in its own ways. In the search for clues to our rudimentary origins it is easy to slip into a kind of ecological snobbery in which the oldest group of primates, the prosimians—the bush-babies, lemurs, sifakis, pottos, lorises, tarsiers, and other bright-eyed, attractive, squirrel- and raccoon-like distant cousins —are thought of only as a reservoir of traits or museums of non-human spin-off, without beauty or importance in themselves.

What, then, is basic to the primates? What are the nuclei around which the ancient primates shaped their diverse forms and behaviors, which have led over some sixty million years to the baboons, chimpanzees, and men? Those hundreds of species of ancient prosimian ancestors are all gone, but they have left a few bones as well as their descendants, prosimian and simian. A survey of the bones and of the living primates reveals several traits in common—the hands, eyes, and the reduction of the number of young born to a female at one time.

The living primates are biochemically more similar to the inconspicuous ground-dwelling shrews than to any other mammals, which is rather good evidence that the most ancient primates descended from the insectivore mammals to which the shrews belong. The insectivores were abundant in those worldwide forests of flowering and fruiting trees, which were rapidly evolving and replacing the older conifer and fern forests. The elaboration of primates seems to have been an accompaniment to the emergence of modern plants. The deliquescent and interlacing branching of these trees made a true jungle canopy, which provided the original home of all primates and was the site of the revolution in the organization of hands, eyes, and holding babies. Leaf, bud, flower, fruit, seed, and tender culms and shoots have all played some role in what one anthropologist has called "the primate patrimony of the flowers."

Hundreds of species of primitive primates came into existence, flourished for hundreds of thousands of years, and vanished. Those prosimians that have survived have been bypassed by the thrust of mainstream primate evolution; they have been left with long ears, claws, whiskers, and wet noses as their emblems of antiquity. The first monkeys arose from among them in the arboreal sea of green, in the leisure, safety, repletion, and perhaps boredom of an endless summer. The jumping and clinging habits of some prosimians, along with the holding of young, helped produce hands from front feet by natural selection, and bigger and better eyes directed forward. Forepaws and eyes instead of whiskers and nose began to be used in testing the environment, resulting in shortened snouts, fewer teeth, and reduced nose and nasal sensory regions of the brain. This broke the ancient bind that tied the hands as mirror images. (Imagine a squirrel-like animal eating a nut with one hand while holding onto a branch with the other: an unexpected eerie ambidexterity.)

Monkeys inherited and perfected this hand independence. They replaced claws with nails to support the fingertips. Special ridges and grooves (the basis of fingerprints) improved the grip, and coil and sweat glands kept the tough palms clean and supple. Muscular and nervous refinement furthered the grasping revolution by increasing precision and dexterity. The monkeys put this combination to work with zest, peeling fruits with their fingers and, with the aid of an increasingly flexible thumb, carrying out the social niceties of grooming, holding, prying, bending, twisting, and plucking.

Clinging was first to branches and then to one another. Even now nothing is more important to primates than holding one's place. The holdouts from this development left bones instead of descendants or belong to the surviving prosimians. In contrast, the ancestors of all modern monkeys, apes, and men combined climbing, holding, and looking as a scheme of life.

In this way the muscular and psychological basis of tool use was prepared. Human-type hands are far older than human feet or brains. Hands and manipulation are coeval with branch-grasping—manipulating one's self through space—and sociality. All animals are social at certain times, but the primates shaped constant togetherness around being held, holding, touching, and, when not in physical contact, holding others in the grip of visual attention. Even handling bits of the inanimate environment always contains this social aspect. Every primate goes through a sequence of clinging to mother, holding and studying objects, hugging and touching other monkeys, and, finally, a more abstract handling of other monkeys, which can be extended into socializing with non-living things. Objects and peers are handled in a to and fro, so that there is always a mix of socializing things and thingifying society. Can we say that the philosophical problems of human tyranny and social injustice and the personification of objects began so long ago? We should remember that the thingifying of others and the socializing of things began in the trees where inanimate objects are indeed organic. Perceiving twigs, leaves, nuts, and other bits of plant life as living, even social, is not so farfetched.

The shift of touch from whisker to finger was more than a change in sense-organ position. Eyes did not see what whiskers touched, but the touch system in the monkeys was associated from the first with vision. The ancestral shrews, like most other mammals, were nocturnal. The shift to daytime activity by early primates included the evolution of color vision and greatly increased visual acuity.

The magnitude of the primate's achievement is measured by the lack of color vision in all other orders of mammals except for a few species of rodents. The most primitive living primate, the tree-shrew, can see color. It probably represents a direct descent from the earliest primate with such eyes. Modern monkeys, apes, and man all inherited this capacity. Oddly enough, other living prosimians, such as lemurs, are color-blind and nocturnal, probably backsliders who reverted to nocturnal life (perhaps in escaping competition with the early monkeys). Those few monkeys without color vision are nocturnal, like their prosimian cousins, having sacrificed it for an eye more delicately sensitive to the motions and forms of objects in the vague grey hues of moonlight and starlight.

Nocturnal, monochromatic-eyed monkeys live in South America. The diurnal monkeys of the New World also differ in their eye anatomy from their relatives in Asia and Africa. The color-sensitive cells in the eyes of the latter are composed of three basic types, and the retina of the eye is said to be trichromatic. The American monkeys have a more primitive system with only two types of daylight receptors, representing a less specialized stage and poorer ability to discriminate some colors.

Old World monkeys are the most intelligent. Vision and intelligence evolved together, and one tells us much about the other. Anyone who has watched monkeys has seen them poring over the details of their surroundings and of fellow monkeys, searching foliage, fur, and facial expressions. Such persistent attention requires more than a good eye in general. In the central area of the retina the receptor cells are more densely packed, improving the resolution of the image in the general line of sight. In the middle of the central area is a conelike depression, the fovea, where the vision is even more acute, and upon which the precise external point of visual attention is projected. All the best daylight eyes have central and foveate vision and go with brains with good capacity to center attention.

Since the colors composing white light do not refract equally as the light enters the eye through the outer cornea and then the lens, different colors cannot be focused at once on the retina. To get the finest, most acute focus there is a reduction of color vision in the fovea. Here only blue and yellow are distinguished. This distinction of "cold" and "warm" is therefore the most basic color perception and suggests an analogy to touch. As day turns to night, color vision ceases and a different receptor system of the retina comes into play, mediating only shades of grey. The bluish colors of dusk are the last to be seen and thus stand midway in the daily cycle of vision between the warmth of the sun's yellows and reds and the cool of evening. At night touch returns to its own, but the first glimmer of dawn finds a huddled form in the blue shadows, a glistening eye welcoming the sun's first rays. The dawn of the new day for mammalian intelligence began when the primates rediscovered daylight; and the new day, to reverse the cliché, had to be believed to be seen.

The architecture of the primate retina is one of the masterpieces of nature. Outside the area of central acute vision the retina is composed of the highly sensitive rod cells that transmit a monochrome world. Thus the center of the visual field is sharply focused and (except in the fovea) highly colored, while the periphery is less sharp and more sensitive. What better arrangement of the eye could there be in animals living in arboreal gardens, where bright patches of sunshine alternate with gloomy forest shadows? It is important for the monkey to know when something moves at one side (a leopard or higher-ranking monkey, for instance) and to see it "out of the corners" of his eyes. After all, the monkeys had lost the wide visual field of the lateral-eyed animals, who see on both sides at once, when they evolved binocular, frontal eye position.

The English tropical botanist E. J. H. Corner thinks that color vision may have first evolved in primates because it was an advantage in finding ripe fruit in the green foliage. Writing of the durian fruits—which are large, pulpy fruits with orange or red skins and pulp and black seeds—Corner says: "On redness their eyes have feasted: with blackness they have been frightened. Redness is attractive and stimulant: with green it is gay; but the combination with black becomes diabolical, long after the horrors and delights of the forest have been forgotten. It may seem a far cry from a tomato to a sunrise, or from a durian to a petticoat, but redness in human experience seems referable to the dim origin of durianism."

Except for fruits and flowers there is surprisingly little color in tropical forests. Like the green shadows of the forest canopy, the primates themselves are rather monotonously colored. Like their mammalian relatives, the primates never developed highly colored hair or fur, though their drabness is relieved by striking patterns of black and white. The brightly colored faces and posteriors of some species are exceptions made possible by specializations of pigmentation and blood vessels of the skin. The most striking are the baboons, who mostly live out of the forest. Their brilliant muzzles and butts are certainly adaptations to visual communications among themselves—and are probably recent modifications dependent on a color vision that already existed among their immediate ancestors.

Thus both color and binocular vision evolved in the three-dimensional world of tree-living monkeys. Color functioned to sort out food objects from the green tunnels. Binocular vision helped to estimate distances between branches, made possible a more accurate appraisal of interpersonal distances, and provided for three-dimensional scrutiny of objects in hand. This relates to the interplay of holding, looking, and leaping—to the eye, hand, and the single infant who grips its mother's fur as she moves through the branches.

There is an important relationship between eye-orientation and the reduced number of offspring. It follows as an evolutionary consequence or logical step on the emergence of the stereoptic leaper, for whom "to see" is inseparable from "to understand," and to whom "to grasp" means also "to apprehend," and among whom "to attend" means both "to watch" and "to care for." All imply communication and learning. They are keystones to the mentality and communal bonds that the higher primates, including men, created.

But something else should be mentioned first, and that is security. Long and complicated individual life evolves only with low death rate. Security for arboreal monkeys could only have come after mastery of locomotor ability in the trees. Before that they must have been relatively easy prey. Most completely day-active or diurnal animals (as well as purely nocturnal) spend their inactive periods in holes. But the monkeys, instead of adapting to hole life, which would have limited their eventual size and brains and drastically curtailed the evolution of apes and other larger primates, retained some nocturnal vision. Although higher primates are classified as diurnal because they sleep or rest at night, their eye structure as well as behavior tells of night wakefulness. Sleeping in the open, they need at least a marginal ability to flee, and even in the peace of their high arboreal gardens, monkeys need enough night sight to adjust their sleeping positions without falling.

No monkey makes light of shapes in the gloom that might be leopards, snakes, or owls. Storms and lightning terrify them. That prime event of the murder story, the scream in the dark, is the primate's ultimate signal of panic. The dark side of imagination generates fearful shapes and bad dreams, infecting shadows with menace, even when the leopards are in fact far away. Such fears are the price of intelligence and the consequence of exposure—the price of sleeping lightly in trees or on cliffs.

Despite millions of years in relative security, with so much less death than among mammals on the ground, monkeys are surprisingly skittish. Their very noisiness and flightiness are indications of their safety. If rabbits had such hysterical reactions when threatened or when one was eaten, the landscape would be churning with demented cottontails. Observers seldom see any predation on monkeys; the death rate is probably higher from falling and other accidents. It is no wonder that their human descendants, with this inherited primate capacity for unfounded anxiety, make good buyers of insurance—and that insurance salesmen prefer to make their pitch in the evening, when the approaching gloom hints of night terrors to come and people are huddled in their artificial caves.

Length of life and number of offspring are inversely related. Such secure animals as monkeys live long and have relatively few young. Among warm-blooded animals, long-lived forms are usually larger. Being bigger, they have room for bigger brains, making possible an elaboration of those tracts necessary for storing information and modifying behavior. So, large size, few offspring, big brains, and learned behavior go together. Longer life usually means slower growth and slower development of the young. This longer childhood, in turn, provides a longer, flexible learning period and delayed sexual maturity. The largest mammals, such as whales, elephants, horses, and apes, are among those with the longest pregnancy and growing stages, fewest progeny, biggest brains, and most intelligent behavior. Large animals, therefore, have evolutionary possibilities not open to small ones. We ourselves are a giant primate and have deep prejudices in favor of large size; it may even seem that all animals would be large and intelligent by preference. But the ecology of animal size requires many numbers and kinds of small species for each large one. The emergence of large primates depended on such a basis of smaller life, whose humble activities together sustain a world that can afford the heavy demands and stable environment of the large.

In the course of evolutionary time different types and groups of organisms rise, flourish, and wane. Success is accompanied by increasing numbers of species, diverse ways of life, elaborate physical forms, and geographic expansion; the wane by a decline in numbers, species, and distribution, leaving odd pockets of relict species whose highly specialized ways destine them to extinction. Each group produces several large-sized kinds which are dependent on the diverse activities of the many kinds of smaller species to sustain a stable environment that can afford their demands. Among the primates such large species include a few tree-living forms, many terrestrial monkeys, the apes, and men.

Since most of the living prosimians and monkeys have only one young at a time, the shrinking of brood size probably began long before there were any large species. Not even primates can hold more than one offspring in the trees at a time. (Of course, there are ways of bearing and rearing a whole litter in trees— witness the raccoons and squirrels, who deposit them in nests and holes.) The monkeys apparently inherited the small family design from the prosimians and then proceeded to explore its possibilities. The secure life requires few young replacements. Small litter size is advantageous to the health of both mother and offspring: there is less strain during pregnancy, and the infant need not contend with a host of brothers and sisters for food and care.

With multiple conceptions the intra-uterine competition rewards the biggest and fastest-growing, and natural selection favors genetic systems for short development timetables. This mode of reproduction emphasizes all the wrong things from the primate point of view. Short pregnancies, many offspring, and a short life span trap animal species into patterns of fixed behavior, limited intelligence, rapid turnover, and high productivity. Monkey sociality presupposed small families with much individuality and strong personal bonds. To achieve this, youthful traits were kept into maturity. This "foetalizing" or "infantilizing" not only stretched the duration of immaturity but modified the adult as well. During immaturity there were fewer "fixed" action patterns, more flexibility, less aggressiveness, rounded chubby features, big head and eyes, smaller jaw and snout, more rounded globular braincase, baby teeth, a modified position of the skull on the vertebral column, slower closing of skull sutures, and so on. Prolonged youth, during which there was an innocent openness to others, made it possible for learning and teaching to take place.

Much remains unknown about infantilizing as an evolutionary adaptation. Is it a true extension of youth or does it depend on new genetic traits and specialized phases of immaturity? Somehow the adults came to defer the fixities of age, the closed, the rigid, the specialized, and the committed characteristics associated with maturity. Primates achieved this youthfulness by refinement of stages (such as "infant," "juvenile," "subadult," "adult," "post-reproductive"), which have only slight counterparts in other animals. The monkeys created the person, first, by giving up litters for single birth, and then by infantilizing. Infantilizing is one of the means by which increased brain size evolved. Since young monkeys have proportionately larger heads than do the adults, the retention of youthfulness meant keeping young head-body proportions—that is, large heads. Primates are the only group in which head size is not predictable from body mass. Hence the large brain is a primate specialization carried forward in turn by our own species.

The reduced number of young made possible the increased attention which each growing individual could receive—and required.

High Society

It may seem strange that animals specializing in individuality are the most social. We think of individuality as the product of a strong inner direction and independence, of solitude as the mother of eccentricity, but that is because we unconsciously recognize both personal qualities and eccentricity from the perspective of a social framework.

Learning, for primates, is a social activity. Monkey life is shaped by instinctive learning schedules for each sex and age.

How to be social or how to communicate is not what the young monkey learns. It learns with whom to communicate and when: whom to relate to as mother, to accept as aunt, to associate with as equal, to dominate, to mate with, to avoid; who is unfamiliar and therefore an outsider, and who will afford protection. Learning is much more complicated than filling in blanks, however. Although there is day-to-day stability in the web of personal relations, over months and years faces change, and so does the rank and position of the growing monkey. No owl has ever been wise enough to ask "Hoo (am I?)" as monkeys ask it, where answers change. The owl's question is addressed to the universe at large—or to itself. For primates the answer is neither in the stars nor in their own navels: the self is real only in relation to others.

The content of what is learned comes entirely from other monkeys by special signals. From the first to the last day of a monkey's life he is immersed in a flux of facial expressions, in waves of sound and posture, a tumult fraught with reactions, intentions, emotions, and, above all, a web of continuity. The infant indicates happiness and discomfort, hunger and satiation, fear and anger, and the need for attention. It may kick impatiently or squirm with irritation. It may smile, coo, burp, and cry with varying intensity. At first mother and infant simply make and respond to such signals; gradually they learn to anticipate, to substitute, to expect sequences, to abbreviate and combine signals. Primates are among the very few mammals who nurse (and some mate) face to face and who communicate with face and eyes. Ear position in horses and cats, lip and brow movements in dogs, serve a similar purpose, but the range of facial signals that can be combined into graded meanings is greater in monkeys. When facial expressions are linked to sounds and bodily postures the repertoire becomes relatively enormous.

Monkeys flush and blush, move scalp and brow, eyelid, eyeball, and pupils; they lift and lower the face, lip-smack, tongue-twiddle, and cheek-wrinkle. By comparison even man is an old stone-puss, apparently having given up some of the monkey expressiveness when he began to use language and initiated strategies of concealment and deception in his communication. Pet monkeys, confronted with poker-faced men who no longer attend as well to faces as they do to print, quickly discover that they must exaggerate in order to be understood, like a man shouting into deaf ears.

Many facial contortions make use of inherited muscles that were adapted by their ancestors to protect or threaten—withdrawing cheeks and lips from the teeth, flattening the ears, closing the eyes or the glottis, all anticipating conflict—over mates, territory, or food. Yet prosimians have limited expression. Their cleft upper lip is adherent to the gums, limiting its mobility. A true face is impossible with a pointed snout. In higher primates the lip is free, the face in a plane, clearing the way to "make faces" to go with sobs, screams, chuckles, and laughs. Monkey joy, rage, amusement, anger, affection, and surprise are inseparable from vocal and facial expression.

For five hundred years the admiration of eyes has challenged poets. Eye beauty seems to be inseparable from the person or the face—there are no songs to disconnected eyeballs, and few to cyclopean monsters with but one eye or to spiders with eight. Eyelids and a degree of opening between them, a tiny vestige of a third lid or nictitating membrane in the nasal "corner," the colored iris and mobile pupil, white sclera (eyeball), tears, wrinkles in the corner, cheeks below and brows above—all combine to make a composition of great flexibility, enhanced by head postures, eye movement, visual convergence and attention. The eyes are a semaphore system so ancient and discursive that we do not have to learn to read it. Except for the excessive showing of white and the ability to shed superabundant tears, the use of eyes as a medium of communication is the invention of monkeys.

Convulsive tear production or weeping is like the convulsion of laughter. Both use the breathing and sound-making apparatus; both are tension-releasers connected to our sense of the incongruent. All mammals have a white sclera, but only the higher primates can roll their eyes and show much white. The function of the white among all primates is to reveal the direction of the gaze, which offers the possibility of a roving line of sight without head movement. Attention can then be paid to a moving individual without staring—which is an open threat. Information on where to look can be conveyed to others, as though saying, "Don't look now, but there's a leopard coming along the edge of the bushes." The prominence of white in the human eye is due to a reduced iris and the elongation of the opening between the lids. Consequently any eye movement in man is more conspicuous at a greater distance, which is an advantage for hunters stalking big game with hand weapons, where silence is essential. "Don't shoot until you see the whites of their eyes" is just a misquote of a much more ancient order, "Don't move when you see the whites of my eyes. I'm watching a very big lion."

Large eyes are part of a baby's appeal. Adults respond to the round-headed, big-eyed, small-chinned features of a very young animal by cuddling it. Neither rabbit nor dog nor any other non-primate responds to such visual profiles of innocence but rather to other signals, primarily olfactory. The attractiveness of all young mammals to people is based on such "helpless" features. It is the bond that links the little monkey to aunts, cousins, and older brothers and sisters who are keenly interested in it from the beginning. Baby monkeys receive wide attention in the troop, and it is clear that adults do not regard them as competitors. In gearing indulgent responses to baby faces the founding monkeys developed a device for getting cooperative, helpful actions as well as protecting the young.

Among the monkeys, not only the baby face but calls, postures, and other infantile behavior tend to be retained until late stages of pre-adult life. This keeps the immature from fierce social entanglements and punishment in a system based on hard-line dominance and rank. The societies of troop-living monkeys—the most aggressively status-conscious creatures on earth—could exist only by virtue of unusually tender concerns for babyhood (and baby's mothers), and the enlargement of that concern as a means of protecting the unsophisticated and of rescuing individual adults from social blunders.

Nonetheless, the time eventually comes when the juvenile monkey takes his place in adult society. What he needs then is good knowledge of each of his fellows and readiness to change with the situation. Humans live in a world so similar it is hard for them to see how unusual monkeys are among animals. For a monkey to cope every day with twenty other high-strung personalities in a semi-stable, dominance-subordinance system, intelligence is necessary, but not just any intelligence. This ancient primate intelligence is concerned with other monkeys, not toolmaking or speech-learning or abstract thought. Some learning—fixed recognition of mother, territorial bounds, the right foods—is permanently achieved in a short critical period. Other learning is reversible, such as conditioning. Learning tends to occur in sequences and patterns, so that, as learning goes on all their lives, monkeys learn to learn. When solving problems for the edification of psychologists they are said to acquire a learning "set" and to improve their capacity for taking notice of earlier lessons.

Learning and memory in animals are always for certain needs. Many kinds of wild animals learn to avoid human settlements, shun gummy tar pits, or stay out of crocodile-infested waters. This kind of learning is a harsh teacher who flunks a large proportion of the class. It is very different from the social perceptual world where every individual is an unsolvable problem, where it would be dangerous to fix one's conclusions on the rank arrangement when tomorrow it may change, or to identify a certain old baboon as "premier" when time will certainly do him in. Nor is it only the hierarchy that changes. Friendship and affections are just as important to monkeys as rank, and these too require the attitude that life is ever in flux and no relationship is ever permanent.

Learning, in even the most fluid situation, is never a simple experience without genetic influence which shapes the capacity and will to learn. Conversely, even the most inherent responses have some environmental aspect. To learn is instinctive. Learning is a part of behavior, precisely marked off by genes, which can and must be modified by experience. The young monkey who is exploring and testing the world is not simply receptive to everything and anything but is seeking certain general categories of signals and social responses. As the monkey gets older these patterns change. He increases and extends his ventures away from his mother, the time he remains away from her, and his involvement with other monkeys—mama-playing aunts and sisters, male baby-sitters, or a play group of peers.

What the monkey knows instinctively is not so much an arrangement of particular individuals as a procedure. Pet monkeys are incorrigible manipulators, amusingly deft and curious. The impression they give of a kind of open-ended wonder is misleading. In view of how important learning is to them, the behavior of monkeys is astonishingly conservative. Their attention is on their immediate environment, not the universe at large. Much is learned by imitation, ranging from what to eat and how to peel it to "following reactions" that keep the group synchronized in the daily round and in emergencies. Like the play of all animals, primate play reveals the spontaneous animal pleasure of movement, muscle use and control, but play is for primates also a schooling where the self is tested and companions sorted, where cunning, audacity, appeasement, insight, and determination are shaped and tried.

Young monkeys, like all primate babies, have an inborn program of development. Each species has its own schedule for social as well as physical growth. For the schedule to unfold, each stage must have the right feedback at the right time from other monkeys, especially from mother—or the monkey may develop serious character flaws that will erupt later in life to impair his social, sexual, or parental life.

One of the main advantages of social group living in animals is that the young have models whose example reduces the amount of their risk-taking. Adults also help protect or rescue juveniles in mortal danger, leading them out, plucking them from the ground, or diverting threats. When this kind of safety

is combined with the relatively safe aerial jungle landscapes of
the tree-living tropical monkeys, the outcome is a high level of
what ecologists and insurance actuaries call survivorship. Only
because of these factors has the evolution of these primates so
favored the affection and patience necessary for learning and
teaching and the slow starting of relatively large mental wheels.

Little monkeys are mother-dependent for a long time and
form bonds with their mothers that last a lifetime. Juveniles
continue to associate closely with their mothers even while the
latter are nursing new infants. This may be the basis for the
development of "mom-worship," which characterizes the societies of higher primates. Nursing females are treated with deference regardless of the pressures of rank and circumstance. All
mothers with small infants have special status or, in some species, are outside the rank structure. Grooming, the *sine qua non*
of social activity, is often patterned along kinship and status
lines, and no one gets more grooming than a new mother. The
monkey deprived of its mother (or mother surrogate) becomes a
psychotic shambles. To have a high-ranking mother is a distinct
advantage on the social ladder. In some species young females
thus have direct entree to the mother's rank, and young males,
who might otherwise be pushed to the fringes of the troop,
have the special privilege of remaining near the troop center.

There is relatively little direct care of small young by
adult males, but as protectors, rescuers, and sometimes as
porters they are never far away. Father figures exist in all
monkey societies. The continued presence of the male in
proximity to females and young is one of the striking adaptations of monkeys.

Most prosimians are still strongly season-bound and so,
supposedly, were the prosimian ancestors of monkeys. Allison
Jolly, an English authority on the lemurs, says that the mating
season in social lemurs "causes maximum disruption of the
social order." In the monkeys all this changed. They elaborated
mating into an all-season activity without shattering society
itself. By unhooking reproduction from an annual cycle they
began to free sexual energy for new social uses. I say "began"

because most monkey species still have a season of birth or at least a peak of births during certain seasons. Nonetheless, the mating game, social relationships based on sexual status or its ritualized forms, and sexual activity continue through the year.

The day-to-day courtship and copulation in most monkey groups—where one or another female is in heat at any given time—has led some writers to see sex as a kind of glue sticking primate society together. This could only be true in part, for monkeys are social almost all the time—as juveniles, as one-sex groups, in off-season togetherness, in scores of things they do that are not in any direct way related to sexual drives. This does not contradict the idea of a kind of diffused sexiness in primate personality; sexuality is not so much a cause as it is a style or condition of behavior. The extended use of sexual postures such as mounting and presenting (offering one's posterior for scrutiny and gluteal delectation) are examples of non-reproductive sexuality.

The separation of sexuality from reproduction was the creation of libido. The new genital glow in family ties, the phenomenon of incest, and the problems of fathers and sons all grew from this eroticism, the diffusion of passion. The sexuality of infants and juveniles, the Oedipal situation and the fantasy life which figure so prominently in Freudian psychology, are the human elaboration of this simian instrument.

Naïvely, one might suppose that so much sexiness would lead to a society completely preoccupied with bodily matters. Instead it produces complicated, intense social relationships. More cerebral and abstract activity than actual sexual behavior seems to be involved. It is a world of indirect physical satisfactions, of impending conflict and threat where fighting seldom occurs. Paradoxically the main emotion seems to be an ambivalent fear-attraction. The young adult must constantly observe the intentions, postures, health, associations, habits, spatial positions, status, and signals of most adults. The successful mastery of all brings the privilege of rank—access to females, food, water, sleeping places, and so on. But the daily events are as much cohesive as competitive, pulling the subordinate animal toward the ones he fears. Appetite and the allure of possession are there as a primitive spur, but acknowledgment and safety in the shadow of the strong are, most of the time, even more active concerns.

A large part of the social life of monkeys is peaceful, with a strong affirmation of cooperative dependence and mutual good feeling. The picture of tense young monkeys challenging the domain of tough old males is real, but this is only one aspect of lives full of long attachments, companionship, play groups, kinship allegiance, sex-group loyalties, love of company, consort associations, and the enjoyment of infants. As one anthropologist has put it: "There could hardly be a greater contrast than that between the emerging picture of an orderly society, based heavily on affectionate or cooperative social actions and structured by stable dominance relationships, and the old notion of an unruly horde of monkeys dominated by a tyrant."

Pursuit and competition are not the most common expressions of primate dominance, which is, after all, a system creating order and safety. Converging monkeys always exchange greeting signals in which one defers to the other. Status gestures initiate and terminate all encounters. Open hostility is rare. The subordinate monkey is ever watchful; his gentle testing of his superior is frequently subtle, a matter of marginal trespass, a carefully equilibrated move.

All of the monkey's sensory areas (touch, vision, hearing) and his frontal brain lobe are connected to a specialized area in the temporal lobe of the cerebrum, the limbic system, which activates emotional life and responses. This association area translates the various modes of sensory experience into the repertoire of social behavior. The intense and many-dimensioned behavior of primates is largely due to their capacity to translate the whole range of information "input" into a single structure of feeling and organization.

Ambition in primates may be in part related to uric acid in the blood, which other mammals break down and excrete. Uric acid is a drive- and intelligence-producing brain stimulant, a substance constantly entering the blood from the metabolic breakdown of proteins. In human children uric-acid levels correspond to levels of drive and performance in school. The mutation that led to primate failure to transform uric acid into other substances may have been a major breakthrough in the evolution of intelligence as we know it.

The subjects of hyperactivity, high tension, and the stresses of attention and responsibility have been receiving increased attention in primate studies. Baboons sometimes suffer from cholesterol deposits and hardened arteries. In laboratory situations monkeys can be driven rapidly along the path to stress diseases, executive-type breakdowns, and ulcers. Oddly enough, monkeys can stand high levels of pressure, shock, and physical torment as long as these cannot be anticipated. The executive monkey, given a switch by which he can prevent a painful electric shock after a warning light is flashed, worries himself into ulcers. Such are some pitfalls of a more planned, organized world.

Certain parts of the brain are associated with the drive to dominate. A monkey with a delicately placed electrode in his hypothalamus, the central base of the brain, bursts into instant fury at the flip of a switch. The electrode overrides another organ that inhibits rage. The normal monkey must learn to defer his rage until he is big and wise enough, and to do so he depends on the second little mass of grey matter in the temporal lobes of the forebrain, the amygdaloid nucleus. Without this organ, which controls the rage centers, instant emotion would always rule. For even further insurance, in the frontal lobe of the forebrain is another network, technically the rostral cingular gyrus, that fine-tunes social finesse, and the monkey (or man) who is deprived of it by lobotomy becomes placid and boorish, treating his companions like inanimate objects.

This aside on blood substances and brain tissues calls attention to the carelessness of describing primate evolution glibly as "bigger brains." Brains do not simply enlarge like shadows. Some brain areas have even been reduced by primates. Among the early monkeys bigger brains meant embel-

lishment of visual and manual areas, and the connections of
these areas to the cerebellum and other parts of the central
nervous system. Areas such as those mentioned in the preceding
paragraph account for the big cerebrum. Becoming a monkey
required brain specialization—for primate social behavior is
surely as specialized as digging by moles, fishing by eagles, or
deep diving by whales.

The mid-twentieth-century view that the development of
the brain exempted certain primates from the rasp of natural
selection, the filters of time, and the certain extinction facing
each species in its turn is negated by the realization that primate
society and communication are highly specialized biological
commitments. Culture is no gilt-edged exemption from nature.
It is a system of information and behavior transmitted by
learning—and learning is not extra-genetic at all. It exists and
is limited according to the directions of the genes. However
crushing to the ego, none of this need detract from human creativity or the brilliance of the mind. It does remind us of ages
of slow and hard-won advance through thousands of generations of our ancestors, some of which were monkeys.

The intense equilibration in the behavior of young monkeys
gradually produced a new approach to rank-order systems. Instead of attack and defense, or even threat and appeasement,
the system was altered to one of special "attention structure."
It was possible, by observing the intentions of others—directed
always to those immediately superior in rank—to fathom and
participate in a society where attention itself became the principal key to relationships. In this, the monkeys invented a style
of mind with unlimited potential, particularly for their descendants, who would redirect it to the whole of creation.

The magnitude of the monkeys' achievement can hardly
be overestimated. They created from togetherness new life
styles. A perceptual world emerged—not simply a sensory
milieu, but an integrated, insightful whole. The primate social
group became the attention structure by which knowing and
learning evolved. Their fanatic heedfulness of space—interpersonal space and aerial space—opened the doors to "time-bind-

ing," a discovery that eventually would enable two primates to signal to each other their separate experiences by their ability to relate events of the past to the present and to use the past as a screen on which a future could be imagined. Manipulation and control were enlarged beyond the social sphere and would be used by their descendants to dominate the natural world. Finally they developed the vocal-auditory system in the same brain lobes as the sense of motion and space, thereby linking doing and saying, the hand and the mouth.

Social space is the context for all spatial learning. A mouse "learns" his habitat space by slowly and cautiously feeling and smelling it out, making deliberate trails. It runs over the familiar part of the path already completed as though clicking off check points, in a more and more abbreviated fashion each time. It extends the trail with nervous, halting, probing labor, like a boy learning his multiplication tables. Being eye-poor, mice and other non-primate mammals connect learning to travel.

Traveling in trees, where noses and whiskers were more or less obsolete and information about spatial-temporal wholes was needed rather than outlines, the monkeys rose above trail-thinking. Eyes instead of body roved. Thoughts wandered instead of creatures. Landscapes began to replace sense data. Yet monkeys did continue to travel on branches. The rudimentary forms were not wholly lost but were transformed into metaphors, regrouped in the unconscious, or organized in ways complementary to vision.

One modification was their divergence from mammalian forms of territoriality. Terrestrial mammals habitually follow familiar paths. They are nose- and trail-oriented, even those with good eyes. Large grazing animals—cattle, deer, rhinos, and hippos—travel customary routes between scent posts, waterholes, salt licks, and feeding areas. There are few if any true wanderers. Even migratory species such as caribou and buffalo move in patterns in the grand-scale terrain of their home ranges. The concept of "home range" as the place in which an individual or a group lives is one of the basic principles of animal biology. The size and habitat of the home range is species-specific: it varies from a few square meters among certain mice to several hundred square miles among wolves and tigers. It is important to distinguish this from "territory," an area defended against entry by others of the same species.

Territoriality is best known among birds. A typical example is the American robin. During the breeding season the male sings from a perch where it can see the whole territory, which, by reason of instinct, it defends by flying out to attack any approaching robin other than its mate. Its territorial defense is most vigorous at the heart of its half-acre. Beyond the bounds it is a sure loser, chased by the neighbor from his domain. After the young are fledged the robins join up in flocks, and territorial defense ceases until the next year.

Among mammals, only a few antelopes and rodents attempt to defend the whole life space from a single vantage point. Most trespass goes unobserved and unopposed. The "meeting" of neighbors is often proxied by their scent posts. Very few mammals reproduce as persistent families composed of one male, one female, and the young—as many songbirds do. Mammalian roles and social organization also differ from birds in their relationship to space.

Very few kinds of primates show birdlike territoriality. There is less territoriality among monkeys than prosimians. The further we ascend the chain of primates, starting from the prosimians, the less territorial and associated behavior patterns appear. In his book *The Territorial Imperative,* Robert Ardrey conjectures that many human social and political problems stem from innate territoriality. Although Ardrey's evolutionary approach is basically sound, there are few territorial monkeys or apes. Except for their instinct to urinate when frightened normal men have lost the scent-making space-claiming of fellow mammals. Hunting-gathering men show little territoriality. More likely, men defend space and invade that of neighbors when they live in overdense populations—that is, as a normal symptom of the social disease of crowding.

Like men, monkeys respond to crowded conditions with

obsessive space-consciousness, extreme attention to rank, and frantic agitation cued by interpersonal distances. A group tends to divide into doormats and tyrants, and aggression leads to killing. Perhaps the first lesson that psychiatry has taught is that such pathological behavior is the key to the normal and that a series of intermediate conditions link the healthy and the diseased.

The creation of society, as we and other primates understand it, was based on hands, binocular vision, and reduced number of young. It required a learning of social relationships that, frequently shifting, favored a range of subtle communications. It elaborated the individual life more distinctly into stages, each with its own physical capacities and social role. Finally, the social group was honed into a rank-order system, re-creating space into interpersonal geometry unrelated to terrain.

The Terrestrials

The primates have been pouring down out of the trees for perhaps as long as thirty million years, a cascade of pre-human and extra-human life. In the perspective of evolution, it is as though the arboreal canopy was a kind of way-station. Having hammered out intelligence as a form of social-spatial learning, the primates, in hundreds of forms, became ground dwellers, and differences from the arboreals developed.

The tree monkeys of the deep forests are more studious, timid, and indecisive than their terrestrial counterparts. Males and females are more nearly alike. The small groups in which they live are stable and homogenous; they move only short distances through the trees. Their social relationships are somewhat simpler, and personal encounters briefer. They are more narrow in their diet. None eats meat. They "monkey" more with non-edible objects. In the trees, life is more casual, more promiscuous, more loosely organized, freer. They are more dependent on a uniform and constant habitat, less able to stand change, to do without food or water, less hardy in general. The arboreals are more defenseless against predators and fluctuation of any kind. In short, they are the stereotype of the monkey: alert, noisy, acrobatic, and humanoid in a way at once companionable to humans and offensive, intelligent but idiotic. They fascinate us by their similarity to ourselves and constantly betray us by their unexpected rudeness, too like ourselves to dismiss, too unlike us to accept.

The movement down from the trees was not simply a path to man but a major flow completing an arboreal cycle. Several lines or taxonomic groups of monkeys have made the transition. Baboons, langurs, and macaques can still climb, but they live as species in different terrestrial habitats, from the forest edge, open woods, and brushy grasslands to rocky deserts.

Open-country monkeys contrast in many ways to their kindred in the trees. To begin with, they are larger; there is a greater difference between males and females, as though in the evolution of ground life consideration was given to size—many little forms or fewer big ones or some of each—and bigness was dictated for males, smallness for females. Other factors are growth rates, sexual roles, protection from predators, length of life, and the body's physical margin of safety against drought and famine. A fact of life in the open is exposure to danger. Another is the reduced variety and uncertain amount of food, which is related to the seasons. A third is that the ground is a different sensory world from the one in the trees, affecting perception of the surroundings and communication.

C. K. Brain, an English anthropologist investigating monkey adaptations to forest and savanna, has compared the African semango monkey, which lives in the forest trees, with the vervet, which occupies the forest along rivers in open country. He has found the vervet much more aggressive than the samango, which it attacks and chases wherever the two meet. The vervets are curious about novel objects in their vicinity, but they do not examine them as intensely as the samangos do. "It is possible," Brain says, "that the less hurried arboreal life is more conducive to a non-material approach than is the case with vervets." The vervets spend more time on the ground. The open country seems to evoke more contemplation of fellows and less of objects, of the scene instead of its details. Perhaps this is an early example of the value of detaching from the forest in order to see more than trees.

Even more striking comparisons of the different terrestrial monkeys have been made by Brain and others. A group of baboons of the genus *Papio,* living in the park lands and savannas, have been contrasted to other ground monkeys living in the grasslands and desert. The savanna baboons (the chacma, olive, and common baboons) live in large troops subdivided into units composed of about six adult males, six or more females, and numerous infants and juveniles. Within these units there is no permanent pairing, but mating takes place between the dominant males and the different females as they come into heat. Subordinate males occasionally mount these females as they start or terminate their receptive periods. The sub-adult males, who are somewhat younger, are excluded from the mating system by threats and attacks. They are constantly wary and station themselves toward the outside of the group, where they can keep all other members of the group in sight. However much intimidated, they remain bound to the group by the protection it affords them, their bonds to their mothers, and their sexual instincts.

Females in these societies develop sexual skin; during their receptive periods the tissues around the anal and genital areas become greatly enlarged. Infant monkeys stay close to their mothers at first; then gradually spend more time each day in play groups attended by adult males. Sometimes, toward the interior of the group, a lower-ranking animal exploits the protective instincts of an old male baby-sitter by taking up a position between him and an attacker in such a way that any threat by the latter is "misinterpreted" by the dominant male as a challenge to himself.

The society thus created is fluid but ordered, with a consistent social geometry, particularly when the group travels. The set of dominance and mating relationships underlies the

formation: infants and females in the center and adult males
nearby but scattered among them, all surrounded by a perim-
eter of watchful juvenile males. Because of their position at
the fringe these sub-adults also serve as sentries, until each in
his turn becomes large, strong, and brave enough to make a
place for himself in the center. Until then, they give the alarm
against leopards and other dangers, bide their time, and wait
for old males to get older.

In the more dangerous and variable grassland and desert
habitats beyond the savannas live the gelada and hamadryas
baboons. Their environment has even fewer of the stable
qualities of the jungle forests, and consequently they have
evolved great endurance against fluctuations in the kind and
supply of food and water, and against variations of temperature
and humidity that would kill the arboreal forms. There is a
fragility about the primeval wet forests that is unexpected, a
delicacy that seems to extend as well to their inhabitants.

There is no such delicacy about the gelada and hamadryas.
If they are more "materialistic," as Brain suggests, they are also
greater opportunists, more ready to shift and change or simply
to survive the seasons of famine and drought. These baboons
eat foods ranging from pine cones to marine jellyfish, from tiny
seeds to antelopes. The more barren habitats seem to offer
scope and challenge for the inquisitiveness of the young and
ingenuity of the old.

The well-known exploratory behavior of young monkeys
is not simply a step to personal growth. In some ground monkeys it is integrated into the behavior of the group as a kind of
antenna. As the monkeys evolved by extending infantile traits
into adult life, they forged new links between young and old.
For example, when unfamiliar food is set out for ground monkeys studied in Japan, the first to try it are the secure young of
high-ranking mothers. From them the eating of wheat and
potatoes spreads to low-ranking youth and finally to the adults.

The ground monkeys have a longer youth than tree monkeys because they need it. There is more to learn, and the
learning is more rigorous. The societies of gelada and ha-

madryas baboons are like tuned instruments, tighter even than the well-arranged society of savanna baboons, infinitely more precise than the small gregarious parties of their arboreal relatives. Although geladas regularly and hamadryas occasionally congregate in very large troop assemblies, the constant group is composed of one adult male and four or five females with their infants. Such harem groups may feed near one another, and among geladas the females may even occasionally intermingle, but the females are under almost constant scrutiny and may be punished if they lag too far behind. They do not have the large sexual swellings when in heat, but they do have colored markings, which, when presented in the monkey fashion of turning the rear for examination, establish their status and usually secure them from harm.

Among these monkeys the intensity of personal interaction is so great, and the temper and strength of the males so prodigious, that both females and juvenile males have marks similar to butt marks on their chests, insignias that inhibit male aggression in that split second when turning tail is too slow and that are gradually lost with age. The males too have exaggerated signals, first in their proportionally greater size, second in the enhancement of size with great manes or cloaks of fur, and finally by the replication of genital skin patterns—in some even the flashy colors of testis blue and penis red on their enormous snouts. These markings—appeasement signals in females and young, authority and threat marks in old males— define social rank at a glance. Life is strung so taut for the female hamadryas that, unlike the gelada, she cannot dawdle at all, and the lifting of an eyebrow by the male will bring her quickly into the group.

The sub-adult males among these open-country baboons are completely excluded from the breeding group. They form all-male groups, which may spend days or weeks separated from the harems. On those occasions when the harems come together at waterholes, or to exploit a rich food supply, or to assemble for sleep, the all-male groups are in closer touch with their kin and with their potential mates. As juveniles, young male baboons are keenly interested in holding infants, and as sub-adults they express this continued interest by borrowing or enticing juvenile females from their mothers and then keeping them. Young kidnaped females are mothered by the young males until they are old enough to mate, and then they become the nuclei of new harems, along with older females that have splintered off from established groups. In time, very old males may lose all their females, but not even this results in a ragged end to the social fabric, for at least some old males move on to a new level of large-group responsibility, acting as leaders of the assemblies of harems, initiating, guiding, and halting their progress. Because of the way in which the harem and all-male groups disperse to feed over very dry and unproductive terrain, then come together again in times of plenty, it is apparent that the tighter, small, one-male group social structure is an adaptation to the resources and habitat.

Beyond the grassland, toward the desert, at the fringes of the habitable environment in Africa, is found another ground monkey, the patas. Along with such monkeys as those that live in the snowy forests of China, the patas may be regarded as a frontiersman of monkeydom. No doubt its distant ancestors originally came, as did those of the savanna and grassland baboons, from the more secure jungles. Oddly enough, however, the patas does not physically resemble the stocky, doglike baboons. It is large but long-limbed, more like the ground-living langur monkeys of Asia. The patas has carried its social organization to the point, perhaps, of zoological eccentricity. Like the gelada and hamadryas, it lives in one-male harems, but unlike them it seldom assembles in larger troup gatherings. The male patas does not stand guard with such heartbreaking ferocity over his females. Instead he removes himself in lofty detachment to some vantage point from which he keeps watch for possible enemies. The bickering among females, settled by the harem male among geladas, is no longer his concern. Instead one of the females becomes dominant within the group. The patas has exquisitely developed facial signaling, expressions that in their primitive form among tree monkeys incidentally accompanied sounds. In his excellent vision and his silence, the patas has, in a sense, come full circle, for the only other higher primate so silent is the gorilla. Thus the most silent forms live on the ground in the deep forest and on the desert fringes, while the noisiest and most articulate live in the forest trees and in the adjacent savannas.

The sounds made by the baboons are much more varied and precise than those of tree monkeys. They are more interspersed with grunts and less like the shrill calls of birds. The glottal noises, the resonances of the pharynx, the use of the tongue and lips are part of a sound mechanism that comes surprisingly close to man's in its achievement of vowel- and consonant-like utterances. This capability is greater among grassland dwellers, who have more seeds in the diet, and may be related to the tongue and lip control necessary to mouth small seeds and other plant parts.

Beyond the seed-eating, there is another gradient extending from the forest edge to the desert, and that is meat-eating. The striving of male against male and the display of huge canine teeth in intimidation are conditions of natural selection for larger individuals more capable of contending among themselves and of defending themselves against predators—and with more potential for becoming predators. Baboons have moved toward the strength, weapons, and temperament necessary for hunting. In their more diverse and variable habitat, through which they roam many times farther than their cousins in the forest, they have expanded their food habits and readiness to try new things. In addition to grass seeds, they eat various kinds of meat. They are ever watchful for nestling birds, infant hares, or crippled antelopes. They have been seen to kill and eat other monkeys, such as vervets, and deliberately to surround and kill the Grant's gazelle, impala, and dik-dik antelopes. The meat is shared exclusively by dominant males. The excluded band of fraternal, sub-adult males is perhaps a prototype of the human hunter-group, which is more far-ranging than the family units. The opportunism and aggressiveness of these groups suggests that they are in an evolutionary sequence that may lead in time to coordinated hunting and altered food habits.

Ground-dwelling monkeys of Asia and Africa all show combinations of traits derived from the more primitive arboreal monkeys, many of which suggest human concerns and behaviors. Particularly conspicuous is the tightness of the terrestrial group, which is organized quite differently from the homogeneous aggregation of sexually promiscuous monkeys flowing through the trees and easing into and out of social liaisons. The ground-living monkeys are stanch establishmentarians with emphatic rank systems and rigid sex codes, living in polygynous families. They have rudimentary consciences, which are shaped during a long immaturity. During this period the young must defer their sexual gratification, equilibrate between crowding the old males and appeasing them, and inhibit their competitive and aggressive impulses.

It would be erroneous to say that in this extraordinary world of ground monkeys we see the forerunners of humanity. They are neither our ancestors nor rudimentary men. In their most specialized details they are not even co-inheritors with us of common possessions, not brethren but others on a course in some ways parallel to our own. The baboons and other terrestrial members of the Old World monkey family of Cercopithecidae are indeed our cousins, but they came down out of the deep forest in their own time and place, a dozen lineages each finding the earth path, shaping and being shaped by conditions of life.

One principle that baboon studies have made clear is that traits are separately modifiable. The anthropoids—apes, monkeys, and men—have many characteristics that distinguish them as a group: grasping hands, binocular acute daylight vision, large brains, expressive faces, upright stances, small litters with slow growth, intense mother-child intimacy, peer and play groups, roles based on sex and age, special juvenile stages and roles, complex and refined social organization, and so on. Although these are mixed in different proportions from species to species, they have come into existence at different times in primate history, and each, to some extent, evolves independently. Celebrated portrait photographers who seek to reveal character in the human face attend to a primate feature that is "ancient monkey," but of different antiquity from the primate hands of a piano player. The ankles of the dancer and metaphorical language of the poet are traits of our human family and genus respectively. A brainy grasper does not have to be a polygamous meat-eater; an upright social hierarchist need never have heard of all-male groups, overhand leaping, or old male baby-sitters. Consequently, men resemble certain anthropoid species more in some respects than in others, and they are unique in the combination and expressions rather than kind of traits.

Another general observation is that the habitat is a direct and powerful influence on the form of society. Primate studies in the 1960s have revealed the interpenetration of habitat and society, correcting the idea that social and cultural processes are independent of the natural environment. The general capacity for social adjustment is a widely shared primate trait. The monkey's ability to coalesce into large groups of several hundred individuals, or to form one-male groups or several-male groups, to split off all-male groups, and then to assemble with neighboring groups without friction, is evidence that behavior of this kind is an adaptive trait with genuine biological purpose.

There is a hidden potential that is not continually visible as behavior. This is revealed when a species of monkey is seen in unusual circumstances or in laboratories and zoos. It is especially true of terrestrial monkeys, particularly those in less stable, open, arid environments. The eminent American biologist René Dubos has observed that man's adaptability to adversity may become a disadvantage when it allows him to pollute and overpopulate with impunity, to survive in a less healthy and less attractive world. Similar toughness and resilience in baboons suggests a common ground, about which those communicative primates have much to tell us about ourselves.

The Apes, Our Cousins

Monkey evolution began in the dense canopy level of some lost tropical Eden. The interlaced tropical limbs serve as three-dimensional paths through which the inhabitants scamper in a three-dimensional mass, like a flock of starlings, but, unlike birds, always clutching the "trail" with hands and feet.

Above and below this bushy arbor of main-traveled paths, the tropical wet forests are more broken. The crowns of the highest trees may scarcely touch at their twig ends. Below the travel lanes, nearer the ground, the gloomy underspace is divided by an irregular geometry of dangling aerial roots, hanging vines and scattered lower limbs, and small trees. Primates travel through these high and low areas by bounding and swinging in graceful arcs rather than by leaping and scampering. The tree limb is still held by the hands, but the body is frequently pendent and upright. Large primates are candidates for the swinging life because bigness is a disadvantage for quadrupeds walking along the tops of limbs. The ratio of branch size to body size pushes the center of gravity of larger, longer-legged bodies farther from their feet and they hang over more on the sides. As size increases, balance becomes increasingly precarious and the efficiency of four-legged branch-running diminishes. Evolution has dealt in at least three ways with this problem: the monkey can remain small; he can increase in size and confine himself to very large limbs; or he can simply slide underneath the branches and hang. He can hang by all four feet, so that he is running upside down, or he can hang by toes, or hands, or tail. Prehensile dangling is the only way a large creature can move among small, outer limbs or among hanging vines.

All monkeys and apes jump, but the leaping postures of quadrupedal monkeys are based on a quadrupedal landing. The front limbs are extended forward, with the elbows more or less under the body. In contrast, the hangers jump for less stable surfaces, which they do not expect so much to land on as to clutch. Their in-flight position shows an overhand forward reach with elbows high and wide, impossible for true quadrupeds because of the more limited mobility of their shoulder joints.

The free shoulder movement necessary for hanging and swinging has caused a radical change in primate anatomy. Although many quadrupedal monkeys are able to break off and drop things down on an intruder, the act of throwing requires the evolution of a swinger's shoulder, elbow, and wrist. Quadrupedal forms have longer back legs than front. Highly specialized swingers—the brachiators, such as the South American spider monkeys and the Asian gibbons—have the reverse. Millions of years of dedication to the pendulous life has led to the total loss of the tail or the ability to hold on with the tail, the reorientation of the head, the shortening of the trunk and hind limbs, and to numerous changes in the details of hands and arms. Equally important have been concomitant changes in the nervous and other internal systems necessary for living the life of a bigger, and therefore scarcer, animal with its own life cycle and social organization.

Among the brachiators are the smaller apes—the gibbons and their close relatives the siamangs. These inhabitants of the forests of Southeast Asia are related to fossil bones found in Europe, called *Limnopithecus,* indicating a wider ancestral distribution in the past. The controlled precision with which gibbons run, swing, and leap through the trees has the same astonishing quality as rapidly maneuvering bird flight. They resemble birds in other ways too: in their beautiful calling and "singing," their small-group, family society, and their territorial life with its symbolic conflicts at the boundaries.

Looking closely at gibbons, one senses not a keen intelligence or receptive mind, but rather that peculiar fixation that narrows the life and scope of all specialists. It is a kind of one-channel living, beyond preoccupation or even fanaticism. Some instrumental musicians and high-wire acrobats convey the same mindless perfection, birdlike, remote from normal experience.

Unlike other apes and man, the gibbons are monogamous,

and males and females are nearly identical. Less glum than larger apes, their life is conspicuously joyful as they greet the sun and one another. They are free from much of the burden of rank striving, the intimidation of females, and the known and unknown dangers that lurk far below. An elongated hand and shortened thumb are typical of specialization for brachiation, foreclosing opposability and therefore manipulation by thumb and forefinger. It would be impossible for gibbons ever to use needle and thread. Their way indeed appears to be over-focused, a kind of mandarin refinement, perhaps beyond survival. Asian people traditionally esteem the gibbons; Malaysians, Chinese, and Thai revere their otherness, and their glorious threading of a different needle between high boughs.

One might conclude from the gibbons that it is the destiny of brachiator apes to develop birdlike personalities, except that the other arboreal ape, the orangutan, is very unbirdlike. A much bigger animal, the orang more nearly fits the ape stereotype—slow, heavy, watchful, and yet nimble. The four kinds of great apes could not have been better designed to confound the stereotype, as each in some way contradicts generalizations about apes. If the gibbon is seldom seen alone and lives a chirrupy, treetop, extrovertive life, its relative is a sleepy, often solitary, vocally restrained, pacific being, who hates to get up in the morning.

The light, lithe, and supple gibbon rests easily on tree limbs, like the monkeys, but this is obviously not feasible or comfortable for orangs, nor for chimpanzees and gorillas, all of whom build nests. The orang is the only one that has been seen to build a nest over its head to keep off the rain. Recent primatology has corrected earlier, degrading views of the orang and other apes. Renaissance savants cast apes as "forest people," hence, depraved, debauched humans. So long as they were uncanny caricatures of ourselves they could never be much studied or much loved by Europeans. Now that is changing. The "solitary" and "silent" orang is disappearing from the books, replaced by an orang that simply speaks softly and whose web of social connections is widely cast. An extensive communications system by means of subtle signals informs orangs of one another's location. In this sense they may be highly social though only occasionally gregarious. Also, there is evidence that small bands of adolescent orangs roam the forest together.

It has been suggested that orangs stay in the trees because the forest floor is extremely wet. This presupposes that large apes have no place in the trees, a theory put forth some years ago that the ancestors of gorillas and chimpanzees descended from jungle trees because they were too heavy. But organisms do not become unadapted and then readapt. Over long periods of time, behavior or anatomy may be modified by natural selection, but the species is always adapted to a particular way of life (or niche), otherwise it ceases to exist. In no sense is the orang yearning to become a ground ape, and his existence must be taken as evidence that heavy bulk does not force apes to the ground.

The chimpanzee too is as modern as ourselves and in no sense our ancestor, though it resembles the human predecessor of perhaps twenty million years ago. Chimpanzees live in the forests and forest edges of Central and West Africa, in main groups of as many as forty, with a core of females and young. They subsist largely on fruit, and the yearly cycle is framed within a succession of different kinds of fruits, ripe at different times at different places in their home range. Mobile male groups temporarily leave the main troop. Sometimes they summon the others to food by calling and drumming. In addition to normal vocal communication between individuals, there is occasional chorusing, especially in the morning and evening, audible for more than a mile. There are bursts of vocalization when groups meet, when strangers or predatory animals are confronted, and during a bizzare display at the onset of rain. The chimpanzee's inability to learn to speak human words is a poor test of its capacity to communicate or to store and assimilate information.

Chimpanzees come and go freely in an open society, and there is much shifting by some individuals. Yet kinship ties are strong, and there is no doubt that each chimpanzee knows and recognizes scores of other individuals. Indeed, individualization is highly developed, and there is experimental evidence that captive chimpanzees recognize themselves in photographs and in mirror images. Their society is characterized by sexual promiscuity, lack of jealousy and competition, and a rank-and-status system in which threat display is reduced by the anxious, peaceful supplications of subordinate individuals through a system of appeasement, reassurance, and status-confirming gestures. That so intensely social a creature should be so cool, casual, and yet vivacious and responsive is a wonder of the primate world—where monkeys bicker eternally, gorillas hunch in introversion or blandness, and humans stagger beneath a burdensome life.

Although chimpanzees have long been known as intelligent, manipulative beings, the extent of their inventiveness in their natural habitat has come to light only recently. Probably the most sensational discovery has been their concept of tools. They carefully select little twigs, pluck and prune them, and carry them along to "fish" for termites and ants. By patiently holding the tool in an opening of the insect nest and then pulling it out and licking off the termites, the chimpanzee engages in toolmaking, tool-using, and even tool-carrying. The probe used for ant fishing is slightly longer than the one for termites.

For years man was "the tool-using animal." This was changed to "the toolmaking" animal when naturalists found that otters, finches, vultures, elephants, monkeys, and bower birds use rocks, probes, clubs, sticks, and berries to extend their physical powers. The theory that the brain of man evolved when he "discovered" tools has been invalidated by Raymond Dart and L. S. B. Leakey, two English paleoanthropologists, who have found tools among the australopithecine ancestors of man—and these had brains no bigger than those of apes.

Tool use is certainly no human invention. Analysis of motor patterns indicates that throwing, clubbing, and incipient weapon use are extensions or derivatives of the general intimidation displays typical of primates. Among chimpanzees, as among men, this skill is improved by experience and practice.

There is skepticism among some experts that chimpanzees could have become so intelligent in the demoralizing depths of the forest. Dr. Adrian Kortdandt, a Dutch primatologist, after photographing a chimpanzee throwing a club at a stuffed leopard, proposed that chimpanzees are actually "post-proto-hominids," regressed manlike forms driven from their more humane pursuits in the savannas by men, and forced for refuge into the degrading jungle habitat, where they remain deprived of their almost-manhood by the depressing effect of the green monotony.

Not only do chimpanzees use twigs and sticks, they crack nuts with rocks, drink from sponges made from macerated leaves, and clean themselves with leaves after defecating. (In captivity they have learned to have tea parties, paint with water colors at a professional level, act, and one was arrested for driving without a license in a Miami suburb.) Like gorillas, they make nests, which could be considered a kind of tool-using. Yet, difficult as it may be for human technologists to believe, tools are relatively unimportant to wild chimpanzees, and their limited use is an erroneous index of their true intelligence, insight, reasoning power, memory, coordination, and sensitivity to complex patterns and situations.

Perhaps even more significant, the forest-edge and savanna chimpanzees are better at tool-using than their deep-forest kindred, and they also eat more meat. Watchers of wild chimpanzees have seen them catch and eat small mammals. Such opportunities come mainly to those chimpanzees living where young antelopes, hares, and even smaller creatures can be easily taken. In zoos they prefer meat. The increased availability of meat in the grasslands, the inclination of chimpanzees to seek it there, and the tendency to use more tools in the open, together suggest a trend in the direction of chimpanzee evolution at the forest edge. Several students of chimpanzees have remarked on their love of variety and novelty and their interest in alternatives to their routine. They take different paths to the same place on different occasions and continuously change their gait and their mode of locomotion.

Captives can learn a sign language of more than 360 figures. This includes learning generic terms representing all specific examples (of flowers for example), increasing their capacity for discrimination (not confusing the smell with the appearance of the flower), and combining signs to make meaningful phrases. Hence they can transfer and arrange signals in new sequences.

Chimpanzees have special "rain dances." They have been seen to watch a sunset for many minutes. Drumming, dancing, nest-making, tool use—these seem to be basic pongid-hominid traits. There are both experimental evidence (using a mirror) and observational opinion of the recognition of self by chimpanzees. They are clearly frightened by the sight of their own dead. "These apes," according to Kortdandt, "have some kind of notion of what life and death are." Perhaps the chimpanzee evokes in us a comparison to ourselves that seems like a recollection.

Like the chimpanzee, the gorilla is a truly grounded ape—not arboreal in general, nor brachiating in particular, like the gibbon and orang. The gorilla and chimpanzee always travel on the ground; but, unlike the chimpanzee, the gorilla does not even climb trees to feed, only to build its nest at night. While small it frolics in the lower branches, but its climbing after that is done gingerly.

Chimpanzees and gorillas are knuckle-walkers, a specialized mode of travel on large limbs or the ground. The hands are used to support the weight of the forward part of the body, with the knuckles folded so that special pads on the middle segments of the fingers touch the ground. Their powerful wrist and digital muscles, modified ligaments and tendons, and joint structure make these apes advanced terrestrials. They can stand and even walk bipedally, but do so only in display or to reach something. Knuckle-walking is easy to dismiss as a miserable, shuffling, half-way-point between quadrupedality and bipedality. Actually it is an efficient way to travel over difficult terrain where men and hoofed animals are forced to follow trails. It combines a semi-erect stance for good visibility with excellent control while walking or running, making use of the long powerful arms, which also serve in defense and picking food.

The gorilla lives in the undisturbed forests of Central Africa on leaves, shoots, and buds. It probably evolved through a chimpanzeelike stage. The groups are smaller than those of chimpanzees—one or two young males, a few females and their offspring, dominated by an old male. Some young males go their own way, although there is little evidence of conflict or aggression. A subtle rank order does seem to exist, about which there is little apparent anxiety or external sign. When threatened, the gorilla begins an elaborate display composed of at least eight distinct phases, among which are smashing and tearing saplings, charging toward the intruder, symbolic feeding, and a climax of chest or ground thumping. Since this intimidation dance was the only part of gorilla life seen by white men in the past, they promptly reacted by taking aim and firing. The lurid tales connected to this giant have all proved to be false; gorillas simply prefer solitude, where their food is not destroyed by cattle or their young stolen from murdered mothers for zoos.

Gorillas call softly, grunt, nudge, and make faces. Like man, they have separated many sounds from gestures. They are relatively impassive and placid, giving the impression of contemplation or uncertainty. Since the shoots and leaves which they eat are diffusely scattered they move randomly. Their food, unlike that of chimpanzees, is not localized within the home range. Neither they nor chimpanzees defend a territory. Mating positions include face-to-face copulation. Like adult chimpanzees, gorillas are enormously strong, and in captivity sometimes injure their human friends by little squeezes, bites, or pushes, which among them would be no more than play or expressions of minor irritation.

The ferocious faces of gorillas are misleading. Their heavy jaws—for grinding stems and munching heavy fruits—are not primitive features but specialized adaptations to life as a forest herbivore. Unlike the chimpanzee, the gorilla has no omnivorous or meat-eating inclinations. It is a beautiful browsing mammal who happens to be a primate instead of an ungulate or rodent.

The gorilla has only about half as much hair per square inch of body surface as most primates. Although this hair is fully formed, unlike the tiny vestigial hairs on man, it is sparse, possibly indicating that the "nakedness" of man is not so peculiarly human after all but an exaggerated ape trait. (In any case, hippos, rhinos, and elephants all have less hair than man, not to mention dozens of species of whales and dolphins.)

Gorillas are sexually promiscuous like chimpanzees, though in both groups females show preferences and certain males have precedence. Promiscuity does not mean frequency so much as randomness of partner. Mating in the wild has not been seen a dozen times. Take away the fiction of ferocity and of carnality, and very little is left of the old stereotype.

The study of the elusive gorilla made by George Schaller, an American zoologist, in 1960, was a dramatic addition to a body of knowledge that ordinarily advances only by small bits. In one way, despite the author's talent as scientist and writer, his book *The Mountain Gorilla: Ecology and Behavior* was a disappointment. It revealed one of the dullest animals ever to be given a book to itself. Almost totally lacking ferocity, the stolid drabs he observed bore little resemblance to King Kong or the apes around Tarzan. The only activity worth giving up bird-watching to see, during his four hundred hours of gorilla-watching, was the chest-and-ground-thumping display, which was not entirely new to science, and even it was rare. Diane Fossey, a more recent gorilla-watcher, who by the end of 1971 had watched wild gorillas for more than two thousand hours, saw not more than five minutes of aggressive behavior—the display similar to that mentioned earlier—which she regarded as mostly bluff. This slender woman reported that she calmly stopped the "attack" of a large gorilla by holding her arms out and saying, "Whoa!"

Among gorillas the daily round of stem-munching and napping is barely enlivened by occasional muffled grunts, their

shadowy movements through the forest, pensive waiting, introverted sociality, care of infants, and the routine evening nest-
building. Judging from the pitifully few instances of copulation, the gorilla must be one of the least sexy primates alive.

The crucial evolutionary transition to gorilla and chimpanzee separates men and apes from the other primates. It is
not yet known whether African apes and the ancestors of men
sprang from a common ancestor who lived on the ground or in
the trees. Along with scores of species of ground-living monkeys,
the African apes and the human line are participants in an
ancient and ongoing movement by primates to the ground. The
progenitors of apes and men achieved an upright posture while
hanging, swinging, and resting, derived from the combination
of overhand leaping and large size.

The intrusion of grasslands and savanna has opened up
the forest of much of Africa, thus providing opportunities for
new ways of life on the ground. Neither in the wet forests of
Central Africa nor in all of South America are there many
terrestrial primates. Of the five kinds of living hominoids (the
taxonomic group of apes and man)—gibbons, orangs, chimpanzees, gorillas, and man—only the last three live on the ground
and only man is a non-forest species. For this reason man seems
to have descended from an eccentric ape who lived at the forest
edge, to be an exception to the rule of ape and jungle association. Yet we know from substantial collections of fossils that
apes and men are relics of a much larger group of hominoids,
many of whom lived in the open.

One of those changes of human perception that occasionally shifts the whole style of human life is underway in the
Western world. It is growing from a new sense of connectedness, exemplified by our openness to ape "humanity." At the
same time, there is a reaction against it, an attempt to discredit
it as anthropomorphism, labeling as illusion the belief that
other creatures have feelings like men that can be understood
by mutuality of experience. Where that reaction is carried beyond reason, the objectivity of the researching biologist and the
preoccupation of the humanist become barriers and psychologi-

cal traps that protect science or human dignity by isolating them. A willing and open attitude is essential for our own benefit, if not for the apes'. After all, apes are anthropomorphs, belonging as they and we do to the taxonomic group Anthropoidea.

Doctrines of racial superiority often rest on unfounded theories of biological or, more often, subjective differences. So, too, species superiority. The tragic figures of adult apes in captivity are exactly what they seem: hopelessly despairing of life, psychopathic, and deformed. Only by denying what we see can we fail to realize the sickness of the zoo, circus, pet, medical, and experimental primate. Movies and animal acts with baby chimpanzees who are not yet broken in spirit perpetuate the fiction of the chimpanzee as a happy and clever rascal delighted to be in captivity.

Although we can never know the subjective experience of an ape, it is probably not as different from ours as we might think. Their inter-individual responses closely match many of our own, and so does the range of emotions expressed in voice, face, and posture.

Captive apes are somewhat more like men than their wild relatives. They get tuberculosis, spinal lordosis, and other human diseases and afflictions associated with life in a cell. They walk more on their hind legs, develop an exaggerated fear of heights, spend more time building nests or other structures, are more fascinated by their own excrement, more interested in killing birds, mice, or other accidental intruders, and in eating meat. At maturity they become sullen and vicious, more introverted, and develop swaying movements symptomatic of neurosis. They may become hypersexual deviants or refuse to mate. There is evidence that they improve at problem-solving and at those kinds of learning directed toward objects instead of other apes. These are also symptoms of human prisoners, and to some extent of urban man in general.

It has been known for at least two hundred years that man was closely related to the chimpanzee and gorilla. The chemical similarity of their gamma globulin molecules (blood serum proteins) is so striking that some experts regard the three as members of the same taxonomic family, separated from one another only by genus and species. Since proteins are the product of gene action, they are indicators of genetic similarity and evolutionary kinship. From the known age of an ancestral monkey blood molecule in fossil stratigraphic studies, it is possible to estimate the rate of mutations producing the observed chemical differences between it and man. When the chimpanzee and gorilla are fitted into this series the separation of apes and men from a common ancestor appears to have occurred only recently in evolutionary time.

Besides chemical and anatomical likenesses, the genetic relationship produces similarities in dentition, chromosome number (twenty-three pairs for men, twenty-four in chimpanzee and gorilla), susceptibility to virus diseases, development and behavior, skin glands, hair follicles, even common parasites. Men in Asia share more species of internal worm parasites with African apes than they do with local orangs or gibbons. The great apes display us as we might have become had our ancestors remained wedded to tropical forests (as the wolves show what we might have become without an arboreal history). By their uniqueness they tell us what we are not. By their continuity with us they become fellows in a common experience.

Our poor relations, the gorilla and chimpanzee of Africa and the orangutan and gibbon of Asia, stand now on the brink of oblivion. We laugh at their impish mockery of ourselves, at their pathological frenzy or brokenhearted despair in captivity. They seem to be the poor not-selves of our tropical dead-end, but they are not. Bell Benchley, in *My Friends, the Apes,* wrote: "I will tell you how they look and act and something about their characters, and I hope you will like them and pity them and laugh with them and with me, until suddenly you will find yourself knowing them as they are; not as low, hideous caricatures of man, but as magnificent animals—noble, loyal and affectionate—virtues to which neither man nor any single beast can lay sole claim."

Men are born human. What they must learn is to be an

animal. If they learn otherwise it may kill them and life on the planet. It is very difficult to learn to be an animal. First man must unlearn his misconception of the animal as a brute. To be an ape is to unlearn the ideologizing of nature.

The chimpanzee caught in a flash of recognition at his mirror image, dancing in a wild ballet in a sudden thundershower, or languidly observing the sunset is our nearest non-human equal. Gone are the ranks of ancestral pre-men and their ape relatives whose self- and world-sentience must have been more or less like ours, some of them perhaps more adept at certain abilities—ESP, pattern recognition, visual discrimination—than we ourselves.

Even the other primates are so like us that they are psychologically almost intolerable. By contrast, we accept easily very different creatures (such as birds or fish) because their very otherness is reassuring. In the apes so many elements of likeness to us are frightening, making an affirmation of connection and responsibility to the apes difficult.

If we can learn to be animal enough to affirm our continuity with the primates, if we can rescue them from the oblivion they now face, we will have established a basis for understanding true discontinuity. By acknowledging what is shared—the only secure grounds on which identity can grow—we would find ourselves.

In our species, knowledge of who we are is linked to origins and beginnings, and it is communicated as a mythology. The first obligation to society by young men and women who are being initiated into adult status is acknowledgment and affirmation of the past, and of its living presence in them as the symbolic embodiment of their ancestors. Being inescapably human, we have not lost the capacity for that affirmation, but we have denied its central content. Because of the imminent extinction of the large primates, opportunity to renew that affirmation is vanishing. Let us protect our cousins from further human persecution, and go on from there to the whole of animate life, and so redeem our heritage. It is not our responsibility to do so because of some higher authority—because we would be angels—but as a responsibility, first to ourselves, and second to this island earth and our fellow inhabitants in a vast and lonely cosmic sea. The anguish of our human tragedy is due more to a delusional system that insists on the exaltation of our species and the failed myths of progress and history than to reality.

3

ON THE SIGNIFICANCE
OF BEING SHAPED
BY THE PAST

The Elegant Refinements of Social Carnivorousness

The popular concept of "man's rise to civilization" projects for the mind's eye a dark struggle with a primordial past, in which men were constantly threatened by a hostile world, followed by the greater margin of safety and enlightened institutions of civilization. Pre-historic man stands sentenced to the limbo of savagery by a conventional historical view which is seldom questioned. Briefly, this view holds that the development of agriculture made it possible for people to abandon the nomadic and uncertain life of hunting and gathering, and that they gladly did so, becoming sedentary. Human well-being was improved and society was stabilized by increasing man's security from starvation, disease, poverty, uncertainty about the future, and the danger of wild animals, storms, and other natural forces. Because food-growing supported more people, the population rapidly increased. The agricultural revolution, it is said, made civilized institutions such as art and religion possible, framed ethic and moral principles, and forged relations among men based on compassion and respect for the rights of the individual.

The objection I raise to these statements is simple: they are not true. For every man whose life was improved by that momentous Neolithic revolution, hundreds lost health, freedom, and social dignity. Because a fortunate few controlled the recording of history, civilized culture became a propaganda machine for itself, which easily manipulated the resentments of peasants and, by redirecting their distorted lives, helped rationalize the genocide of hunter-gatherers on agriculture's enlarging frontier. It is a tragedy euphemistically called historical destiny, economic progress, or the inexorable surge of the political state. Yet, from the beginning, agriculture failed our species, and now, after fifty centuries with scarcely a word raised against its mythology of virtue and security, it is failing the modern world, failing to nourish it both physically and spiritually.

Important to our ecological reawakening is an understanding of the hunting-gathering people: first, as forebears who have constituted more than 99 per cent of all human time and all human lives; second, as people who still live today in remote parts of the world according to pre-agricultural traditions; and third, as profound aspects of ourselves.

On Being Well and Well Fed

The most authoritative estimates of the history of the human population show some increase in human numbers from forty thousand years ago until about five thousand years ago, then the fearful exponential curve whose thrust still rushes upward like a rocket. Because the start of this upswing coincided with the beginning of centralized agriculture, it has generally been supposed that it was the result of increased food production. The logic is that of the pig-breeder who assumes that the fruit of his sty will be limited only by the amount of corn he puts into it.

If this were true, then the quantity of food must have been the factor that limited the population of all pre-agricultural people. Yet the study of living hunter-gatherer societies shows that some of them have times of hunger but that starvation is uncommon; and that their environment can support more people than inhabit it. Of more than a score of such societies whose foods and nutrition have been studied, all use more than fifty kinds of plants and twenty kinds of animals. From such a broad base something is always available. The living hunters who are most vulnerable to starvation inhabit the most difficult environments, the Australian deserts and the Arctic North. They are certainly not typical of Pleistocene men. Even there, hunter-gatherers are vastly more secure and competent than one is led to believe from the hungry, hapless wanderers described in film and fiction. Desert aborigines consume a surprising variety of plants, and Eskimos, who seem to have nothing but blubber and snow, get salads from the gut of slain herbivores, such as the caribou. Of course, certain foods are preferred to others, and the least liked are used only when others are unavailable. Like all omnivores, such people can readily turn to alternatives as the season or other conditions affect availability.

Nor does the evidence from paleo-anthropology support the view that food was the bung in the barrel of human population growth before the dawn of agriculture. Had it been, fossil teeth and skeletons would show the deformities of starvation, and campsites would not be littered with the remains of marginal food plants and animals. Except for local vitamin deficiencies there is little evidence of deprivation or the kind of environmental pillaging seen among starving people today—consumption of leaves, leather, and each other.

Most populations of hunters were not and are not limited by food supply. Studies of living hunters not only refute starvation but reveal that food-getting requires a relatively modest investment of time and energy. By African Bushman standards, the "work" of a typical hunter requires no more than about three hours per day or three days per week. Hunter-gatherers show a lack of concern about finding food, since they seldom fail. They are characteristically neither anxious nor future-oriented. When these people were first encountered by Europeans this nonchalance was sometimes interpreted as defective lack of foresight and intelligence. Modern men could not at first comprehend that people could exist who did not worry about tomorrow unless there was something wrong with them.

That famine was uncommon—and often unknown during the lifetime of an individual—is consistent with the general principle of ecology relating size to population density and stability. In general, large animals are found in numbers below what is possible in terms of the food supplies; while smaller and shorter-lived forms occur in densities approaching whatever the productivity of the habitat will allow. Among many large herbivorous mammals, such as the deer, antelope, and rhinoceros, the available habitat is divided by them into territories, which are in turn related by courtship and mating behavior to reproduction in such a way that the number of young each year is related to the number of territories. Large predators, like wolves, lions, and tigers, are characteristically fewer in number than the potential of the environment without establishing defended territories. Their very low birth rates—or, more correctly, replacement rates—seem tuned to keeping each species rare rather than to "maximizing" its numbers. Some biologists believe that, while the quantity of food may not limit these larger species from year to year, the population size and replacement rates are set genetically by the worst food years that occur over a long time. Long-lived animals, whose behavior is guided by social learning and who require stable and dependable inter-individual relations, would be disastrously affected by sudden high death rates.

Modern man sees hunger and starvation as a stage on a scale of diminishing food supply, of which continuous satiation is the opposite extreme. Satiation is the ideal and norm for the herbivore or potato-eater, who must take in massive amounts of carbohydrate foods to get enough nourishment. Hunger, however, is a normal state for carnivores, who have empty stomachs most of the time. In spite of men's food habits, which are not entirely carnivorous, they behave demographically like carnivores. Insofar as man is a carnivore, he is healthier when he does not eat much. Medically, people who eat less—even who border on malnourishment—feel better, have less organic failure, and live longer.

The anomalous position of man in the ecological community is that, physiologically, from the neck down, so to speak, he is an omnivore whose diet is about three-quarters plant products, like a bear or boar. By looking only at his gut one might predict that he is a kind of oversized raccoon. Yet the patterns of life set by hunting-gathering peoples are centered on the eating of large mammals. Behavior and culture are more wolflike than bearlike. No other omnivore engages in the group hunting of large, dangerous prey.

On Birth Rates and Death Rates

The carnivore-like traits of hunter-gatherers carried over into population size and density: few and stable in number, unaffected for years at a time by weather, disease, predation, or other fluctuations in the environment. This means that in the past the number of humans was limited by the birth rate, not the death rate. Men did not—and living hunters do not—reproduce at their maximum possible rate or live in saturation densities. It is not clear how this was accomplished. In the life of constant tragedy and frequent death we imagine for them, it is easy to picture a rush to multiply, an anxiety to keep up with continuous losses. This fantasy is given a veneer of verisimilitude by the assumption that modern medicine has greatly extended human life. This also is not true. The capacity for longevity in man is not an accident but an expression of the realities of life during his evolution.

It is true that the death rate of infants among pre-industrial peoples is much higher than among our own, but figures on average length of life among hunters have been distorted because of infant deaths, giving a misleading typical life span of twenty-four to twenty-eight years. Actually the age-group composition of modern hunter-gatherers is much like our own. For those surviving the first three years, life expectation among hunters is about that of Americans today. Though death may have claimed 50 per cent of the infants, this did not much affect the continuity of individual associations composing the hunter group of about twenty-five, nor did it threaten a people shortage.

Today among all peoples there is a prenatal mortality rate of perhaps 75 per cent—that is, three-quarters of the embryos conceived die, most of them before the woman knows she is pregnant. This is a service to mankind, for incompatible gene combinations are thus removed. This important function of early mortality was, in the past, extended through the first years of postnatal life. The death of infants, though sorrowful, was far less so than the death of children or adults. Indeed, it is not easy in our present swarming numbers to realize the impact of an adult death on a group composed of about twelve adults. It has been observed by anthropologists that the tribal collapse of North and South American Indians was due less to the actual mortality caused by the white man's diseases than by the social deterioration following so large a loss.

A 50 per cent mortality rate among the newborn is a gift of life and health to the survivors. The modern medical reduction of that rate is an enormous alteration in human biology that we, as a species, may not be able to afford.

The birth rate in hunting-gathering societies is kept down by a variety of means, including contraception and induced abortion. Children are nursed by their mothers into their third year, and there is evidence that prolonged lactation inhibits ovulation, preventing further pregnancy. Social customs surrounding marriage do not exploit the human biological potential. The average age of marriage ranges from two to ten years beyond that of peasants. The total number of young born during a lifetime is smaller for most hunter-gatherer women than for their farmer counterparts. Infanticide is also practiced. In general there seems to be no great egotistic or familial pride in large families.

Recent studies show that the menstrual cycles of women working together tend to become synchronized. Apparently this is brought about by aerial-borne hormones, or pheremones. Such substances are not consciously detected but affect the physiology and behavior of those within smelling distance. If this were true among a group of the six or seven adult women of a hunting band, its consequences might have been far-reaching for birth limitation. It has been widely observed by anthropologists that menstruation was taken into account in both social, ceremonial, and practical life. A corollary is that the female cycle harmonized with the general round of life. If all the women ovulated about the same time, appropriately scheduled hunting forays away from camp or taboos or other deflections from copulation would have greatly reduced pregnancies. If such arrangements existed they would probably have come into being pragmatically rather than deliberately.

Studies of family size in modern societies also suggest a diminishing return of human quality in larger families. Large families seem to have a higher percentage of mental defectives, such as mongoloids. The first-born usually has the highest IQ throughout his life. If the mother is older (say, thirty instead of twenty), the IQ differential of the first-born is even greater over the second. Whether the reasons are genetic or environmental are not important here. Also, there is a higher probability of male children among early births, of female during later. (In a society with very small families where the mothers reproduce at an early age this would produce a preponderance of males, which would tend to reduce the reproductive rate of the group as a whole.)

Through successive pregnancies a woman accumulates increasing responsiveness against foreign tissue—that is, antibodies that attack the foetus. The probability of embryonic reabsorption or spontaneous abortion is therefore raised with each birth. This functions as a built-in device for limiting births—or, one might say, as a sign that the norm for the species is being exceeded. Thus small families appear to be superior in terms of quality of offspring and likelihood of survival, and probably reflect the species-specific state of the basic human family in a hunting-gathering ecology.

For all primates and all humans the tender loving care of children is normal, though in man its precise expression varies from culture to culture. In a farming civilization, the political state brought new pressures, a new sense of competition, and different motivations for parenthood. Farmers went for quantity. They wanted field hands, heirs, living evidence of paternal virility and maternal fertility, recruits for armies, replacements for losses into slavery, candidates for sacrifice, new bodies for the villages, and scions to honor and care for them in their old age. Such were the peculiar needs of tillers of the soil. Their culture gave this drive for more offspring its status and symbolic content in the formulation of a mythology that greatly emphasized fecundity. Rural societies have traditionally encouraged the desire for children and more children. They blessed big families and praised people who have a way with children, especially women whose lives were given exclusively to reproduction. The centuries have added military motives and sentimentality to this religious zeal, which has cloyed the reality of motherhood, paternity, sexuality, and morality with an emotional single-mindedness scarcely short of fanaticism.

Since the increase in human numbers from Paleolithic low densities was not the result of an increased food supply, the connection between the first farming and the burst of population probably lies in the alteration of the birth rate. An interesting parallel to this is found among certain macaque monkeys in Japan, who ordinarily live at population numbers well below the carrying capacity of the available food and space to support them. When additional food is added by men, their numbers increase. Apparently their reproductive behavior is altered in subtle ways that result in more macaques. For man, an increased carrying capacity of the land due to tillage was not the causal factor if the population was not already pressing food resources. Instead a dramatic cultural change must have altered society's regulation of its own generation; or, to put it from the standpoint of the hunters, the ancient ways, with their customs and norms of behavior, were shattered. The human species moved closer to realizing its innate capacity to increase, its biological breeding potential prompted by an enlarged plant-eater's psyche.

To Be Few Is to Be Wealthy

No one thinks of a herd of bears, a drove of tigers, or a flock of eagles. Our image of these animals is as individuals, as part of a singular grandeur, whose uniqueness of powers and spirit would be degraded by their gathering in crowds.

This is not simply a romantic notion. Solitary and small-group species are different from group animals. In addition to freedom from death by starvation, very different spatial relationships, self-regulation of numbers, low mortality rates, and population stability, large predators are free from epidemic disease. Men living sparsely are also less vulnerable to widespread contagious diseases. Many disease organisms simply cannot exist where the hosts are in such low numbers that transmission is impeded for months or years. Unable to endure the long wait between victims, or in larval stage in an intermediate host, they bear no acute epidemic threat. Their spread and virulence depend on ready transfer by host-to-host contact and on their ability to produce many generations in a short time—a vast proliferation that gives rise to new genetic strains.

This does not mean that species with small numbers are entirely free from internal infection. All get parasites from their food. All are subject to some communicable diseases. But it does mean that hunters have fewer parasites that might weaken and kill them or limit their populations. Low levels of communicable diseases and parasitic worms are indicated from the study of human fossil feces and from studies of living hunters. It appears that many of the diseases of modern man may not have existed for pre-agricultural people, and the number of human diseases has increased with world population. Disease organisms are associated with high human density not only because of the increased ease of transmission and contagion, as in measles and smallpox; but also because habitats have consequently been altered, favoring certain types of pathogens (disease-producing organisms), such as the cholera microbe, which flourishes in sewage-polluted water, or the malaria germ, transmitted by the mosquito. Malaria, which has probably killed more people than any other single cause, and many other infectious diseases are the heritage of agriculture. The early hunters had natural countermeasures to disease already present in their environment, in their bodies, and among the many herbs and other medicinal organisms known to them. The two factors in this were low population and the complexity of the ecosystem. The two tend to occur together since men deviating from hunting-gathering homogenize their surroundings as well as increase their numbers.

In view of this, is it possible for modern drug-diseased man to get closer to the hunter's situation without sacrificing what is valuable in modern pharmacology? The answer is yes, by retaining more of the natural environment. The richer the natural environment in kinds of plants and animals, the greater its chemical and microbial diversity. It may seem at first more rather than less dangerous for people to live in habitats enriched in germs, and of course this luxuriance does increase the number of kinds of potential disease organisms. But this is more than offset by the controls that organisms impose on one another, with the result that the diversified natural community offers greater stability and health to all its populations.

If the evolution of the human mind took place in a world of human sparcity and small group life, it follows that the human mind malfunctions in areas of high density. The point is controversial because of man's adaptability and his inability to recognize social pathology; he has little with which to compare the conditions of his life except other distorted communities. Superficial studies have been made by crowding people into a room and giving them tests, which show that they are not affected, but mental disease takes many months to appear.

As in much of human biology, the real tests take many generations, require a control group, and so endanger human life that they cannot be done experimentally. Studies on other animals reveal that where groups of rabbits or rats are squeezed together the individuals begin to develop behavioral symptoms related to tissue changes in their nervous and endoctrine systems. These include failure of maternal behavior, increased homosexuality, and widespread social withdrawal to the point at which individuals become pathologically isolated. In such a "behavioral sink" there is an odd tendency for exaggerated clumping, for animals that normally move about during the daily course to sit in one place.

No one is quicker to admit that humans are not rabbits or rats than the people conducting these studies. But the parallels to human behavior in areas of population concentration are too conspicuous to be overlooked. Scientists are increasingly able to identify individual neurosis and social breakdown in animal groups, and their relationship to altered spatial distribution. The cat, for example, is an unusual mixture of a solitary carnivore-hunter with modified territorial boundaries during the daytime and an intensely rank-ordered social being during the night. When cats known to one another are artificially crowded but are provided with all their other material needs, the system collapses into a snarling tangle of tyrants and doormats.

Since human physiology and behavior are much more like those of other primates than of other animals, the recent lessons learned from primate studies are instructive. By the end of 1972 more than twenty species of non-human primates, mostly monkeys and apes, had been studied in their natural habitat. Ten of the same species had also been studied in zoos or other confinement. In every case the wild forms were described as generally peaceful and affectionate, sensitive to friendly, cooperative relationships, each kind with its own way of avoiding harmful physical conflict. In no species was the top-ranking individual in a group dictatorial. In all cases, where the same species were studied under crowded conditions (with plenty of food and water), their social organization as well as their immunity to disease deteriorated. Maltreatment of young and violent attacks on doormats by tyrants increased as much as ten or twenty times over normal.

Insofar as he is a carnivore, man's sensitivity to density may be even greater, and there is evidence that social breakdown, followed by violence and murder, is related to this. Recent studies by sociologists in Chicago were set up, with the variables of social class and ethnic group controlled, to ascertain the effects of the single variable of density on the birth rate, death rate, juvenile delinquency, and mental disease. There were shown to be positive correlations, not simply in numbers of people per acre but in terms of the way in which space was subdivided. The number of persons per room was found to be more important than rooms per housing unit or housing units per acre.

There is nothing romantic or even figurative about space requirements. They are real, and overcrowding may menace human health long before its other effects are evident. They are innate and have little to do with cultural expectations or the kind of interpersonal distances that individuals establish between each other during conversation or other social interaction. The mental health problems related to space should not be interpreted simply as an argument against cities but as a criticism of the way in which urban and non-urban space are organized.

As the industrial states send medical missions to pre-agricultural people, the latter are perceived through the window of recorded history: threat of plagues and pestilence, the memory of horrible epidemics, a recent past full of suffering, sickness, and violent death. Part of the problem is surely the failure to distinguish between primitive pre-peasants, like the Papuan inhabitants of New Guinea, who suffer much of the debility of the agricultural revolution, and true hunter-gatherers—Pygmies, Bushmen, and certain other African tribes, Fuegians, particular groups of the upper Amazon and eastern Brazil, a few American Indians, Eskimos, the Borneo Punan, small groups in Siberia, India, and southeastern Asia, and Australian aborigines. These groups, except for those at the mind-breaking fringes of the human habitat in equatorial wet forests (without adequate large mammals to hunt), are among the world's most isolated people, and yet they are humane, generous, and hospitable. They suffer little from mutual aggression or from unredirected aggressive instincts resulting in "manager diseases" like renal atrophy, high blood pressure, and gastric ulcer.

On Species Rarity and Individuality

It has generally been claimed that modern Western religion or political democracy discovered the importance of the individual. More exactly, this was the pseudo-discovery by consciousness, for evolution defined this long ago. The primate order, to which man belongs, has carved out a way of life based on the intense interaction of individuals. The large carnivorous mammals the world over also live in such a personal cosmos, having the capacity to function in isolation and as group members. Human ecology emerged with the addition of the knife edge of carnivore cunning to the elegant foundation of primate sociality.

To belong to a species whose members are few and unique is a relative not an absolute good. Personal individuality is useful only until synchronized activities are necessary—cooperation, mutual defense, reproduction. Beyond that eccentricity isolates and non-breeds itself into a genetic dead-end. Most animals have small margin for individuality. In the courtship of ducks, for example, the sequence of signals and responses is very precise. Deviations breaking the chain upset the whole procedure. Idiosyncratic ducks would simply disengage themselves from the flow of generations, wasting the energy the species invested in them. Species with large populations endure in spite of iconoclasts; a sparce species composed of prima donnas would die of eccentricitis.

The larger carnivores and primates, and man in particular, have circumvented this limitation on individuality by their capacity for learning. Among them, learned behavior is an adaptation for imitation and conventionalizing. The capacity to learn and remember similar patterns of behavior evolved with increased genetic diversity, which otherwise would have been destructive. Strong cultural standards were necessary to guide what was learned, in order to protect the species from the disrupting effects of individual variation.

The relative amount and effect of individual variation depend on the size of the population. As man's ancestors evolved from a tropical brush ape toward a steppe carnivore, their numbers per unit area probably diminished and were broken into smaller and more isolated sub-units. Such a pattern was ideal for rapid evolution of larger brains, making increased learning possible, which in turn allowed for the retention of high genetic diversity, or polymorphism. The evolution of the capacity for culture was not, therefore, a biological means toward the idiosyncrasy of belief and behavior but toward overall difference. Human individuality and rarity were achieved because essential social activities could be coordinated in small groups of very different persons through a common system of beliefs and values.

Several leading philosophers of human evolution have contended that the peculiar human approach constituted a major breakthrough in the history of life, and they see man as heralding new modes of existence as revolutionary as the first invasion of land by aquatic amphibians. Caution is needed, since man is not the end of all evolutionary change, but only the terminus of one small branch, contemporary with and not descended from all other living species. Since complex behavior, nervous systems, and learning are widespread zoologically, one might ask, in the light of the alleged importance of man's advance: What are the ducks, zebras, pandas, and so on waiting for? Are we to assume that they are rushing toward expanded individuality and consciousness as fast as the evolutionary machinery allows?

More humility is needed in our perspective. The combination of species rarity and individuality based on a highly specialized life cycle and exceedingly complex brain is new and dangerous, and may not succeed; indeed its extinction is already threatening. Most kinds of animals are probably already as intelligent as it is possible to be in their particular niches; further refinement would simply diminish their survival rates. It is both erroneous and wrong philosophically, I think, to assume that all creatures want to be men or that human consciousness is the cosmic pass toward and through which all life must make its way.

The idea that learned behavior is an adaptation that makes us seem more alike while our genes become more different is the reverse of the usual view, which is that our biological natures are like great identical stones all cut from the same quarry, and that the seemingly enormous range of human and cultural differences is the result of flexibility or plasticity. In part this error was due to the poverty of primate studies and in part to our ignorance of learned behavior as a means of unifying behavior.

When human population dynamics broke down with the subversion of hunting and gathering, the latent genetic diversity previously hidden or controlled by tight social conformity was released. Just as the "goofies" poured out when the domestication of animals broke the balanced genetic systems of their wild progenitors, a thousand "goofy" ideologies have been exploding since agriculture shattered the life ways of the hunting clan.

Written history of the last two centuries has put its emphasis on personality, on those heroic leaders of the state who champion the departure from tradition by coupling political power to idiosyncrasy, and on creative genius as sources of culture. Yet the traditional (learned) behavior of higher animals and the study of pre-farming cultures indicate that most change is destructive. The fundamental characteristic of a culture, which is a biological adaptation, is the conservation of persistent styles and themes, which its members accept and support, however brilliant they may be individually.

Perhaps, as the philosophy of history becomes more deeply affected by anthropology, modern history will itself be the best evidence against the idealizing of social change. The world population is now more than five hundred times what it was during the late Paleolithic. In this perspective it is evident that the political form of the state is less important in human freedom than the inexorable effects of population size.

On Population Density

Large human populations tend to degrade the environment, both as a source of food and as a medium of biological richness. Complex brains are an adaptation to biological richness and therefore require interesting surroundings. Over-high densities affect men directly and through the environment. Apes in zoos and men in dungeons develop symptoms of mental and social deterioration: seething dominance hierarchies, withdrawal, sexual perversion, hostility, intolerance, and group psychopathology in the tormenting and ostracism of selected scapegoats. Below a certain point of crowding the cause of this breakdown is not density as such. So many people per square mile is an abstraction, since people have never been randomly dispersed. Men always live close, in intimate groups, whose size is deeply ingrained as a species characteristic.

In our species there appear to be two basic levels of clustering: the single group or band, and a geographic network of such bands, the tribe. Studies of living hunters throughout the world and of paleo-anthropological evidence from the Pleistocene show a consistent, universal size average for the living unit of about twenty-five. Tribes range from a few hundred to fifteen hundred but many are around five hundred. These two cluster sizes are so widespread that they probably represent basic human biology, group equilibrium systems that are psychologically satisfactory, settled upon during thousands of years of adaptation to the hunting-gathering life.

Among such people as the remote Venezuelan and Brazilian Indians, this band-tribe pattern of life was, and still is, the basis of a highly adaptive genetic system, preserving heritable variation within the species and fostering micro-evolutionary differentiation—that is, differences between local groups that are passed on by genetic inheritance. Its biological wisdom is expressed in the way in which it helps to limit population and stem communicable disease.

For such groups the rate of evolutionary change and adaptation can be a hundred times greater than that of a larger population. Obviously the present expansion and amalgamation of world populations deprives our species of this small-group evolutionary advantage, an advantage that may be important to future survival if any kind of worldwide catastrophe lies ahead, manmade or otherwise.

Another advantage of the band-tribe arrangement is the individual's personal acquaintance with all other members. This trait—widespread among all mammal groupings—is especially important in the lives of all higher primates.

How and why did such group sizes begin, and how were they related to hunting? Perhaps twenty-five was the largest number of people who could be regularly fed from a single bison, horse, or reindeer. A life unit of this size may have provided just enough adult males (about six) to stalk and kill a woolly mammoth and keep the carcass from hyenas or other fierce scavengers, while some individuals rested or butchered or assisted in transporting the kill. It may also have been the minimal number to fill the major social roles.

It has been called the "twelve-adult group," and it has been recognized not only by anthropologists but by mammalogists as typical of large primates and some other large mammals. Perhaps a larger group would tend to fragment or to develop conflicting cliques, while a smaller group would be less efficient in the storage and use of important traditional information.

This size may also have been adapted to the patterns of camp establishment, sanitation, and mobility—that is, an appropriate number of people for the size of the region to be hunted and gathered over from a base camp. Such an area might have been expected to support two dozen people for a certain number of days or weeks—the residence period, which was important for the social-cultural activities or for the proper development of the young. More simply, the band may have been the optimum number of people able to occupy comfortably a cave or ledge shelter.

The size of the tribe also remained stable because it fitted the needs of the bands. The tribe was sufficiently large to prevent deleterious inbreeding, as long as it had peaceful connections with other tribes, and yet it was sufficiently isolated to foster its own uniqueness and adaptation. By exogamous marriage the bands within the tribe maintained family and kin connections. The tribe stabilized occasional band disasters by providing a haven or replacements; in addition, the larger related cluster of bands yielded a regular increment of individuals with special talent and leadership qualities or occasionally produced an unusually wise old person whose genius would benefit the whole tribe.

In view of the highly dispersed small-group geography of hunter-gatherers, the whole tribe might occupy between five thousand and fifteen thousand square miles, an area defined by such terrain features as the basin of a watershed, a uniform geological or vegetational region, or combinations of parts of such major features. This contains band home ranges, and in this area the particular details are landmarks which, through systems of ceremony and myth, become part of the identity of the people.

If the human group size best for mental and physical health is about twenty-five, how do people survive in cities? The answer, in part, is that one function of this group size in shaping human behavior is in terms of familiarity. In spite of the actual number of people, each person strives to participate in a small group, and his circle of relatives and friends forms an abstract band totaling about the magic number. In the city perceptual screening devices enable the person to limit his contacts. This may account for the mechanical behavior of those in public jobs or the attitude of inhumanity or non-involvement by people on the street with those in distress.

Among hunters and gatherers the band is a mix of ages, sexes, familial relationship, and personalities. In effect the group is given, not chosen, and each member must make adjustments to the wide range of difference in human personality and potential.

Ancestors of the Hunting Heart

Most of the basic traits of our species are not "originals" but have come into existence at different times in the history of the primate order. Thus we share visual traits with all who have descended from ancient monkeys, and a shoulder girdle with those descended from now-extinct apes. The characteristics of the family Hominidae have been traced from the late Miocene or early Pliocene periods, about fifteen million years ago.

Hominid Forebears

There was then worldwide geological and climatic change that favored mammals in general and apes in particular. More than fifty species of a fossil group called dryopithecines are known, which include the ancestors of modern African apes as well as man. The most numerous of the fossils belong to the genus *Proconsul,* monkeylike "semi-terrestrial" apes weighing about forty pounds, some species of which apparently roamed the parklands in small omnivorous bands. Certain features of the jaw discourage the conclusion that they are in the human line, although their rather generalized anatomy suggests an approximation of the appearance of man's first terrestrial grandfather.

Another sub-group of the dryopithecines is distinctly

more apelike. Of these, some, specializing in fruit-eating, were antecedent to chimpanzees; others, subsisting on forest foliage, may have fathered the gorillas. A third group is known primarily from a few jaws and teeth as *Ramapithecus*. The curved pattern of lower jaw teeth, tooth eruption sequence, small canines, and palate have qualified it as the earliest known ancestor of man. Its remains have been dated at fourteen million years of age. In that period it lived in warm savannas and prowled open oak countryside in search of plant foods, bird eggs, small animals, the fresh victims of accident or predator, helpless young, and the disabled and diseased animal cripples.

Large canine teeth are common among apes and terrestrial monkeys; there has been widespread speculation as to how and when the large canines of human ancestors were lost (or never existed) and why. It is possible that the proto-human line may have completely bypassed large canines and massive jaws. But even so, the question remains: in what ways are huge canine teeth beneficial to apes, and, if beneficial, how did pre-men manage without them?

Several answers have been proposed. One is that the use of these daggerlike teeth for defense against dangerous predators, such as tigers, was outmoded by the use of rocks or bones as tools. This theory carried more weight when *Ramapithecus* was unknown and the "loss" of canine teeth could be correlated in later pre-human forms with the manufacture of weapons.

Another answer is based on the observation that these canines are used more frequently for display than for slashing dangerous predators. The canine teeth of male baboons are much bigger than those of females, and male baboons compete more intensely with one another than do females. In several species there is a male "yawn" threat display that is both challenge and bluff. The bigger the teeth, the more "battles" are won without fighting.

When the progenitors of men began to hunt large game, cooperation became more important to success than competition. Teeth were less effective than sticks, bones, or stones as weapons against game. Clubs could be put away, but teeth were a persistent threat, inadvertently endangering the peace and cohesion of society—as carrying loaded guns does today. As the pre-human psyche increased in aggressiveness, hand-in-hand with carnivorousness, a minor conflict or irritation might cause wounding of the old or young, endanger the pair-bond of mates, or the fraternal bond of the hunters, or accidentally undermine a friendly, established status relationship.

Still another theory is derived from correspondences between teeth and food habits. *Ramapithecus,* with grinding molar teeth, may have been essentially granivorous; he scrounged the grassy fields, munching corms, culms, stems, and seeds. Corms are bulbs and culms are grass stems, which may have been gritty from soil or contained abrasive silicates. It looks therefore as though one of man's early ancestors went through a root-grubbing, cereal-crunching, stem-biting phase in which large canines were a disadvantage.

Grain-eating would have been as important an ecological episode in the food habits of hominids (the various species of man) as the later development of meat-eating. It would not only account for hominid tooth patterns but would have enlarged the habitat of the ramapithecines into prairies and plains. Here natural selection would have improved their bipedal ability. Seeds provided new concentrated energy sources as they came into the proximity of the hoofed animals and baboons, the smaller of which would become the first deliberately stalked prey.

Ramapithecus is a stage of pre-human life between forest-edge fruit-eating apes and open-country proto-human predators. Its remains have been found in Asia, Africa, and Europe, and this wide distribution indicates a successful, adaptable animal. When more is known about its anatomy, it seems likely that intermediate or transitional features other than the small canine teeth may be accorded to these late Miocene hominids.

In view of widespread tool use among animals, especially higher primates, *Ramapithecus* was very likely a tool user. It was probably larger than its ancestor apes, and slightly slower maturing and longer-lived; it was a shorter-armed, longer-legged "Oak Ape" who commonly carried young, tools, or food. It would be a mistake to project upon *Ramapithecus* much detail without more evidence. Earlier, contemporary, and later open-country, granivorous primates are also known.

Evolutionary thought has been hampered in the past by the belief that no specialized primates could have given rise to man. Earlier in this century no hominid remains were considered general enough to have been "in the main line," so that for a while all the paleontological specimens down to Neanderthal man were regarded as "a side branch" of the family tree. The mysterious originals were always missing. The illusion of a pure generalized form has finally been given up. It originated largely from the idea that an apelike jaw was too specialized to be reduced by evolution, and ancestral forms were considered to have been vague, undeveloped creatures, incomplete, waiting to become men. They were referred to as "savanna waifs" who were "kicked out" of the forest because they were so helpless, delicate, and defenseless against animals and storms, who had to invent culture and civilization in order to survive.

It is time to bury the nonsense of the "incomplete animal." As Julian Huxley, the eminent British biologist, once observed concerning human toughness, man is the only creature that can walk twenty miles, run two miles, swim a river, and then climb a tree. Physiologically, he has one of the toughest bodies known; no other species could survive weeks of exposure on the open sea, or in deserts, or the Arctic. Man's superior exploits are not evidence of cultural inventions: clothing on a giraffe will not allow it to survive in Antarctica, and neither shade nor shoes will help a salamander in the Sahara. I am not speaking of living in those places permanently, but simply as a measure of the durability of men under stress. Several evolutionary developments have made this possible: highly specialized skin, central nervous system, and self-regulatory physiological systems. Man's ancestors were neither helpless nor incomplete.

In our family, the Hominidae, there are three genera, *Homo* (living men) and two extinct ancestral forebears. The oldest genus in our family line is *Ramapithecus*. Between *Ramapithecus* and *Homo* lies a span of perhaps ten million years, occupied in part by an intermediate genus, *Australopithecus*. Our pedigree, as it is now understood, although a continuous line of descent, is arbitrarily subdivided into these three genera.

There were undoubtedly several species in the genus of our distant ancestor *Ramapithecus*. *Ramapithecus brevirostris* is the species most likely to have been the progenitor of the earliest *Australopithecus,* which in turn also developed more than one species.

One of these, *Australopithecus africanus,* is regarded as the probable antecedent of the human line. Leakey considers the earliest species of our genus to have been *Homo habilis,* which, as might be expected, is intermediate in bony structure between *Australopithecus* and the second human, *Homo erectus.* Thus, by way of *erectus,* do we come to *Homo sapiens,* the three-hundred-thousand-year-old species to which all living men belong.

The physical characteristics and ways of life of each of the five species in the three genera have become increasingly known from accumulating fossil evidence. Each went through a period of evolutionary transformation, at the start of which it resembled its immediate ancestral species and at the end of which it graded into its descendant species. Each added to and subtracted from a pool of genes that has continued through time.

In the course of these transformations our line has increased in body size; improved its bipedality and running; graduated through seed-gathering, scavenging, small-animal killing, to the pursuit of large mammals; increased the brain size; elaborated tools—including the use of fire; developed language, shelters, clothing, and made other changes in human ecology. In retrospect it is easy to look back on this sequence as though it were inevitable, and, by projecting it forward in time, to see a future for man already written in the stars. Perhaps the paleontological perspective is especially seductive, for it has certainly led such eminent savants as the French philosopher Teilhard de Chardin to see life as a stage on which man plays the lead, in a drama moving inexorably toward a denouement in which angelhood is recovered for the species. We misperceive our branch of the tree of life as the main trunk. Even the extinct hominids—other genera and species of dryopithecines besides *Ramapithecus brevirostris,* other australopithecines besides *Australopithecus africanus*—were far from inconsequential failures; they existed for a long time, contributed in unknown ways to the enrichment of the planet and the evolution of life, and proceeded to the inevitable end of all species.

The significance of being shaped during this almost inconceivable length of biological time is that it implies a degree of inherent biological control over our lives which we are accustomed by our culture to reject. The idea of "biological determinism" has been so persistently denied that we have nearly crippled our appreciation of the organic factor in our lives. By identifying culture as the opposite of instinct we are in danger of putting the idea of culture at the center of a fantasy world.

Inherited Behavior Patterns

Because of the past, the norms of the modern human organism, at every level of being, reflect the conditions of life during its evolution. Although we are each whole individuals, each basic element of our being has its own origin. The present shoulder and arm complex is older than the hip and leg structure. Man was a runner after he was a swinger. (This does not mean, however, that the shoulder girdle was not affected by the later evolution.) Chimpanzees throw rocks with an overhand motion, as do human females. In human males the throwing musculature and behavior were modified and specialized during Pleistocene hunting. Not all boys and men throw equally well, or better than all girls and women. Learning, custom, the conditions of time, place, and experience do modify and sometimes magnify differences already inherent in individuals. But this does not disprove the genetic and evolutionary origin; it only illustrates what is gradually being accepted of all innate behavior: much variation is built-in and determined by genes, but these genes require a facilitating environment for their proper expression.

Our origins would have been merely of academic interest if it were not that all behavior patterns—running, throwing, the two-dozen grouping—are more than dim reflections of out-moded customs from the ice ages, trivial souvenirs from the youth of our species. They are expressions of our physiological and psychological structures, continuous with muscles, glands, and the brain, imperatives for normal health.

Many of these do not have to be exercised in order for us to survive. Boys may be prohibited from throwing; people can live in solitary cells. Nonetheless, optimal human health demands the use of these muscles and glands in functional equivalents of the environments in which our primate forebears and the human organism evolved. Failure to find or provide the environment does not end human life but introduces stresses that injure individuals. A good example of this is vascular failure. Hypertension, thrombosis, and arteriosclerosis are symptoms of the malfunction of a system that is not properly used.

Statistics show that modern, sedentary men suffer twice as many heart attacks as active men, with four times as deadly an effect. Men who are 15 per cent overweight are twice as likely to be victims, and men are five times more vulnerable than women. The human cardiovascular system evolved as part of the physiology of hunters, who regularly ran for their lives. The title of Laurens van der Post's book on Kalahari Bushmen, *Heart of the Hunter,* is not simply metaphorical. Men ran after and ate horses more or less consistently for some four hundred thousand years. The outcome of this is more than a love of horseflesh; it is a runner's body.

This does not mean constant activity. The hunter is less compulsive than the peasant about work. A typical Bushman hunter "works" two or three days a week, during which his total running time is not more than a few hours. The incidence of thrombosis among this group is extremely low. The implication is clear: an hour or so a week of jogging plus occasional sprints is the normal exercise for every male individual.

Forty years ago an American physician, George Crile, traveled around the world studying the relationship of certain organs of large mammals to their habits. Shooting and dissecting giraffes, lions, camels, musk oxen, and many others, Crile and his assistants examined and weighed the heart and vascular systems, brains, thyroids, and adrenals. Trying to prove a theory concerning the role of oxygen in metabolism (which has since been discredited), he accumulated more data on these organ systems than all previous studies together. Crile recognized a relationship between the relative sizes of the organs and the animal's energy expenditure. These differences were related to the animals' ecology. For example, most of the cats (lions, tigers, leopards) hunt by a combination of stealth and short, high-speed charges, seldom farther than a few hundred yards, while the canids (wolves, coyotes, wild dogs) hunt by relentless pursuit over long distances. Crile observed that man's circulatory and endocrinal systems were like those of the dogs, indicating that he had evolved as a hunter by endurance and strategy rather than fleetness and surprise.

Man is a distance runner as a consequence of hundreds of thousands of years of chasing antelopes, horses, elephants, wild cattle, and deer. Everywhere in the world men are still running in sports and games. The Tarahumare Indians of northern Mexico traditionally ran down wild deer until recently; now they play a grand-scale form of soccer covering many miles and lasting for several days. When men do not run they are likely to die prematurely from dysfunctions of the heart and vascular systems, or to suffer disabling chronic illness from stress diseases associated with the adrenals. After half a century of treating heart and circulatory problems with diet and medication, the medical profession, with the endorsement of major life insurance companies, has at last begun to acknowledge that men must run to live. They have abandoned "regular moderate exercise" such as golf and tennis and now recommend "stressing the system" and "system overload." Calisthenics is inadequate by itself. One wonders how many middle-aged men have died from stroke or heart failure, mistakenly thinking that "getting outdoors"—walking, hunting, fishing, golfing—would keep them in normal good health.

Almost all weight-control programs for normal people attempt to counteract the effect of lack of appropriate exercise on the assumption that diet alone will mitigate the disabling effects of a life without rigor. Associated with such a degenerate daily regimen are vascular and heart disease, joint and skeletal problems, neuro-physiological, psychological, skin and other organ-system deterioration. Good nutrition is useless without adequate activity.

For our species, evolution suggests three important activity sequences to offset premature aging and the pathological effects of our over-anxious and underactive culture. No machines, belts, or calisthenics are necessary, though stretching and bending are important for women. The three sequences utilize sets of muscles associated with the origin of human physique. The first is swimming, the second hanging and swinging, the third running.

All must be undertaken at stress levels, to overload physical systems temporarily. A typical daily regimen for modern man would be as follows: swim steadily for five minutes, rest; hang head down and swing from ropes or bars by the hands for five minutes, rest; run for ten minutes. Women should modify this plan by reducing the running to five minutes, preceded by five minutes of stretching or dance. By exercising at maximum capacity the individual can gradually increase his performance up to a plateau, which becomes an individual standard.

This program stresses vertebral segmentation and muscle complexes whose origins are associated with fish, primate, and hunter-gatherer. It should be begun during adolescence and continued daily throughout life. Modern adults entering it from sedentary backgrounds will suffer, but will improve slowly, depending on their age. No one is too old or too soft to begin unless he has a congenital defect or degenerative disease which has progressed to the point where intense activity endangers his life.

In a commercial society everything that people do and need is exploited for profit. In the late 1960s jogging became fashionable in the United States. But it will survive fashion and fad simply because those who run will be healthier and live longer.

Species that travel long distances have metabolic systems based on generous energy storage, primarily as fat. The best-known examples are birds, whose weight may increase as much as 30 per cent prior to migration. Mammalian carnivores glut themselves after a kill because they may not eat again for several days. Large predators gorge when the chance arises, sometimes twice on the same kill. Like long-distance migrants, they have efficient means of storing energy as fat. Normally they do not continue to store beyond a certain point, partly because of a tightly regulated metabolism and habits established in wild conditions, partly because there is no more to eat, and partly because in the interval between meals they will run it off. In zoos their lives are often shortened by overfeeding. There is increasing evidence that, short of malnutrition, underfeeding, which would be recognized by occasional hunger or even brief periods of intense hunger, is far more healthy for man than overfeeding.

Whether our primate and carnivore habits threaten or help us depends on how we use them. The apes and monkeys are incurable nibblers and snackers. They live salad lives. Apes have been seen munching fruit before getting out of their nests in the morning and before going to sleep at night. Foods low in protein and fat require high-volume processing. That is why hoofed animals and gorillas are large bellied; they need voluminous storage space and very long guts. The mechanics and chemistry of digesting plant foods are slower and more complicated than digestion of meat; not only are most plants lower in food value than meat, but tougher.

Man is a fat-making, fair-weather carnivore who can eat

more than three pounds of meat at a sitting. He is also a primate snacker, a connoisseur of ripe and unripe berries. He has the best of two worlds—until he begins to confuse them. Then he not only fails to draw down the stored fat but begins to switch his snacking to fatty foods. Without heavy exercise some of the fatty substances are eventually deposited inside major arteries, more or less irreversibly. Tropical primate fruit-eaters pick and choose, then discard half-eaten morsels. But men "wolf" their food, gorging not once a week but, after their vegetarian instinct, several times a day, becoming gluttonous snackers.

Since the body can convert any kind of food into fat, the problem is not simply too much meat, eggs, and other direct sources of animal fat. Diet alone (or "weight control") cannot prevent the ensuing syndrome of breakdown and failure, though the latter may be delayed long enough so that the individual dies from other causes. Even when not overweight, the non-running gluttonous snacker undergoes deterioration of muscles, joints, bones, lungs, body metabolites, coordination, disease resistance, and psychological function. Cause and effect are often connected through intricate, sometimes obscure psychosomatic chains.

There is still another complicating factor in human food habits. Before men became eaters of flesh on a large scale, but after their ancestors had moved out of the heavy woodlands and the savannas intermediate between trees and dry grasslands, their attention turned to nuts, grasses, and tubers—plant-storage organs high in fats. Their use may have been a necessary stage between chimplike fruit-nibbling or gorillalike stem-and-leaf-munching and eventual meat-eating. Man and his ancestors have long used these high-energy foods. Potatoes, cashews, and corn are good for the runner but dangerous for a non-hunting (non-running) individual who likes to eat between meals.

Patterns for women set in the evolutionary past are different from those set for men. Women, who have not run after large game, have fat-storage systems that do not overload their vascular organs and contribute to heart failure. The rhythm and physiology of their life are so different from those of men that it is almost as though they were another species.

Evolution of Sexual Dimorphism

The gender differences, or sexual dimorphism, of humans, as among all organisms, are a compromise between opposing selective forces. In general, among animals where social roles are strongly differentiated, so are musculature and appearance. Roles are related to habitat. Among the monkeys both sexes of most tree-living forms are very similar in appearance, and social behavior, while terrestrial monkeys and apes are much more dissimilar in these respects. Male gorillas and chimpanzees are more than 100 per cent heavier than the females. Within a single species of baboon, which is found from forest-edge habitats to barren country, there is more dimorphism among those living farthest from the trees, and more pronounced dominance of the males over the females. Strong dimorphism is associated with intense male hierarchies and extended pairing. The more intensive the rank-order system, the more open the terrain, the more aggressive the males and submissive the females, the greater is the physical difference between the sexes.

If the differences between human sexes are compared to those seen in the range of primates, some educated guesses can be made about the habitat, social organization, and role differentiation during the long period of Pleistocene hunting-gathering. As man-the-hunter emerged from his hairy forefathers, he retained face and chest hair patterns, which emphasized sexual difference. Beards, like manes in lions, intensify dissimilarity and trigger spontaneous feelings of awe, submission, and intimidation. Modern races of men who have lost the beard-growing ability, such as Polynesians or American Indians, commonly substitute tattooing, ornaments, or cosmetics.

The differences in role that are signified by external appearances are mainly those connected with food-getting. In the early dawn of our genus, or of its australopithecine precursors, there may have been no home base to which groups returned at night, and the prey was small- to medium-sized animals eaten on the spot. If so, the group moved and stopped as a whole, and the foraging for tubers and nuts as well as the killing of porcupines and antelope calves was participated in by all. But among *Homo erectus* and *Homo sapiens* the men departed from a base camp or a field camp, hunted large, dangerous mammals, sometimes for many days, and returned with meat. The very young and old probably remained behind. Women and children foraged during the men's absence.

Not only did this affect the kind of natural selection for physical traits, but new pair-bond mating patterns came into existence, stabilizing couples during their separation. Copulation intensified by orgasm and preceded by erotic play, emphasizing female postures and anatomy, became an intrinsic part of a pattern of life whose rhythms were dictated by the coming and going of the hunters.

The dramatic specialization of non-reproductive sexuality by the hunter-gatherers seemed to demand not only increased dimorphism and incitement signals, but culturally defined gender exaggeration. Our species developed the instinct for cryptandic cosmetics—that is, the universal penchant for self-decoration, for coiffures, body rouge and paint, jewelry, clothing, and other means of grooming—to enhance sexual traits. The advantage of these devices over extreme anatomical divergence is that they can be temporarily employed (for the return of the hunters) and, perhaps more important, local groups could develop unique cryptandic fashions or skills which lent themselves to the many fine social distinctions of totemic clan differentiation.

For a million years under conditions of the hunt women lived—and because of their biology still live—geographically more circumscribed lives than men. They have a poorer sense of large-scale spatial relationships and direction and are not good throwers or runners. They probably have superior social intelligence and inferior strategic cunning than men. These differences are genetically controlled and are part of the personality of all living women, taken as a group. Women are less subject to heart attack than men because of the way in which female hormones regulate fat deposit in the circulatory system and elsewhere. Their body fat deposits differ in location and somewhat in function. Even the psychological differences between men and women were shaped originally by the conditions of life in a hunting-gathering society.

It is perhaps not accidental that there is a large proportion of women among the students of wild apes. Examples are Jane Van Lawick-Goodall with chimpanzees, Dian Fossey with mountain gorillas, and the women whose part in husband-wife teams has been significant. Women in some measure share with the apes a pre-hunting perception and psychology, even a musculature, from which men are excluded: a world of frugivorousness and pensiveness, at once more intensely social and more tranquil than that to which man's symbolic carnivorousness led. Perhaps these similarities evoke an empathy which gives women an insight into and an advantage in studying, even joining, ape groups.

In a time of increasing confusion over gender differences, the evolutionary past provides a meaningful perspective. Admittedly the line between specialization of role and arbitrary social oppression as seen today is not easy to determine. But to distinguish between what is genetically given and what is cultural bias it is necessary to consider dimorphism in its psychological as well as social and biological aspects. The reality of innate temperamental as well as bodily differences does not justify just any social-status distinctions. Male chauvinism based on evolutionary determinism is reprehensible. But it is futile to pronounce, at the end of fifteen million years of hominid evolution, that men and women are alike. It is typical of the ideological approach to life to suppose that by political action we can make the human organism whatever we want it to be.

Among living hunters, men make the major decisions relating to their activity as hunters, explorers, and symbolizers, while women dominate in matters of children, diet, and social relations. An over-all gender-based, dominance-subordination ranking does not exist among them. Hunters are not patriarchal authoritarians like cattle- and sheep-keepers. They perceive gender as the outcome of a cosmic philosophy of complementarity. Personified male gods of the sky and sun and female deities of the soil or sea, to whom omnipotent powers are attributed, are the fixations of planters and herders. Humanized gods among hunter-gatherers are seldom absolute rulers and are usually envisaged as benign, ancestral figures.

The past, having shaped our species, holds the clues to normal function. The cell, individual, and society all tend to create and adapt to the kind of environment in which they work. Versatility of cultural form may seem to imply that for man the environment is relatively inconsequential, but in reality environmental requirements are greater and more exacting for humans than for most other species. Men need, in their non-human environment, open country with occasional cover, labyrinthine play areas, a rich variety of plants, animals, rocks, stars; structures and forms numbering into the thousands; initiation solitude, transitional and holy places, a wide variety of food organisms and diversity of stone and wood, nearby fresh water, large mammalian herds, cave and other habitation sites, and so on. Beyond the ecological and psychological constants needed for normal human health there must be an environmental margin of security to allow choice and to contribute to the individuality of experience and learned behavior.

Post-industrial men do exist without these things and in an enormous variety of social arrangements, but they live in constant crisis, stress, and poor mental health. Men are not free to create any form of society or any kind of environment they choose; they are free only within the bounds shaped by the past which is present in them.

A wide flexibility of behavior requires suitable environmental diversity. If an omnivore concentrates his attention on a single kind of food he will injure himself and his environment. If the runner does not run he will die of heartbreak (and so will the antelope). If sexually dimorphic forms subordinate the values and role of one gender to the other or deny their dimorphism, they hamper individualizing (or individuating) processes and cripple the social and ecological life of the group.

It is sometimes said that higher complex creatures like humans do well in a changing world. In truth, such species, with flexible, learned behavior and diverse social forms, require a stable natural environment. Since modern forms were created by the past they depend on environments like those in which they were shaped. This is, of course, a highly heretical opinion in a society whose myths enshrine progress and change —a society puzzled by the decay of the quality of life and threatened by self-destruction. It is also said that "nature is change" and argued that such is the essence of evolution. But this observation, often used as a justification for arbitrary control of the environment, distorts the fundamental aspect of evolutionary change, which is its tempo. The dramatic alteration of planetary life over hundreds of thousands of years requires great stability of life cycles, individual experience, and social organization. Without such continuity and seeming changelessness over the shorter term, life and environment would be too chaotic for the delicate processes of evolution to operate.

On Aggression and the Tender Carnivore

Animal aggression is inseparable from its opposite: fight-inhibiting, cooperative, and compassionate activity. All animals are aggressive at some times, even the most placid vegetarians— witness the combats between big-horn rams. Fighting between members of the same species is very different from the killing of prey by predator, and psychopathological fighting is very different from normal conflict. All animals are predatory (or parasitic) since they obtain and eat other organisms. Carnivores, which eat meat, must catch, kill, and dismember their prey. Man is in part a carnivore: the male of the species is genetically programed to pursue, attack, and kill for food. To the extent that men do not do so they are not fully human.

Within their own species and societies, all animals are occasionally competitive, irritable, and antagonistic. Assault against their own kind, as when stags lock antlers over hinds or house cats thrash young adults as initiation into the brotherhood, is always subject to precise restraining signals that inhibit or deflect attack. The animal world is full of appeasement signs and diverted aggression, which allows the escape of beaten rivals. Among men the instinctive response to submissiveness is general enough so that the exact signals by which the defeated says, "Enough!" may be modified by local custom.

For modern humans the question of whether or not man is by instinct a killer has been misleadingly centered on war and on the political ends to peace. Since men do kill en masse, this might seem to be a very unusual species-specific behavior, or else something that a biologically peaceful and cooperative creature has learned to do—that is either innate and instinctive or learned and cultural.

Neither alternative is correct. War is the state's expression of social pathology. Ecologically, it is a breakdown in the distinction that a healthy species makes between inter-species and intra-species behaviors, and in the use of organized predation. It occurs where men cannot regularly hunt and where population densities are too high. In a Frankensteinian fashion it fuses elements of the primate rank-order system, as the basis for military organization, with the cooperative yet lethal talents of the human social carnivore. Every facet of soldierly conduct honored and reinforced by the military for the past fifty centuries is a perverted form of the desired qualities evoked in the ancient initiation rites of adolescents: fidelity, idealism, skill, and courage.

The main episodes of war—cooperative murder—can be seen in caged or stressed predators of any kind. The particular behavioral components of excess killing by predators and murder of one's own kind are all normal in the food-getting context. But among neither free-living animals nor hunting-gathering men is war an inherent trait that was at some time in the past a regular part of daily life. Among all carnivores, individuals occasionally kill other individuals. Sometimes it is an accident of uncontrolled rage, but usually it is the outcome of a chronic disturbance that has led to instability in group composition. Among those primitive groups in which prestige is gained from the daring murder of a member of another tribe, there is usually evidence of abnormal stress. The socially sanctioned expression of violence is an attempt to cope with pressures deforming and threatening the human condition after more peaceful expiatory measures have failed.

The expression of normal, infantile "primary process" thought (desire for omnipotence, immediate gratification, unrestricted emotion, and acting out feelings) is safely submerged in myth, its tensions released by the telling, or, on occasion, may be called upon in time of need to give credence to delusional belief systems. These are acted out in socially organized spectacles of violence, such as ritual mutilation, torture, and execution: desperate, shocking (and usually successful) measures to readjust the group neuroses by means of scapegoats.

When a group is threatened by disintegrating forces such as sudden mass mortality, acute deprivation, alien invasion, unusual climatic events, widespread health or nutritional disorders, or the failure of important social and religious institutions, it normally reacts this way. Essentially, the pain-and-trial-inducing activity, with its shock and horror, operates much like the self-inflicted pain that keeps a man from collapsing under intense physical or psychic stress. Like the captured spy in the story who clenches broken glass in his fists in order to avoid yielding secrets to his torturers, society controls its fear and injury by induced, controlled trauma. Its mass psychopathology is channeled, limited, and spent with the least possible damage.

The incidence of mental disorder leading to mutual slaughter is perhaps the best evidence that the human cerebrum is near its tolerable limits in size. In the past it may have surpassed that equilibrium and have been reduced by natural selection, reversing the trend toward enlargement. Among certain Neanderthal fossils the average cranium was slightly larger in volume than that of modern man. There is evidence of accompanying cannibalism and ritual murder. The great burst of human achievement among the Aurignacian peoples that came later was perhaps a reflection of successful backward evolution.

The crisis of mental overreaching does not end there. Hyper-complexity is determined by function as well as by volume. A changed environment may render the brain unfit. A brain of razor-sharp keenness useful in a world of human rarity may be too large in a world of billions of people. Today the symptom of the overdone head is no longer the scapegoat ceremony, however; it is the insanity by which mass society delivers itself into military hands. Hunters and gatherers, by contrast, do not make war.

An altered population density is not the only environment incompatible with a large brain size. In the interior of New Guinea there are people who have been much written about and filmed in recent years. The men engage in chronic inter-tribal war in the form of more or less organized spear-throwing and ambush. Their lives have been described as "an unending round of death and revenge." Their culture is dominated by ferocious sorcery cults whose grisly fantasies serve less as a safety valve than as perpetual machines of fear and hate. In spite of their celebrated primitiveness these people are not true hunters. Like the tropical forest peoples of the upper Amazon, they lack large mammals to hunt. Psychically, yam-harvesting is no more a suitable occupation for them than supermarket-shopping is for a man in Detroit. As among industrial men, their deprivation has psychotic consequences. It is no surprise that the inhabitants of New Guinea, descendants of far-off hunters, now isolated in a land without large prey, mutilate themselves (although they have no automobiles for this purpose) and vainly display their lifelong frustration in a furious search for alternatives to the hunt.

Certainly no other animal exhibits anything like the degree of intra-specific killing and maiming that occurs within our own

species. That wars have continued despite the variety of political forms that have been tried through the ages of written
history suggests that something more fundamental is at fault
than systems of ideas. The New Guinea spear duels and the
Big Power missile race are equally biological malfunctions—
instinctive, but pathological. As in other forms of mental illness, the true causes are submerged in unconscious obscurity,
shielded by conscious images and ideas that are the opposite of
the truth—such as the stereotype of the farmer as a man of
peace. Modern war is attributed to failure of belief or will, or
failure of leadership, or failure to contain the animal and
archaic savage beneath our skins. In fact, the swords of war
are hammered from plowshares. To consider goat-breeding and
soil-breaking virtuous is self-deception; war emerged with the
shift in ecology, which produced the arrogant concept of land
ownership and the struggles for resources, space, and power.

The seeming contradiction between the aggressive and
peaceful attributes of the carnivore-hunter requires a somewhat
closer look at carnivores in general. As has been noted, fighting
is normally ritualized (becoming somewhat like a dance) among
members of the same species, and most injury and killing within
the species is psychopathic. Between-species killing among large
predators is rare—in spite of the staged displays of fights between lions and tigers, bears and lions, by circuses and irrespon-
sible nature-film makers.

The large carnivores are few in kind, few in number, and
highly intelligent. Their attention, unlike that of plant-eaters,
is fixed on roving prey rather than on rooted plants or place,
"thatness" instead of "thereness." Apes in captivity become
visibly agitated when the food dish is moved, but coyotes and
lions do not. The size of mammalian carnivores is inverse to
their fecundity and is proportional to the relative amount of
learning in their behavioral repertoire.

Carnivore-hunters are sound sleepers. Sleep, associated
with complex nervous activity, is divided into specific phases in
big-brained animals. One phase, dreaming, performs functions
known to be necessary but not fully understood. The content

and structure of dreams in man are related to both individual and species experiences, so that the analysis of dreams provides a unique insight into environments and activities "expected" by the organism and may help reconstruct the daily life and ecology native to our species.

The various kinds of hunting animals are not usually competitive. In a given area different-sized species live in hunting sets or clusters with a spread of hunting styles, habitat, food preferences, and daily rhythms. Wolves and lynxes occupy the same habitat but hunt very differently and kill different species of prey. Wolves track, surround, and attack from the rear, while cats stalk, ambush, and attack from the front. This picture of an integrated set of predators, each playing a part in the whole ecology, minimizing competition, with cautious and deliberate procedures, belies the image of the rampaging bloodthirsty killer or the fictional creature that "kills for the pleasure of it." The common analogy between a berserk murderer and a predatory animal simply is not true.

The ecology of all hunting involves a strategy that has been called "the prudent policy of predation." In the evolution of predation there are long-term considerations that outweigh sheer killing efficiency. It is to the predator's disadvantage as a species to maximize the kill if this is detrimental to the stability of the prey population, and therefore to future generations of predators.

The prudent predator is not an exterminator. It plays a role in a self-regulating system, taking a yield of the prey only up to a level of the replacement rate. Within this limit predation has the effect of increasing the birth rate of the prey by removing the old, the crippled, the non-reproducing, whose places are taken by vigorous individuals. In a sense the carnivore is using the prey to manufacture food for itself from plants. The efficiency of this transformation never exceeds about 15 per cent because the herbivorous prey has already used most of the energy from the plants it eats in its own metabolic activity. Its body tissues represent the remainder, but in order for the carnivore to take this without harm to the prey species it must be harvested in the right stage of the prey's life cycle.

The predator, of course, has not consciously figured out this complicated equation. Nor has the human hunter, in spite of his superior intelligence, for he usually lacks the information needed to adjust his hunting to top ecological efficiency. Like all hunters, men therefore take a pragmatic approach. Since to harvest too few or too many is detrimental to the system in which predator and prey are complementary, the hunters adopt a mode of operation that achieves the same end that mathematical analysis would indicate: a certain predator population density (usually well below reproductive potential and the actual carrying capacity of the environment); a shifting harvest of different species of prey; and a choice of individual prey whose loss will least affect the continuity of the prey population, mainly those animals with the highest probability of dying soon from any cause, particularly the old and diseased. In most carnivores the ability to make such a choice is the outcome of instinct and experience; in man it is these plus the empirical taboos and rituals that restrict the hunt.

The strategy of the prey is to separate as clearly as possible those animals that will perpetuate the species and sustain group behaviors from those that are defective, senile, and degenerate. By providing some animals that transmit the energy of plants to carnivores, the prey can more effectively insure the survival of those who are the gene bearers of future generations. The prey is also engaged in the longer-term objective of sorting out bad genes and poor genetic combinations by shunting them out of the gene pool and thereby improving the quality of the species.

In considering man as a carnivore, the essential fact is that he became a large game hunter as he became human. The omnivorous, scavenging *Australopithecus* was intermediate in the transition. The later Ice-Age hunters of the genus *Homo*, with their exquisite tools and cooperative tactics, stalked the largest living land animals. The last of the Paleolithic hunters raised the art of hunting to the center of a complex philosophy of life. Throughout, the basic principles of predator-prey equilibrium were never abandoned.

4

HUNTING AS A WAY OF LIFE

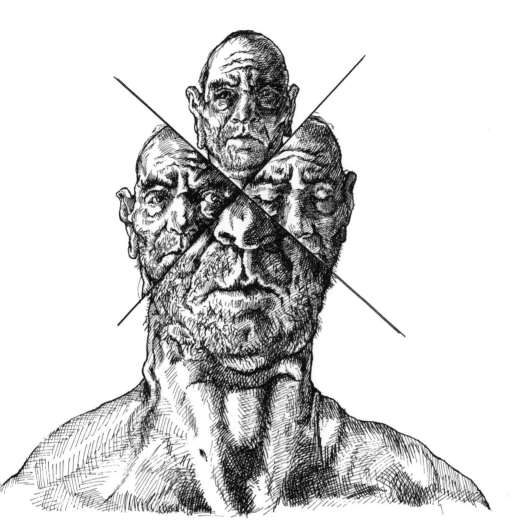

The Band of Hunter-Gatherers

It is widely believed that urban life is more complex than the
hunter's world because it is organized on a class basis, with
specialized occupations, while the latter is more egalitarian,
and each man and woman is capable of the full range of his or
her activities. But town society is only more complex in this
sense as the abstraction of an outside observer. It is not more
complex from the standpoint of its individual members.

Urban life has a special kind of sensory opulence in the
diverse scenes of human embroilment—in the human stream on
the streets or in public buildings, in the range of amuse-

ments to divert and entertain. This something-happening-every-minute is not equivalent to genuine environmental richness and depth of human relationship. To urban man the range of the hunters' daily experience may seem small and boring, but his boredom is not a true reflection of the measure of sensory richness and diversity of possible experience in the hunters' camp and habitat. It is only a measure of his own insensibility to the textures of nature and tribal life.

The typical hunting band is composed of human family units in the broadest sense—blood kin in various combinations. There are very few solitary women, and there is frequent polygamy. While relationships are strongly affected by personality, the band structure is hardly the free-love affair dreamed of by back-to-nature romantics.

Society based on kinship is universally conservative and stable. Oddly enough, the most flexible bond seems to be marriage itself. The divorce rate is higher among known hunters than among modern Europeans and Americans. Even so, the hunter society is stable because the so-called extended family—composed of uncles, aunts, cousins, siblings, grandparents, clan brothers, in-laws—is sealed by customs and obligations, only a few of which would be affected by divorce, disagreement, or death. If a high divorce rate seems difficult to reconcile with the conservatism of "primitive people," the reason could be that modern, educated people think of all pre-industrial societies as being alike. But not until the rise of agrarian cultures was marriage subjected to the chains of public opinion, civil law, and institutionalized religion. It is that notion of the marriage bond that misleads civilization's perception of hunters.

For hunting-gathering people the natural environment is firm. The kin structure is stable because the individual is born or initiated into a group as durable as the plant or animal species taken by it as a totemic emblem. Given the reality of flux in all human society, this link to the natural throws people into closer intellectual and emotional recognition of the one constant in their lives, the terrain with its enduring natural community. Nature is an outside reference to personal identity, surviving all social discord, a stable base in the turbulence of life.

Of course, the environment itself changes. What is important is not whether it changes but whether the changes are patterned and how much change occurs in one lifetime—the speed of change relative to the rhythms of human reproduction. Frequent unpredictable change is socially and psychologically destructive. Like an addictive drug, it may, however, become tolerable and even desirable.

Competition among hunters is a derivative of individual difference and pride of skill, not an aggressive striving to acquire spoils or dominate. Members of the group differ greatly in ability, not only in the chase, but in sensitivity to the location of plant foods, in finding shelter, in toolmaking, in dancing and all the other social arts. Superior ability contributes to general prestige. Being thought well of is important. There is no accumulation of trading goods, property, children, food, or other material signs of success. Such things cannot be stored. Personal status plays only a minor role in routine protocol. In the distribution of meat, traditional formality extends the kill along lines of kinship and clan tie to every member of the group. Other things are freely given, and esteem is gained in the giving. Sharing is built into the life style. Among bands there is a constant give-and-take of vital goods through hospitality and gift exchange. Generosity is a social virtue. When kinship is extended by inter-band marriage, so are reciprocity and mutual aid.

Rights in the kill belong not only to the hunter whose spear is in its heart, but to the first to see it, the first to wound, the first to give a serious wound, the owner of the weapon used in the final blow, and to the hunt leader. Customs designate who gets what organs and cuts of meat. This specialized adult male activity, symbolizing social relationships, was developed by men who hunted large mammals and had a home base, if only for a few weeks or a season. Other primates do not transport or share food.

To have a home base is to have a place to care for the

injured and sick, who might otherwise be abandoned—as they are among baboons and wolves. Here they undertake tasks for which they are fitted.

Conscientious care of the weak and disabled did not leap into the human heart from nowhere. As the patterns of sharing and care emerged, the group came to depend on those too old or infirm to hunt or gather for the performance of certain tasks. Old people, like old apes and baboons, came to be respected for their experience and wisdom and were voluntarily followed as leaders. Respect for the aged is a widespread trait among hunting peoples, though not unique to them. Among peasant and industrial societies it is much more variable. Some provide only the shell of respect; many give security but only token status.

The old are storehouses of clan custom and lore, of the mythical stories which contain the deepest beliefs, the days important to ceremonial celebration and to the movement of game, the phenology or seasonal calendar of the life cycle of plants, the details of ritual procedures and the roles of participants. They know from long experience and oral tradition how to deal with rare events—severe drought, strange disease, unfamiliar terrain—that no young member of the group ever confronted. Perhaps beyond all else, the old are wise in the intricacies of human personality and in personal knowledge of the whole arc of the life span along which other members of the group have moved lesser distances. Their knowledge is shared through ritual ceremony, learned as part of normal education. In some societies the total period of such instruction for young men lasts many years. In parts of Australia, a young man may be twenty-seven before he can marry.

Most hunting societies are polygynous gerontocracies—that is, men marry one or more women and there is voluntary acknowledgment of the leadership of the old. Roles and status are determined by age, sex, and temperament. Initiation into adult society spans many years for men, fewer for women. In a typical group men might marry at twenty-five, women at fifteen. (Among farmers, men marry at around nineteen, women at sixteen.) Older men with prestige and seniority marry the younger women. In some groups the first wife of a younger man is an older widow. This arrangement is possibly another factor in population limitation.

At first glance it may seem that post-hunting societies rescued women from an unfair and unequal status, but such is not the case. In hunter-gatherer cultures the women were relatively free from large families, slave-like labor, and lackey status; farming was a lifelong commitment to toil and drudgery in which the wife became part of a taxpayer's property.

Since marriage is deferred for younger men, there is an all-male sub-group, reminiscent of similar situations among open-country baboons. Individuals share residence quarters and the common experience of their age class. The bonds thus formed are likely to take on overtones of homosexuality; one might say that all institutionalized one-sex groupings among men depend to some degree on libidinal instincts. Perhaps natural selection exploited the sexuality of early men to forge the strong loyalty needed when confronting an angry bear or mammoth. But such bonds, if too extreme, could interfere with subsequent marriage and social responsibility, even the continuation of society itself.

Perhaps the cryptandic devices affected by the women are the means of countering the homosexual tendency of young men. In addition to body decoration are those species-specific sexually evocative physical characteristics and traits that are part of the human but not the primate picture. Most of these can be covered and obscured or emphatically displayed: breast, aureola and nipple, red lips, blushing, long eyelashes, ear lobes, odors, fat-rounded hips and buttocks, beardlessness, naked torso with pubic hair, and so on. To the several theories of the purpose of the first clothing (a way of carrying emergency food, for warmth, as badges of status) should be added its function as a veil or frame of the ultimate icing-on-the-cake of sexual dimorphism, permitting the turning on or off of those traits as though they were cryptandic.

The focused intensity of these features displayed with appropriate behavior neutralizes the long-standing and exclusive bonds of brotherhood and serves as signals in the pair-bonding of the human couple, which is surely one of the most powerful specializations of human biology. Pair-bonding does not destroy the fraternal bond but rather balances it with a new phase of life, the two together forming alternating modes that thereafter will constitute the whole rhythm of life. By establishing a pattern of mate fidelity the hominids escaped the incessant tension and strife of the baboon troop, freeing both women and men to be confidently absent from their mates.

Many of the age-group characteristics of people are in some way adaptive to the integration of hunting-gathering societies. Women generally age rather abruptly, so that there is a period of middle life when women seem older than men of the same age. It may be argued that calling a women but not a man of fifty "old" is simply another example of a double standard, another holdover from the inequity of the Victorian past. But I think that such differences are worldwide and that a man of fifty may be in fact more youthful because males have no equivalent of the relatively abrupt menopause, which alters female physiology, behavior, and appearance.

The menopause, in a Pleistocene perspective, is apparently adaptive both biologically and socially. By the age of forty women are producing an increasing percentage of genetically defective ova, which could lead to deformed or mongoloid offspring. Undertaking the rearing of children, even if normal, is increasingly difficult. The mother may not live to "launch" the child as an adult, or to educate it as a young parent and to be known to its offspring as a grandparent. Nature has not arranged to kill off women at this age (as it does most animals before they become barren) because human society evolved with a role for older women that adds to the total well-being and stability of the group.

It has been generally assumed that the changes in appearance accompanying the end of fertility—changes in skin and its underlying fat and muscle structure as well as the rest of the large list of other symptoms—were simply the physiological consequences of the broad hormonal changes accompanying the cessation of the menstrual cycle. But is all that necessary to accomplish infertility? Consider instead the changes in the social role of the woman at that time that might be signified and enhanced by changes in appearance and temperament.

Even though men marry late and some widowhood is inevitable, there are no unmarried female adults (and certainly no prostitutes) in hunting societies. In some households there are two wives, one of whom is usually much older than the other. Their roles are likely to be somewhat different, and that difference is the basis of household compatibility. The older woman is by no means demeaned by her non-sexual role, and in some groups the wise old women are the most prestigious members of the band. As already mentioned, some older women find their second husbands among the younger men. Perhaps the attraction that still exists between young women and middle-aged men and between middle-aged women and young men is due to these ancient social accommodations to the uncertainties of life. In any case, the "old" features do not prevent the widow from marrying the young man. In summary, the dramatic change in the middle-aged woman's appearance and its lack of an equivalent in the male is correlated with the occasional presence of two wives of the same man and the rarity of the opposite—two husbands of the same wife.

There is little political power as we know it in the polygynous gerontocracy. The typical hunting-gathering clan does not have a chief—or, if it does, his function is usually advisory. No one is accountable either to a higher executive or to a subordinate. Every adult male is a member of a council of the whole. In some groups this is much more formally arranged than in others. Charisma is always important. Leadership is sometimes exercised simply by strong personality and the willingness of others to follow, though they are free not to do so. Needless to say, an unwise man is not voluntarily followed long.

While it is difficult to generalize because of the great diversity of hunters, force, authoritarianism, and tyranny are not their way. Opinion and esteem are important. Integrity is recognized, and prestige is given, not extracted by force. Serious problems are discussed at such length that the decisions become obvious to all. Leadership is due to personal traits, not an accident of birth. Where especially well-endowed individuals have more than one wife, they leave the most offspring. Such a genetic-social arrangement accelerates evolutionary adaptation and flexibility.

The informal affirmation of leaders without political affinity is difficult for men of modern states to comprehend. "Take us to your leader," is the stereotyped greeting of modern man to primitives. For American Indians the demand to "bring out your chief," put by some white military officer, brought confusion and tragedy because the chief was not empowered to make commitments and agreements of the kind expected in military parley.

Among hunters personal relations are part of a formal framework. Arguments and disagreements are kept within the framework, where rudeness can be socially sanctioned and nondestructive. One is inclined to think of Paleolithic hunters and, say, eighteenth-century French nobility as opposite poles in codified behavior, but the manners of the latter were sometimes cynical posturing, employed as a way of disguising brutality. Among primitives formality is less a ritual acknowledgment of class rank and submission than a courteous deference paid as a token of esteem.

This distinction between the system dominated by a threat and that of natural courtesy is central to the difference between class and totemic societies. It may surprise modern adolescents, who see the rejection of all formality as the means to self-realization and personal growth, to learn that cynegetic men are not anarchistic cults of idiosyncratic rebels or revolutionaries bound by ideology or love.

Restraint is also part of the body of standard etiquette. Moments of parting and reunion, of injury or death, events that would evoke among us expressions of tender regard, pain, or despair, are abided in relatively stolid silence by these usually emotional hunters. It is a mistake, however, to suppose that

people who do not react to such events with operatic display
are lacking in moral sense or are numb and insensitive.

Hunting societies define personal responsibility differently
from us. Instances are known in which unfortunate individuals
have been abandoned. Infanticide is sometimes practiced. This is
not due to lack of affection, for love is widely expressed among
them in certain ways. If these practices are morally hard for us
to accept or comprehend, we ought at least to remember that
such events are rare compared to the horrors and cruelties of
the civilized world, where 59 million people were killed vio-
lently by other people in the 125 years preceding 1945. In an
overabundant human population the small group is always
expendable and its members unconsciously know it. A member
may not be abandoned, and if consequently they all die it is
only a tiny glorious scene in a romantic play where the continuity and wisdom of the tribe will not be lost because these are
stored in books. The same books generate the readiness to die
and kill, so that experience is yoked to sentimental expression
and ideological romanticism. These, both in their philosophical
and literary origins, make it easy for us to judge others as un-
feeling.

Courtesy links bands of hunters. When they meet, usually
at the boundaries separating their respective areas, they are
peaceful and cordial. Because of the quasi-territorial face-off
and because the serious matter of mate selection and marriage
is frequently a part of these meetings, they are highly charged
affairs. Tensions are buffered by fixed procedure, by more or
less formal ceremony and contests of skill and courage. These
vary greatly, allowing for all kinds of personal involvement and
conflict within the overriding rules conducive to harmony.
The meeting is cause for celebration; dancing, information
exchange, companionship, courtship, and trade are carried on.

Since hunters are bound by instinct to several hundred
square miles of familiar terrain and have no motives for enlarging their domain, they are not normally at odds with neighbors.
Unlike farmers, their population is not chronically under-

spaced. Since men are not by nature territorial, hunters do not
repel invading cattlemen, which ultimately works to their
destruction. In the final squeeze hunters may fight desperately
and suicidally—justifying further invasion and repression by
the invaders—or die of a broken spirit, as other men in captivity sometimes do. The hunter, unlike the farmer, cannot
move on to some other place. His mental health and orientation
are inseparable from the particular features of his terrain. This
is the real "territorial imperative."

The Venatic Art

A century ago it was thought that boys playing at hunting were
unconsciously re-enacting the adult pursuits of ancient hunters.
It is more likely that boys do the same as boys in ancient
hunting-gathering societies did, which is a special kind of practice. Among them all, play hunting has the same relationship to
hunting that love for mother has to adult love: grounding in a
fundamental context combining action and implicit thought.

Play has a physical aspect, of course: skill, dexterity, endurance, coordination, and with it a constant expectation, an
awareness of what must be done next, the kind of flow that
comes with drill and practice.

Childhood training undoubtedly had phases in Paleolithic times, as it does now among hunters. Miniature hunts of
insects or small animals are interspersed with the rough-and-
tumble of games. Captive animals are widely kept by children;
it is a way of getting at their behavior and taxonomy while
still too young to go hunting. Every animal brought to camp
for butchering is a lesson—in language, anatomy, perception—
and an exercise in thinking.

Tutorial direction in the use of weapons is associated with
special exercises to develop body position and sets of muscles.
Much is learned from stories, from the talk of adults, from the
legends intended to educate in the best sense of the word.

As a boy in the Missouri Ozarks, I knew boys who were

considered to have fewer "advantages" than I, who hunted but had no guns. They did have dogs and all the flintstones the hills so abundantly provided. I admired them then, but I now appreciate more deeply the range of their skill. They knew where and how to see; they could find a squirrel in the top of a post oak when only a few whiskers or part of a leg showed. They knew how to make it move and keep it moving, and, most astonishing of all, could throw and hit the fast-moving squirrel fifty feet overhead. I believe their independent, alert confidence was not only revealed by but was directly associated with their knowledge and skill in hunting squirrels and other small animals.

The childhood training of hunters is not so much practical training as the opening of spiritual doors by leisured and generous people. Nothing that men do comes so close to fulfilling the promise that the imagination builds in youth as hunting. The boys I knew had no work more onerous to do than chopping occasional firewood or feeding a few pigs. Years later, after working in the local factories or on the farm, they became dull-eyed and defeated. After they could afford guns they could still get excited about hunting but in a sad way, turned in on themselves, puzzled and querulous.

This is not the defeat of innocence and enthusiasm by age and knowledge. It is because drudgery and toil had blunted them and, worse, their life style had failed them. Hunting had put a premium on physical good health, on sensitivity to environment and to the nuances and clues in a delicate and beautiful world, on independence, confidence, persistence, generosity, and had given them a powerful sense of the non-human creation. In their adult lives only one of these—persistence—was rewarded; the others were destroyed.

Childhood programing is by no means all the training given in a traditional hunting society. All the elements of the hunt must be learned. There are at least four parts in a typical hunt: scanning, stalking, immobilization, and retrieval. Scanning is based on a knowledge of the science of animal life. The hunter must know the habits and habitat and the characteristics of each animal of both sexes at every stage in its life cycle. He must know the clues revealing its nearby presence even before he sees it—tracks, calls, feces, smell, the alarm signs given by other animals, or the browsed condition of plants. There is so much to know that the hunter can go on learning all his life. The extent of what can be learned is far greater than that of human social knowledge, and this is why nature is the best model for the evolution of social consciousness and organization.

Stalking is the approach to the animal once it is known to be nearby. This includes calling or luring as well as following. It means monitoring the prey's movement and predicting where it is in the local terrain, and what the effects of weather and wind conditions might be. "To stalk" suggests the creeping of cats, stealthy and low profile. The use of the earth and the vegetation as cover, the mimicking of the prey or other animals, the speed and type of movement, the knowledge of when to rush, all are complex elements in a mosaic. The kind of prey, which one of the prey to pursue, the season, the routes of escape open to the prey, must also be considered. The distance to the animal is always critical, because as the hunter approaches the flight distance the prey will flee as soon as it senses the hunter, and as he gets closer the prey may attack.

Immobilization usually means killing. Even for men with spears this is at close range and tests human cunning, strength, skill, and cooperation. The thrown spear may be lost if it is simply hung in tough skin or wasted in a non-mortal wound. In some hunting the spear cannot be thrown and is thrust to impale the prey. To appreciate the skill and courage that this requires it is necessary to watch men hunting large, dangerous mammals; or to stand with wild elephants on an open African plain (preferably with no vehicle or other escape) and imagine oneself a hunter. Such an experience enlarges one's understanding and admiration of the Paleolithic hunter more than any book.

Immobilization does not always mean immediate killing. The animals may be driven or captured first to avoid transporting the dead carcass or to put the hunter in more favorable terrain. Animals are also stampeded into pits, over cliffs, into swamps, into a cul-de-sac, or taken by snares and log or rock droptraps.

The retrieval of heavy game from the site of the kill or from secondary camps set up for butchering and drying sometimes requires relays of additional help. The carcass or its parts may be carried, floated, boated, rolled, or transported in a skin bag—which comes with the kill. Once killed, a large mammal is not usually moved whole, partly because of its weight and partly because some is eaten, at least ceremonially, on the spot. Retrieval includes distribution, preparation, and consumption of the meat according to customary procedures, which are likely to be elaborate.

Hunters the world over eat certain parts of animals fresh and uncooked, other parts cooked. The use of fire may be the only universal trait that distinguishes men from other animals. Its earliest use was probably for protection, warmth, illumination, and driving game, not for cooking. Heating meat is more important than cooking it. The same is not true of some roots and vegetables, which are otherwise indigestible.

These elements of the venatic art have been listed as though, together, they were elementary routine based on planning, imagination, and cooperation—which indeed they are. But they are also integrated into social and religious life. The variety of spiritual attention given by different tribes to all the steps of hunting in its many forms is immense. In all cases, however, men are engaged in more than a merely physical foodgetting activity, for in hunting they are immersed in their most deeply held spiritual and aesthetic conceptions. Spiritual preparation for the hunt often takes several days; both ceremonial and practical details of daily life are prescribed. Exceptions to a formal style of hunting are found in areas of collision between hunting societies and civilized technology, where cultural deterioration has led to the breakdown of customs and to wanton killing.

The magic and religion in primitive ritual reveal fundamental components of the hunter's attitude. The organized ceremony simultaneously serves not only a magic and a religious purpose, but ecological and social functions as well. It is aimed at maintaining equilibrium in the total situation. The whole of life, corporeal and spiritual, is to be affected.

Part of the prey, at least, is killed ritually and eaten sacramentally. By following the prescribed style the hunters sacrifice the prey in evocation of events too profound for understanding. By its own self-imposed limitations the ritual hunt embodies renunciation in favor of a larger context of interrelationship. If the preliminary solicitation is effective and the traditional procedure is followed the hunt is successful. Unlike farmers who must labor in the fields and who earn by their sweat a grudging security in nature, the primitive hunter gets something for nothing.

Formalities keep before the hunter the immanence and mystery of a world not created for him alone and over which he has only partial control. This is perhaps the main difference between his personal vision of existence and that of those who have superseded him.

Cynegetic Man

Modern men are no smarter, kinder, or more creative than their forebears of a quarter of a million years ago. Man has been fully human far longer than can clearly be comprehended or history allows. Men's bodies and minds, personality, and institutions are adaptations to a way of life. The word "hunting" is inadequate to describe that life, as it evokes only images of a manner of food-getting. For a much more comprehensive term that does not carry the prejudice and hostility of the last ten thousand years the word "cynegetic" is used.

Cynegetic men, being small in population—hence a rare species—have highly personalized lives. Living in small groups, each person becomes fully matured as an individual and uniquely valuable to the group. Cynegetic people are leisured, generous, hospitable. They do not stockpile possessions or children. Their only private property is personalty. Among them, social reciprocity and sharing are normal events, not a charity. The aged are active, revered members of society. Their world philosophy is polemical, conservative, and normative, not opportunistic, progressive, or existential. The men are deeply attached to place and home, yet are mobile and free of defensive boundary fixations. Among them leadership is advisory rather than executive. Action is taken by consent. Their populations are not expansive. Group aggression, plunder, slavery, do not exist. There is no political machinery, little feuding, and no war.

These are fully technological men, evolved and individually involved with the manufacture and use of tools. Tools and art came into existence with the emergence of human consciousness and are part of the rise to personal consciousness of each individual. Because he is a hunter, he is the most deeply loving and profoundly compassionate animal. Generally he is free of communicable disease and famine. The past and future are not sources of anxiety because of the stability of the natural environment and because the rate of cultural change is small. The concept of time is that of simultaneity, which engages every individual and all of the past in complete attention to the present.

Such a view of time is not intellectual; it is inseparable from perception itself. Cynegetic man lives in an event-world, which has the fleeting quality of sound. Much of his ceremony and celebration is in song, dance, and oratory. Privacy does not exist because the world is a presence. History for him is a wondrous rhetorical tale inseparable from moral poetry and from the accumulated wisdom and mythology of the group. Paintings and other symbolic objects are connections between different parts of a cosmic reality or different levels of meaning, open to all, not private property.

For cynegetic man nature is a language. I do not mean only that he is a skillful reader of animal behavior or meteorological events but that nature functions as a syntax. Travel across the terrain, the internal anatomy and relationship of animal parts, the taxonomy and classification of plants and animals with its concept of species, the *objet trouvé*—all are steps in the normal maturing of consciousness and mentality.

In his relationship to other individuals, and in his ecological relationship to the whole of his environment, man the hunter and gatherer has a great advantage in that the social and environmental perceptions necessary for his way of life are similar to those in which man evolved, so that his life style is the normal expression of his psychology and physiology. His humanity is therefore more fully achieved, and his community more durable and beautiful.

In no other life style is personal experience more ecstatic and authentic. The word "authentic" keeps ringing through the pages of *Meditations on Hunting,* by the late Spanish philosopher José Ortega y Gasset. The cynegetic life is authentic because it is close to the philosophical center of human life. It constantly contrasts two central mysteries: the nature of the animal and of death. These are brought together in hunting. All other ways of life weakly confront the wild or are designed to avoid it altogether.

It is the rich perception and intensity of experience of the world that, Ortega says, is associated with the hunter's attitude:

> When one is hunting, the air has another, more exquisite feel as it glides over the skin or enters the lungs, the rocks acquire a more expressive physiognomy, and the vegetation becomes loaded with meaning. But all this is due to the fact that the hunter, while he advances or waits crouching, feels tied through the earth to the animal he pursues, whether the animal is in view, hidden, or absent.

Thus his attention is locked into a "mystical union with the animal, a sensing and presentiment of it that automatically leads the hunter to perceive the environment from the point of view of the prey, without abandoning his own point of view." To modern man, who thinks of neither predators or prey, this may seem at first trivial, but it is central to thought itself. The hunter, Ortega continues,

> . . . will instinctively shrink from being seen; he will avoid all noise while traveling; he will perceive all his surroundings from the point of view of the animal, with the animal's peculiar attention to detail. This is what I call being within the countryside. Only when we see it through the drama that unfolds in the hunt can we absorb its particular richness. Articulated in that action which is a minor zoological tragedy, wind, light, temperature, ground contour, minerals, vegetation, all play a part; they are not simply there, as they are for the tourist or the botanist, but rather they *function,* they act. And they do not function as they do in agriculture, in the unilateral, exclusive, and abstract sense of their utility for the harvest, but rather each intervenes in the drama of the hunt from within itself, with its concrete and full being.

The hunter is the alert man, in whom the attention is different than in those occupations where it is focused only on the objects or points that have a predetermined utility or attraction. Ortega uses the term "countryside" in a way that the ecologist might use "habitat," as distinct from the idea of a landscape—an external scene of nature or an aesthetic artifact created by the romantic imagination. It is the landscape that the tourist seeks, spaces upon which his gaze glides. "It seizes nothing, it does not perceive the role of each ingredient in the dynamic architecture of the countryside." The farmer, the miner, and the businessmen who stand behind them also tend to look at points and leave the rest unattended. The farmer sees only "what is good or bad for the growth of his grain or the maturation of his fruit; the rest remains outside his vision and, in consequence, he remains outside the completeness that is the countryside."

The hunter's look and attention are completely opposite to this. . . . He does not look tranquilly in one determined direction, sure beforehand that the game will pass in front of him. The hunter knows that he does not know what is going to happen, and this is one of the greatest attractions of his occupation. Thus he needs to prepare an attention of a different and superior style—an attention which does not consist in riveting itself on the presumed but consists precisely in not presuming anything and avoiding inattentiveness. It is a "universal" attention, which does not incribe itself on any point and tries to be on all points. There is a magnificent term for this, one that still conserves all its zest of vivacity and imminence: alertness. The hunter is the alert man.

What Ortega speaks of is not the same as the appreciation of wild land as a national park. The aesthetic perception of wilderness as scenery has relegated it to the categories of space and use, to the canons of taste. If it is fashionable today it may be unfashionable tomorrow and is therefore without abiding value.

All past landscapes of human history, says Ortega, are obsolete except one. Except for the hunt in wild lands, their reconstruction or a return to them yields fictitious value. "Hunting is the generic way of being a man, a permanent availability. Having no history, it is the only form without historical supposition, hence the only past form to which man can return."

The humanized terrain, he adds, helps us realize that:

Only on the hunting ground, which is the first countryside, the only "natural" one, can we succeed in emigrating from our human world to an authentic "outside," from which history represents the retreat or anabasis. But it is clear that we cannot get "outside" . . . if we stay located and anchored in our habitual terrain. It is not for nothing that the words which in Indo-European languages signified "countryside" also meant "outside," and they are precisely those that meant "door." Countryside is that which is beyond our habitation, whether it is a house, a garden, a park, or a hacienda.

. . . cultivated countryside is land already exhausted by humanity to the point where that humanization of the countryside has served as model and name for all the more specifically human ways of life: *the culture*. To walk, then, through an orchard, sown field, or stubble field, through an olive grove laid out in diagonal rows or a methodically planned grove of pin oaks, is to follow man traveling within himself.

The idea of the hunter's attention, as Ortega implies, is not limited only to hunting. As "ecology" is used frequently as a metaphor for "interrelationships," the hunter's kind of "attention of a different and superior style" has broad implications. Philosophers, Ortega says, often use hunting terminology to describe their mental activity—Plato uses the word *thereutes* and Thomas Aquinas *venator*.

. . . the only man who truly thinks is the one who, when faced with a problem, instead of looking only straight ahead, toward what habit, tradition, the commonplace, and mental inertia would make one assume, keeps himself alert, ready to accept the fact that the solution might spring from the least forseeable spot on the great rotundity of the horizon.

Like the hunter in the absolute *outside* of the countryside, the philosopher is the alert man in the absolute *inside* of ideas, which are also an unconquerable and dangerous jungle. As problematic a task as hunting, meditation always runs the risk of returning empty-handed.

There is a sense in which metaphors on hunting to explain mental activity are not metaphors at all, and we must take care not to suppose that the true reality is the metaphor. We may use "walking," for example, as a metaphor on the careless assumption that no man actually needs to walk in order to know what is meant. Man's genetic constitution provides that all men will instinctively learn to walk at about the age of one year and will continue to walk the rest of their lives. This instinct was selected for in our pre-human ancestors many millions of years ago and passed on as part of a genetic heritage. But unless each man learns to walk as an infant, at the time indicated by his genetic program his muscles will atrophy and legs become useless, and he will never know what it means to walk. He will remain a cripple throughout his life, a ward of those who have walked.

To hunt for an idea can never be fully understood—or fully practiced—by those who have not hunted game. Ortega, like many other students of the traditions of hunting, is careful to note that many philosophers and other great men have been hunters. Indeed, there are certain activities that have been preferred by leisured people in all places and times: hunting, dancing, racing, and conversing. It is no accident that these are precisely the "true vocations" of primitive hunters, who, like the aristocrats, make no distinction between leisure and life.

In mass societies dancing is reduced to repetitively sterile forms on public holidays; games are degraded in style; and conversing suffers from the mental fogging of boring work. Farmers and other mass men know little of the empirical wisdom of sportsmanship, which is the voluntary renunciation of mechanical advantage, handicap, or rules which accompany the use of modern weapons. For the true hunter success must always be problematic. The free function of the prey's instincts is the prey's game. Men with only hand weapons do not need to invent stern codes to insure that hunting is a challenge rather than an amusement. The hunter's confrontation of the enigmas of death and animal life inspire attitudes of honor and awe expressed in ceremonial address.

Because hunting is "a deep and permanent yearning in the human condition," says Ortega, there is a chronic fury in all people to whom it is denied. When the uninitiated are allowed unexpectedly to hunt they trample its subtle rites, ignore its awe and uneasiness about inflicting death, and disregard the necessary relinquishment of the supremacy of the overarmed as necessary homage to what is divine and unpredictable in nature.

When the French peasants, who were denied the right to

hunt by the *ancien régime,* were released from this restriction by the revolution, they brought their crippled ecology back into the field, merely slaughtering the token wild animals that remained as though these were merely livestock to be butchered. They hunted as they had lived, and without the hunt they had been brutalized, though their yearning for it was as strong as ever.

The idea of the hunt as metaphor applies to man's search for knowledge and is therefore vulnerable to being invaded by its analogies—to hunt with microphone or camera, for example. It has been argued that by these other ways allow for the play of venatic talents—scanning, stalking, "shooting," and retrieving—without the cruelty of death. But photography, as a substitute for hunting, is a mockery. It is platonic hunting, says Ortega, "and Platonism represents the maximum tradition of affected piety."

> One can refuse to hunt, but if one hunts one has to accept certain ultimate requirements without which the reality "hunting" evaporates. The overpowering of the game, the tactile drama of its actual capture, and usually even more the tragedy of its death nurture the hunter's interest through anticipation and give liveliness and authenticity to all the previous work: the harsh confrontation with the animal's fierceness, the struggle with its energetic defense, the point of orgiastic intoxication aroused by the sight of blood, and even the hint of criminal suspicion which claws the hunter's conscience. Without these ingredients the spirit of the hunt disappears. The animal's behavior is wholly inspired by the conviction that his life is at stake.

One does not hunt in order to kill, he says, one kills in order to have hunted—for authenticity. Yet something further should be said of the kill, which Ortega has overlooked. Hunting requires that certain parts of the prey be eaten. The loss from our culture of the hunter's attitude of the sacredness of eating is perhaps one reason that we have mistakenly come to think of killing animals as shameful. Hunting disturbs moralists because it enjoins men to be joyful in killing. Some Christian philosophers see in the prodigious amount of death in nature a shocking "waste" of life. They say, in effect, "I acknowledge this vast slaughter as the way of nature, but it is man's unique responsibility not to condone it and join it; he should not only avoid participating in it but reduce it, as far as he is able." This view, whether it sees the natural pattern as a consequence of evil or simply as absurd, is a denial rather than an affirmation of the world, and affects an ethical bravado that gives the illusion of elevating man above the rest of nature.

A denial of reality, this "ethic" is the epitome of the philosophy shaped by farmers and herders over a period of fifty centuries. If it could be acted upon, it could be tested, but men die when they do not eat, and the futile attempts of fanatics to avoid killing by shifting their attention from cows to rice results in more killing, since each rice grain is a living organism. By removing the killing from sight, as the modern slaughterhouse does, what in the hunt is the essence of connectedness and transcendence is made hideous. Vegetarianism is a dream of innocence, a fantasy of compassion. The mystery of life does not reveal its secrets to bean-eaters as opposed to bison-eaters.

One of the things known about man is that he is not a pure herbivore but an omnivore, who occasionally eats large mammals. To correct or "elevate" him to herbivorousness may seem desirable but amounts to little more than a gesture, not so much of grace and goodness as of mannerism and arrogance. "If you believe that you can do whatever you like—even, for example, the supreme good, then you are, irretrievably, a villain. The preoccupation with what should be is estimable only when the respect for what is has been exhausted," comments Ortega.

But why, one might ask, should we affirm this horrendous ecology with its killing, of which we are part, and whose ultimate purpose we cannot fathom? Without that knowledge how can we ethically or religiously do anything except oppose it? For most of us this kind of reaction is probably associated with our hope for everlasting life, not only for us but for all other people, our pets, and even all creatures. It is difficult, in this framework, not to see predators, like those foxes which eat the farmer's chickens, as bad, and to generalize that all predation is evil, including that by man.

Because war and hunting have been confused, since both involve killing, it is difficult not to regard them both as reprehensible. Yet distinctions between them were made for thousands of years. Ecologically, death leads to life, not in a hazy and obscure way but in the eating of the prey. Among hunters the fallen prey is universally cherished and honored both for itself as a thing of beauty and in the solemnity and meaning of its death. Ceremonial salutation to the prey, and to those larger forces that it represents, are more than social conventions: they are the ritual occasions for personal witness. The rage of the hunter is necessary; he must not be overwhelmed by awe when he needs all his strength to drive the spear home. Afterward there is a quiet time, often a formal, reverent acknowledgment, a supplication, a thanking, or other ritual, in recognition of the relationship of hunter and hunted. Ortega says, "the greatest and most moral homage we can pay to certain animals on certain occasions is to kill them with certain means and rituals." I would add: and to eat them.

Men must eat them to live. Men must also eat them because it is wrong to waste the life of the prey. Moreover, the symbolic function, which is after all what is uniquely human, turns on the metaphor of taking into our bodies that which we confirm. All religions have dietary laws and take symbolic eating seriously. Long before the emergence of the potato-eaters, before the insult of the domestic animal, and before the symbolic cannibalism of Christian communion ceremonies, ritual ingestion was practiced.

Truly religious people know that there is no such thing as "merely food and drink." That is a phrase by which the consume-and-accumulate society disguises its cupidity or by which its philosophers separate the spiritual and corporeal and denigrate the natural. To such a society the hunter is a paradox: he neither stores his meat nor is anxious about tomorrow. For him the hunt has a transience, an event-quality, which is the essence of being. It is the symbol *par excellence* of life, which is used—and uses him—in the process.

Although it has long been fashionable to describe it so, the world of the hunting and gathering peoples is not a vale of constant demonic threat and untold fears. It is a life of risk gladly taken, of very few wants, leisurely and communal, intellectual in ways that are simultaneously practical and aesthetic. Most pertinent to our time, it is a life founded on the integrity of solitude and human sparseness, in which men do not become a disease on their environment but live in harmony with each other and with nature. The ways of the hunters are beginning to show us how we are failing as human beings and as organisms in a world beset by a "success" that hunters never wanted.

Toolmaking as Natural History

It is assumed that the machines of today have no precedent in the pre-industrial past, and that the invention of the wheel marks the inception of human ingenuity, before which men had the misfortune to be, in effect, crippled. Neither of these ideas is true. Man did not even discover the art of toolmaking —he inherited it—and his ability in this regard is probably not quite as good as it was about twenty thousand years ago. The most successful tool ever made, older than *Homo sapiens* and still in use today, was the hand-ax—so called because it was not hafted (tied to a handle) until about thirty thousand years ago.

Men are descended from a line of technologists going back beyond their species and even their genus. Long before *Homo* appeared, the australopithecines used tools to kill, to dissect, and to eat baboons. Sticks, rocks, shells, and bones may have been employed earlier by their ancestors, the chimpanzee-like dryopithecines. Pre-men were using tools while their brains were the size of gorilla brains, before language or hearth-fire.

Therefore it is impossible to assign toolmaking to culture as opposed to human nature. The use of tools is a legacy from primate ancestors. The neural feedback system of hand and eye in connection with a tool is sometimes said to have been the unique human means of evolution, but this system for the examination and manipulation of the world is more primate than human. The drive to invent, improve, and complicate tools, which is so much a part of modern technology, is clearly separate from the capacity to make tools.

Hunting and gathering peoples strongly resist modifying or changing tools, replacing them with new kinds, innovating, or producing them beyond their own needs. This seems at first out of keeping with the idea of technology, but that is because the notions of progress, expansion, and opportunism that are attached to the idea of industry are just that—attached. The obsession with technological improvement and the more general yearning for substitution and future orientation are not innate. Indeed, men who hunt resist technological progress vigorously and with good understanding of its implications. Yet idealists who see nature and technology as incompatible are wrong. It is only the fashion of rapid modification, not the use of tools as such, that has set modern technology on the road to social and environmental destruction.

The capacity to learn to do brain surgery or play the piano may represent final touches added by our species. If so, the activity responsible for that final and delicate perfecting is probably the making and using of tools by early man for killing, dissecting, and utilizing animals. Tools associated with the seasonal harvest of domestic grains and preparation of plant materials are gross by comparison. The "good hands" of the hunter is not a familiar image, yet he is the surgeon. Tuber grubbers and soil tillers have hands calloused, arthritic, swollen, and otherwise deformed by their work.

The degree of dependence of men on tools is apparent in hunting. Even a medium-sized antelope has a very tough skin.

The lion or wolf tears through it with bone-crunching car-nassial teeth, using powerful jaws and neck to tear it open. If it were possible to obtain the prey without using a weapon, a desperate man might then laboriously chew his way into the carcass, and he could pull most of the soft organs loose, but he could not easily butcher for transport or even eat the rest of the carcass. With a sharpened piece of flint, however, he can not only open the body and cut it at the joints but finish butchering it in order to transport and distribute it.

The cutting tools used by the very earliest men of the genus *Homo* were preceded by cruder stone implements, the pebble-tools, rounded but hardly altered from natural form, which were in use for hundreds of thousands of years. The earliest tools were kitchen implements. These have been found near habitation sites, and they have characteristic blow marks on the stone indicating that they were used to strike—probably seeds, plant materials, and bones. The use of wood, bone, and teeth as tools may have been even more ancient, but few such artifacts have been uncovered. The idea of a "Paleo-lithic" or "old-stone" age is based on what remains today, not what may have preceded the use of stone or have been the predominant materials used. Tools may mislead our estimates of the true antiquity of toolmaking if the oldest have indeed vanished.

Very broadly considered, this has indicated a progression from primitive to more complex tools and an increasing variety on a rising tide of craftsmanship. Tools improved from basic core types (made by chipping off the opposite sides of an oval stone) to the flake tools (in which the flakes themselves were finished), to the blade tools of the more recent Paleolithic. There emerged an exquisite body of work of a very high caliber, knapping (chipping) techniques so refined that it takes many weeks of practice and instruction for a modern man to master them, and, indeed, some of the techniques have been lost. In *Tools of the Old and New Stone Age,* Jacques Bardaz, an American expert on the subject, has said: "The extent of this skill is quite astonishing, and despite the examination of millions of prehistoric stone implements by archaeologists and extensive experimentation, the full range of the ingenuity and skill of prehistoric stone knappers is yet to be completely shown."

The Mousterian tool kit (a hundred thousand years ago) contained some 73 different stone tools, the Aurignacian (twenty-five thousand years ago), a variety of about 240. As the use of stone increased, so must the time required to teach the techniques.

How this relates to contemporary skill in working wood, bone, horn, and other organic materials is not known. With occasional regressions, the evidence is that man developed a cumulative variety of stone tools, though some of these could have been successors to those once made of perishable materials. A cumulative increase in tools does not mean an increased rate of invention—it could simply mean the continuation of invention. In view of the enormous number of people who have lived in the twentieth century, compared to the small populations of the distant past, if the number of inventions is tallied in terms of the number of man-years lived, the rate of technological change may not have changed since about three hundred thousand years ago. The significance of this is that if a tool change is made once in every ten million man-years it would constitute a rate of change of one tool each twenty years in a population of 500,000 hunter-gatherers but 350 changes a year in our present world population. The important point is not only that the rate of invention may be fixed by our biology but also the danger that our ability to cope with change may also be biological.

No one group of men had access to the total accumulation of human invention. Different groups had different tool kits, assemblages based on cultural origins and on particular local needs and materials. Within a human group, different tool assemblages depend on the type of camp: home base, butchering, vegetable processing, preparation, or other specialized site.

Because the artifacts from such sites often run into the thousands, researchers have been using computers to calculate the relative frequency of the nearly three hundred kinds of tools found in archaeological sites. Insofar as the abundance of a tool indicates a measure of its use, the computer may show that the different proportion of scrapers to sickles indicates that tribe A spent 10 per cent more time flensing the skins of wild goats and 6 per cent less time reaping wild grains than tribe B. When this information is corrected for the relationship of campsite relicts to the habits of living hunters, pictures of the daily life of different groups of ancient men may be reconstructed much more accurately.

Except for hearths, it is difficult to estimate the importance of fire as a tool. The first hearths may be a million years old. There is firm evidence that they have existed for seven hundred thousand years—long before the earliest fossil remains of our species—and excellent evidence for four hundred thousand years. We owe the discovery of fire, then, to *Homo erectus* or even the older *Homo habilis*.

African paleobotanical studies have suggested that for a very long time men have set fire to grasslands, perhaps as part of their hunting strategy. This would have affected the relative numbers of plant and animal species, the extent of vegetation—such as savanna, forest, brush, thorn forest, grassland—and the location of boundaries between them. Probably nowhere in the world is there a greater diversity of plant associations than central Africa, though we cannot assume that man-set fires caused it.

The making and keeping of fires, the occupation of caves, roughly coincided with the expansion of our ancestors northward into the cooler climates of Europe and Asia. Where caves were available they were then occupied for the first time on a steady basis rather than occasionally, as among the more nomadic bands of older australopithecines. Men must have competed for the caves with large members of the cat and dog family (some now extinct) and with other large predators such as bears. Fire would surely have been a decisive margin in this struggle, though we must not project upon them our will to dominate. Men lived alongside cave bears for a very long time. Fire must also have a factor in easing men's fear of the dark, which is characteristic of both primate and prey.

Other shelters were probably built very early in the history of our species. Twenty-five thousand years ago hunters were living in villages near Dalni Vestonice in Central Europe and Tomsk Kostenki in Eastern Europe. The oldest house known— some three hundred thousand years old—was recently uncovered at Terra Amata near Nice, France. It is so sophisticated a structure that the full impact of its existence on the modern mind has not yet been felt. Made of wood and skin and oval in shape, 49 by 26 feet, it was occupied in the spring and summer. Under and near it were found 35,000 objects or fragments, including wooden bowls and ocher for coloring. The floor was covered with skin rugs, and its interior was divided into a hearth, a toolmaker's atelier, and other spaces.

As archaeology probes further, current ideas in many other areas may also undergo change—such as that mathematics, geometry, and astronomy were discovered by scribes, tax collectors, and mariners of the early irrigation dynasties of ancient Mesopotamia and Egypt. Lunar notations have already been found on Paleolithic materials from the Azilian period in Spain, from the Magdalenian of Spain and Russia, and even from the Aurignacian and Gravettian of Europe and Asia, all before civilization and the beginning of written records.

The Totemic Vision

Visiting the Paleolithic sanctuaries today, one cannot hope to capture more than intimations of the human past, a glimmer from some distant world awesomely remote, but a remoteness within which our own personal core of being is held. It is unintelligible only because we want words, no more truly foreign than oriental music to Western ears.

Like all other creations of hunting peoples, the Paleolithic cave sanctuaries of Europe and Asia were only grudgingly accepted by official modern culture as major productions of mankind. For decades experts denied that the painting and sculpture could have been done by "primitive" man, and other pedants grudgingly allowed them to be the childlike scrawls of a simple magic for insuring a supply of game. Even in 1970 Paleolithic art was still being compared to the work of small children.

Cave Art

To the casual visitor the walls of these caves seem at first to be decorated indiscriminately with a mélange of irregularly scattered figures, and for many years the experts also saw them as disorderly accumulations of centuries. The observer can easily be misled by his knowledge of modern art, in which the idea of creativity is associated with art for art's sake or with the unconventional and arbitrary whims of a rebellious genius. Those who have looked more carefully have found a meticulous and elaborate system of forms and ideas in the many drawings and in the thousands of decorated objects as well. This implies an underlying metaphysics and cosmology.

The modern French archaeologist André Leroi-Gourhan, in a lifetime of study, explored 66 of 110 known caves. He mapped 2188 animal figures and innumerable abstract signs. He found a development of styles stretching across thousands of years, from which he concluded that Paleolithic art was not a beginning of human creativity but a culmination of a vast and enduring institution that may have included most of mankind. By studying the number and exact location of the different animals represented, he found an underlying scheme.

All the animals and signs belong to two basic categories. Even the most abstract, geometric forms are part of the pattern, linked to the realistic figures by intermediate forms. The fundamental concept is that of male and female; to this division of life the whole of the art is subordinated. The distinction is not in the gender of individual animals but in the assignment of each species to a category. For example, the bison is female, the horse male. Each painted panel is an association of com-

plementary species and their abstract signs. The basic groupings are:

$$\text{man} = \left\{ \begin{array}{l} \text{ibex} \\ \text{stag} \\ \text{lion} \\ \text{bear} \\ \text{horse} \end{array} \right\} = \text{spear} \qquad \text{woman} = \left\{ \begin{array}{l} \text{bison} \\ \text{oxen} \\ \text{hind} \end{array} \right\} = \text{wound}$$

Pairs or groups of pairs are often flanked by accompanying
individuals of another species.

These panels with their themes of complementarity and
accompaniment occupy central chambers in the sanctuaries.
Entryways, passages, and rear chambers are dominated by individual male animals and male signs. The female signs range
from naturalistic vulvas to ovals, triangles, and rectangles; the
male, from phalluses to barbed signs, strokes, and dots. There
are sketches of the "vanquished man" or wounded human, and
of manlike figures, sometimes with animal antlers or tails, who
appear to be injured. Dangerous animals such as the bear, lion,
and rhinoceros are found only in the most remote sections of
the cave. In some parts of France and Spain bison predominate
in the central chambers; in others aurochs (the wild oxen) or
mammoths.

In addition to the tools for painting, engraving, and
sculpting, archaeologists have uncovered torches and lamps.
Series of bas-relief forms and sculptured plaquettes sometimes
accompany the painted and incised figures. Handprints of
women are outlined with the mineral pigments of the kind
used to execute the major drawings, and there are footprints of
groups of young adolescents.

The majority of sculptured and painted figures are found
in areas of the caves so far from the entrances that it is very
unlikely that they are merely the decorated surfaces of lived-
in space.

Near the cave entrances and beneath overhanging cliffs
there are signs of habitation: tools, bones, jewelry, hearths,
and other artifacts commonly associated with occupation sites.

Here the drawing and sculpture are different. Isolated bear skulls and sculptures of animals have carefully placed "spear" or "dagger" holes in them. Hundreds of scrawled animal figures seem to be imitations of the master drawings. There is evidence that these were shielded from view by post-and-skin tents, suggesting ritual use and perhaps a subordinate religious shrine.

Covering a period of almost 20,000 years, from about 34,000 to 14,000 years ago, this complex body of cave art is the most ancient, continuous, and possibly the most revealing product of human creation. Leroi-Gourhan likens it to Romanesque art (as opposed to the arbitrary iconography of modern art) with its many figures, repeated stylized details and fragments, and duplication of symbols, which fill the space available. In caves from Russia to Spain the key scenes are similar, showing a unity of idea and purpose. Some modest little caves have but a single set of signs, rural chapels in a widespread religion whose most profound expressions are the great cathedrals of Lascaux and Les Combarelles.

Missing now but very likely used in ritual ceremonies implied by the paintings are objects made from wood, feathers, shell, skins, and the finer, more perishable bones. The recovery of jewelry and objects archaeologists call "wands," made from teeth and bone, suggest the possible richness of occasion. Large containers of ocher have been found, attesting to a variety of colors. One can only imagine the elaboration of painted body, song, chant, dance, and mime, all part of the panoply of the great rituals of the Magdalenian period, the highest point of Paleolithic culture, ceremonies evoked by the duality of life, gender, and the paradox of death as the source of life. Combination of pairs of females flanked by males and the arrangement of spear and wound are the oldest symbols of the theme of copulation and death, the great round united by the deepest mysteries of experience, integrated in a cycle of life's renewal.

In guessing at the nature of that lost culture and its conception of the universe, archaeology carries us only so far. What further can be guessed must come from our knowledge of the working of the human mind. One significant detail of some of the cave art is the use of natural masses, lines, edges, and curvatures of the cave wall and ceiling. Again and again, the surface contours of the limestone define the morphology of the painted animal. Here, the profile of a horse is given by the stone and followed by the artist; there, the belly of an auroch. At Lascaux, a falling horse is breaking its back on a shoulder of rock jutting from the wall on which the painting is done. As the natural relief of the floor, wall, or ceiling become hip, hock, or hoof, the figure and the stone seem to interpenetrate. Stone and flesh blend, so that the figures seem to stand halfway between what is given and what is made, to be as much discovered as created.

The Duality of Life

These cave figures belong to a larger class of transitional objects, the first of which in the life of every person is the mother who, during the prenatal and early postnatal life of the child, is both part of and yet separate from the child.

The cave is the containing space in the earth metaphor of the mother goddess. As an image of the female reproductive tract the cave leads to the source of life. We are told by psychiatrists that all normal perception and a stable mental apparatus later in life depend on "good mothering." In his personal rebirth as a religious individual who has become sensitive to spiritual reality, to cosmic purpose and order, and to the symbolic dimension of physical surroundings, the young person requires a good mother earth.

It is possible to misinterpret this return to the mother as an anxiety-driven retreat from real life. An anthropomorphic concept of Mother Earth can indeed reflect a pathological regression in which men obstinately cling to symbols of security or yearn for the lost fetal unity. Whether this "love of nature" is normal or perverted depends on whether it is the end of adult maturation or a stage in the mental development of the adolescent. That the complex and necessary process of adolescence may malfunction is one of the risks of our highly specialized human mode of maturing by stages that in some way invoke, emulate, and build upon what has gone before.

The return to the womb-cave of mother earth is fraught with primary process thought; that is, the yearning for identity, immediate gratification, and existence without subject-object separation in a mythic world where symbol and symbolized are the same. During childhood this infantile form of thought gradually makes room for its opposite: perception of separateness and limitation, a rational awareness of sequential events, and the denotive working of symbolism. Every human mind has this double aspect, which rises to a level of threatened collision or split as the new powers of cognition in the service of language come into their own. This is a critical time in the development of the individual mind (or, if you wish, psyche or ego). It is precisely at this point that the hunter's ceremonial initiation of the adolescent into adulthood is a biological adaptation. Only an integrating system at this crucial time can prevent the psychosis that accompanies the denial and failure of one or the other of these two poles. This integrating system is based on the transitional-object prototype.

While the mother herself is the first and most general of these, later transitional objects in the life of the infant are parts of the mother's body, such as face and nipples. The infant proceeds to discover its own fingers and toes, the bottle, a rattle, a blanket—objects that function for a time both as parts of the self and in some way not-self. As part of the self they are self-creations. As part of the not-self, they are found and other. They are intermediate between the person as maker and searcher, as omnipotent and finite, making possible the realizations of self-limitation. The transitional forms reduce the anxiety of this discovery and continue to serve in one form or another in the twenty years of sorting out self and not-self. In the child's later relationship to the inanimate environment will be employed those psychological forces that were first used in relation to its mother and the rest of its human environment. The transitional object is a substitute environment propelling the individual into a new level or plane of awareness. A full awareness of the cosmic "fitting together" may be a temporary state, constituting, for example, in adolescent initiation ceremony, the moment of a peak experience.

Life as an *Objet Trouvé*

The initial discovery of the caves by Paleolithic men must have been a compelling and awesome experience. Living perhaps at the mouth of the cave, they ventured deep into it and were in some subtle way transformed by what they felt there. Such is the peculiar power of the found object—which, in the caves, was to be exploited with marvelous insight and subtlety as time passed.

The pure *objet trouvé* is the unique cowrie shell, the singular gem, feather, piece of coral, tooth, or mineral, which communicates in some way beyond the usual. When such objects are incorporated into a human construction, such as the addition of a neck-chain to a piece of coral, an arrangement of pieces of driftwood, or the drawing of the eyes of an owl on a head-shaped rock, their significance is raised to a new level, as though the finder had completed a fragment of a sentence.

The *objet trouvé,* modified or not, is a fragment of the universe that more or less embarrasses us today, for we are no longer a society of amateur naturalists who can hide a strange instinct behind scientific purpose. Yet, like Victorian gentlemen with their cabinets of birds' nests and quartz crystals, we continue to bring the objects home if they are portable and to make photographs and drawings of them if they are not. We exhibit them. Something, it seems, is to be learned or revealed or confirmed—one cannot say which. They are catalytic in our perception, though we do not know just how. *Objets trouvés,* which uniquely relate man to nature, are worn, traded, scrutinized, imitated, and treasured. Neanderthal man apparently collected such objects. Australian aborigines keep a collection of such stones for religious purposes. Yet the fascination does not depend on religious custom. They are common as well among people who do not formally incorporate them religiously.

They stand in a special relation to human sensory and perceptual systems, intermediate between human productions and the given world of natural objects. They anticipate human productions; not just any products but art forms. Therefore the *objet trouvé* is a substitute (or natural) work of art, anthropologically a precursor of art, which is followed by the transitional object, whose physical qualities relate the symbolic and the real, as in the cave figures. Modified *objets trouvés,* these are tangible expressions of both natural and human processes of creation, linking the given and the created, transforming, with the help of ceremonial action, opposition into connection and relationship.

If the Paleolithic sanctuaries were in fact instruments for buffering the adolescent's inherent predisposition to split mentally, and instruments of an immanent theology of relatedness between opposite psychic forces, then the caves must also have a male dimension, complementary to the symbol of the great maternal body, just as there is a symmetry between female and male figures within them. That these caves may be perceived as masculine lies in the nature of visual experience. The caves are archives of visual images, records of group memories parallel to the memories of an individual. The individual is aware of his own head as a dark space bound by the cranium. Our thoughts, our visual and auditory experience, and our recollections of the past seem to illumine that space. Visual memory seems to be made up of photographic stills, flashing into vivid illumination in consciousness. An actual cave may be perceived as an externalized replica of the cephalic interior. Its interior is a model of the head, its contents representing the mind and memory.

Cave art is a memory bank, giving concrete form to the images of a mythological dream time which the individual knows from narrative accounts. The desire to see is associated with the wish to see the past and is synonymous for most people with the desire to know. Cave images are probably the visual counterpart of myths transmitted orally, answering such questions as "Who created the world?" and "Where did men come from?" Language is the magic that makes possible the re-creation of the cave images in the dark cave of the mind. The visual and verbal body of symbols identifies and binds the group.

Fire and Cave: Transitional Objects

The lamps and torches found by archaeologists in the sanctuaries prove that fire had functions other than warmth or cooking. Even when light and heat are needless and there is no danger from animals, men still gather around an open fire at night. As the hub of a social group, it has great antiquity and force in all human life. Fire is like the ranking individual of a primate group, the focus of attention, power, and authority. The destruction of the fuel and life of the fire represent the antitheses of life and death. As the symbol of life and consciousness, fire is a transitional object by which the warmth and motion of the living body are seen as qualities of the inanimate universe. It is symbolic, therefore, of three central themes of human experience: the livingness of the inanimate, the eventual death and annihilation which is the destiny of all life, and the reality of consciousness and thought.

Paintings seen in the light of the fire became special instruments for calling insight to attention. To go into the cave for a sight that reveals men's connections to the cosmos is the ritualization of insight. This play of ideas presupposes an organism with a personal history of play as a child, who already understands conventionalized style and repetitiveness, and who knows that movements, postures, and sounds exist that resemble familiar social forms but that are, nonetheless, very different from the practical routines of daily life.

Devotion to Tradition

Though it is commonly said that primitive men see themselves as "part of nature," Paleolithic hunters did not and modern hunters do not "identify" themselves in a sense of merger or union with nature. The main thrust of their education and culture is the opposite: to clarify and emphasize their identity—not as an apartness so much as the precise definition of sets of relationships. The images of art play a role in this. It is for this reason that art has been called a love affair with the world and that the art object is seen as a love gift. Fidelity is a pre-condition for mature love relationships—among people or between men and the world. Twenty thousand years of cave art did not endure because of mystic union with nature or because of innovative genius, but because of genius in devotion to a tradition, a tradition that used art in the education of perception, sensitivity to otherness, and the bold affirmation of that otherness.

In recent times the romantic period in art (c. 1700 to 1900) has been regarded as evidence of a growing and renewed love for nature. In some ways, such as the shift toward organic metaphors and away from static object or space concepts, it revitalized human ecology. Its celebration of the "noble savage" implied an attempt to recover human virtues spoiled by civilization. But the "good behavior" it celebrated was closer to child-like innocence than to mature understanding and acceptance.

The identity-formation ceremonies of hunter-gatherer peoples suggest a parallel to romanticism's recognition of the importance of the individual. But the difference in the ancient life-ways described and the theme of personality in literary romanticism is wide. The latter produced a cult of politics and art based on inspiration, characterized by disdain of discipline, adulation of departure from tradition (considering this creativity), provocation of emotion as an end in itself, and celebration of individuality as personal taste, talent, and personality. It organized devotion to "great" individuals. This has been academically expressed many times in the yearning to know exactly who painted the bulls on the walls of the Paleolithic cave at Lascaux. The impact of romanticism on the adolescent, especially those getting a humanistic or liberal arts college education, has been to create unattainable heroes and ideals and to encourage the self-indulgent, private, existential imagination. Romanticism erected a façade of words-music-images, emotion and scenery between the individual and natural reality. It created the illusion of nature as landscape and nostalgia for a nonexistent past—in short, a way of rejecting reality.

Cave art, as a transitional object, in conjunction with its religious use, was precisely a way of accepting reality. Fidelity to a tradition and a sense of connectedness to a real outside world are related, for both rest on a conviction of order and participation. Cave art was probably associated with holy ritual, which was inseparable from certain phases of adolescent initiation. Explication of the cosmic order of creation came at the right moment in the life cycle, for the sub-adult attention to religion and search for a larger identity are pre-timed by genetic development. Readiness to leave the ways of childhood and the desire for ritual tutorial and symbolic thought are part of human biology, to which society responds and by which a new, more mature self and a wider universe unfold. Just as the creation of art is a love relationship with the world, the creation of culture and society is a loving mastery of the ambivalence of self and not-self. All love relationships begin with the mother and mature in the wisdom of the father. Cave men wisely celebrated this homology.

The Love-Death Figure

The whole of man's hunting endeavor must be understood as a symbolic, cultural, and social activity. Though he is a highly capable social predator on large, dangerous mammals, he is singularly without the nutritional necessity of eating meat. He is a polished runner and stalker who eats meat as a sacrament, and for whom bodily renewal by eating and mating are united religiously in the flesh. Hence his hunting and mating combine unusual behaviors.

The symbiotic interplay of the hunt and love, of predation and copulation, is a primal motif, surely preliterate, and older than the agricultural theme of the cycle of birth and death, regeneration from the decay of life, and the dead as a source of the living. The spear's interpenetration of the body and the flesh as the source of all new life are the iconography of venery —at once the pursuit of love and game.

The poetry of the love-death axis reaches us through the philosophy of totemism, the world's most ancient system of thought. Totemism postulates a world in which social groups of men and the society of natural species are logically equivalent. The most conspicuous relations between species are food habits and food chains, while the connections between the human sexes and groups are defined by marriage. Consummation for one is the act of eating, for the other copulation. Both lead to a unity or affinity, but provision is made to insure continued distinction and difference and counterbalance merger and assimilation. The central theme of parallel and interlocking food-and-marriage rules is the poise between coming together and keeping identity. The rules specifying which animals may be eaten, which parts and under what conditions they can be consumed, are not simply parallel to rules of incest and kinship: they are part of a single fabric, woven into symbolic expression, in which the given world of animals provides a rhythmic form with which the man-created forms of society resonate and interplay. Although we may think of eating habits as largely fixed by nature and marriage customs as human inventions, the perception of them by members of a traditional society is that both are given, since both change little during the individual lifetime. Eating and marriage laws are therefore reciprocal and they may be regarded as springing from the same basic order or source.

The relationship between them does not depend on intellectual symbolism. Both have to do with the most profound of life's passions, the demonic moment of the kill and of orgasm. These two powerful expressions are related. Both lead to life and to death, which, like maleness and femaleness, represent a fundamental polarity.

This suggests in a somewhat poetic way the mature wisdom and health that shaped the totemic vision. The deranged are unable to feel either, or are obsessed with death or sex and incapable of unity. Feeling for the complementarity of the hunt and love (or death and sex) may have existed much earlier in human experience than its formulation as a religious scheme. The pair-bond between man and woman and the pursuit of large game entered human existence together in the prehistoric past. The bond was an intensified expression of pair preference, the repeated but temporary companionship of two particular individuals during the female's monthly oestrus. The hunt was a refinement of the casual pursuit of small game that happened to be at hand.

The development of the human menstrual cycle is an intrinsic part of human origins. The monthly cycle inherited from ancestral primates was modified by the gradual increase of the period of sexual interest along with the retention of sexual-releasing signals and the enhancement of the erotic state. By extending sexual activity longer after ovulation and starting it sooner before, the asexual part of the month was slowly extinguished from both ends, and sensory signals tended to replace the older hormonal cues. The males who, in the ancient primate manner, had previously shifted their attention from one female to another as their libido bloomed and faded remained longer in companionship with favored mates. The menstrual period may have become the only part of the cycle without copulation. If so, it is possible that, in the earliest days of our genus, the lunar cycles of the women of the group were perhaps synchronized. There is evidence even today of such synchrony among women working close together. Such timing would have reduced strife and conflict by stopping all sexual activity in the group at the same time.

It is well known by anthropologists that hunting-gathering people have strong customs concerning blood and, more particularly, taboos regulating female activity, sexual and otherwise, during menstruation. The association of menstrual blood and the idea of a bleeding wound is inescapable and, together with genital anatomy, became the cornerstone of the symbolism of sex and hunting, love and death. Older, post-menopausal women would probably not have survived unless they played some useful role in the life of the species. Undoubtedly one of their roles during the ritualization of venery was that of intermediary or even executive in administering menstrual and sexual rules.

There is a danger in all carnivores of confusing the two kinds of veneral aggression, loving and hunting. Among men particularly, it is important to protect other humans from malfunction of the hunting instinct. All carnivores, including men, have unmistakable signals saying I-come-in-peace. Perhaps the razor's edge separates assault from love, requiring female postures that can instantly deflect attack. The female, whether the target of redirected fury or the sexual prey of the wild huntsman, has not only to deflect his violence but to entertain it.

Prototypes of this situation occur throughout the animal kingdom, where, among many reptiles, birds, and mammals, the first steps in courtship are attack and deflection. With a sinuous movement, the female lifts her head, flashes a color, gives a call, or produces an odor—and the attack is instantly transformed into part of a dance, which will elicit a new response from the female. A courtship has begun with a beautiful set of signals initiated in the style—for a moment the reality—of aggression.

Our species built the choler-to-fervor use of passion into daily life. The wrath of the most dangerous animal can be transformed into a mighty compassion by the female, the perennial tease, who quickly learns to draw the male's anger in order that she may change it. This may have been a major factor in the evolution of continuous sexual receptivity. The woman's special morphology is then brought into play as eros-inciting signals, emphasized by modified submission postures, such as that called "presentation" by primatologists. The morphological signals also include the breasts, which do not diminish when dry and are thus readapted to a new use. The pubic triangle is probably hairy for this reason. Mankind is almost unique among animals in the use of the genitalia themselves to stimulate. For the same purpose are those culturally refined, eroticizing, cryptandric features, which have already been mentioned, such as jewelry, bound feet, bustles, hair arrangements, cosmetics, perfumes, and tattooing. (The most arresting attitude the woman can take is to face the angry man naked except for her jewelry. Perhaps it is not surprising that hoodlums' "molls" are either overdressed or have nothing on. They are the extreme response to the extremely aggressive men of modern society.)

It is difficult to arrange in order of time the origin of all these behaviors and traits. Somewhere in the vicissitudes of a million years of hunting and the reworking of a primate heritage, there emerged a new sensitivity. The emotion scale from hate to love may be like a tree whose very high crown indicates a very deep tap root, a great depth of aggressiveness in a single being balanced by a lofty tenderness that is unmatched elsewhere in life.

In daily life the mysterious processes of redirecting our native ferocity may be at work in emergent ways. It is an axiom of Christianity that this redirection is done consciously and deliberately; in the Greek way of thinking, this can be done only by striving for humane, civilized behavior. In truth, this is as innate, as instinctive, as aggressiveness.

The human hunter in the field is not merely a predator, because of hundreds of centuries of experience in treating the woman-prey with love, which he turns back into the hunt proper.

The ecstatic consummation of this love is the killing itself. Formal consummation is eating. As all human hunters have always known, the kill must be eaten. Otherwise both are disgraced. Those who say, "Well, it is all right for primitive hunters to kill because they must do so to eat," are only half right. The prey must be eaten for ethical not nutritional value, in a kind of celebration.

On a superficial level, the meat is a relish that makes the main dish tolerable, a festive release from a routine of tubers and nuts. Symbolically, it is a re-enactment of the emergence of man from herbivorous ancestors and the dark of ignorance, as love between man and woman is a re-enactment of the discovery of love as a continuing bond, a passion engendering compassion and affection, prefiguring the feeling for and affirmation of other species and the world. This is one reason that the difference and otherness of the genders is important and "unisex" a perversion in a normal society and possibly an extreme perceptual adaptation in a stressed society needing to reduce its birth rate.

I have suggested that the carnivore whose attack is stopped by appeasement experiences a change of feeling. In courtship the appeaser is not a true prey but the human female. What then does she feel? Humility and adoration perhaps? Something has been added to the fear grimace with which a subordinate monkey allows itself to be mounted. Face-to-face copulation, as among humans, some higher apes, and probably extinct species of hominids, coincides with a new psychology. Sexual intercourse has become the most powerful imaginable experience of relatedness. One might almost say that it comes close to ceasing to be reproductive behavior (which could be taken care of much more simply with oestrus; fertilization once a year could be accomplished with one-fiftieth as much copulation). Supine in the act she may be, but the woman is more a partner and less an object. The male does not simply penetrate her; he is engulfed. He is also engulfed in the sacred cave, in the ceremonial confrontation of the symbolic gender of animal art.

The vast body of painting, engraving, and sculpture, of which the associated orations, dance, and ceremony are lost, does not document the origin of humans culture or the beginnings of art. They are part of the archives of a fully mature body of thought on the profound themes of human life.

5

THE KARMA OF
ADOLESCENCE

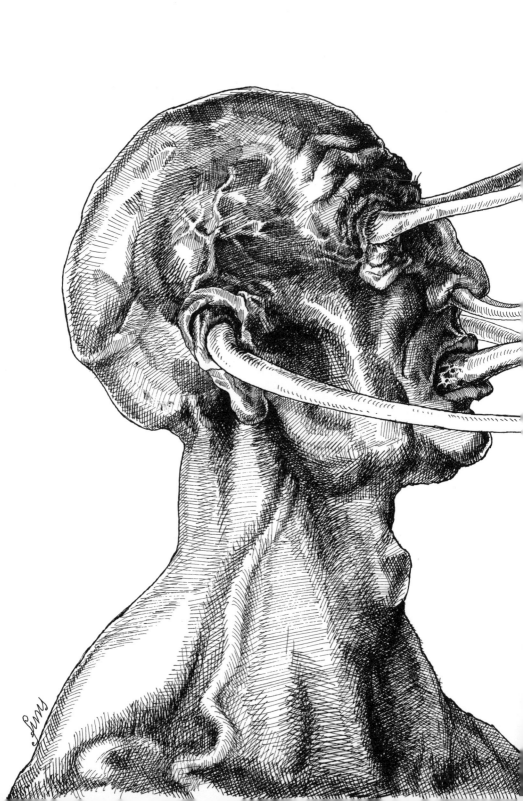

Self and Not-Self

It has been said that, because man lacks unusual physical features, he is an unspecialized species, or a generalized animal; that his brain enabled him to modify his behavior or make tools in substitution for biological evolution of the kind that produced the penguin's adaptations to the Antarctic Ocean or the giraffe's ability to browse in the treetops while standing on the ground.

This view was based on a misunderstanding of how specialization modifies particular functions of the central nervous system. Indeed, it was wrong even about physical characteristics: the human skin, foot, eyes, pharynx, heat-regulating system,

[177]

hand musculature, maturation schedule, mammary tissues, and sexual dimorphism are but a few of the specialized details of the human body.

The life cycle of our species is especially unusual—and extremely specialized. Certain aspects of protracted postnatal growth—or ontogeny—are biological adaptations to conditions of life in the past and make sense only in the perspective of man's niche as a hunter-gatherer. They have been inherited by man from his evolutionary ancestors.

From ancestral primates came the extraordinary gift of a long youth, with continued dependence of the young adults after weaning and unbroken association with adults throughout life. A prolonged dependent period was gradually evolved through natural selection, and no species of primate has since traded back this slow uncoiling of the curve of individual life for the quick leap into maturity.

The primates are unusual in the degree of longevity and in kinship as the kernel of sociality. Old bass eat young bass, and robins drive yearlings away from home territory forever. Extended immaturity could be good for any species only as part of a larger ecology to which adult behavior is keyed, so that the species is modified in many related ways and society is thoroughly reorganized. The population composition by age groups cannot be altered independently of rates of growth, birth, and death. Such an evolutionary twist can be afforded only by those rare species who are large, secure, complicated, and relatively free of the kind of fixed action patterns that rule the lives of bass and robins.

There are relatively few animal niches where evolution can work in this way. Galápagos turtles have a stretched-out life span, and so do elephants and horses, locusts and clams. But the stages of their lives are not so well defined as among primates. In most animals immaturity is got through as fast as growth will allow: a few months of dependence, separation from the parents before full growth or maturity is achieved, and—presto! new adults.

The life cycle of the individual developed by the higher

primates was based on a graded series of stages, each with its unique traits. The social group as a whole is as dependent upon the peculiar features and contributions of each stage as upon the presence of adults themselves.

Because of the characteristic social status of each age group and of the importance of age, health, and temperament in the individual's status, the organization of primate society is like a large, complicated building with many floors and many rooms through which a succession of individuals moves. Exactly who is to the left and right, above and below, is important to each individual. The personalities of those surrounding him affect his position at any given time. His own personal qualities, age, sex, size, and experience, also play a part.

Adaptable response to such a society requires constant attention and adjustment. The young primate does not have to learn how to respond to other individuals, nor *what* the complicated structure of society is like for his own species. These are part of the coded information he inherits. What he learns and relearns constantly is to whom to respond appropriately and when to do so ("when" in the context of events, not the calendar of life). Similarly, human children do not have to learn to walk or talk, though their skill in doing them will be imperfect at first; they learn where to walk and what to say to whom.

In man very specialized adaptations to the phases of the life cycle have evolved. The mammalian-primate brain seems to have followed the paleontological principle known as Romer's Rule, which says that when an organism develops new organs it makes them from the tissues of the old whenever possible. This means that many of the characteristic mental events of adult life are derived from those of youth. Certain behaviors in the years of childhood are a kind of replay—in a new key and with new harmonies—of infantile behaviors. For this reason it is necessary to examine parts of the mental life of the very young before some peculiarities of the older can be understood.

That the life cycle is extremely specialized in man can be seen from its effect on the composition and organization of human populations. This characteristic is obscured by the effect of modern medicine, which mistakenly is credited with longevity. Medicine is largely occupied with combating the diseases of modern man, which have come into existence in the era of medicine itself. In any case, medicine is simply making it possible for more people to realize the potentialities of longevity and diversity of each phase of life, as evolved in man over the past two million years or so.

A long childhood seems to be reason enough for its own existence, but nothing comes that easily to any species in its tenancy on earth. However it may seem to the harassed and hurried modern man, the gift of long youth is not a gratuity against later burdens and responsibility. It was not "designed" by primates as a recess from life. The period of learning to learn in monkeys requires about five years in the larger species; the great apes need ten. Our species did not double that period simply for the fun of it.

The purpose (or, as the biologist should say, function) of this long immaturity broken into sub-phases in man is an adaptation to a way of life, to the ecology of a special kind of hunting and gathering. Yet it is not related to a direct advantage in the quest for food. If the life expectancy of a Paleolithic man, upon reaching the age of twenty, was sixty years, and if he was mature at the age of twenty-one, then 35 per cent of his life was spent in immaturity. Because of the incompetence of the young as providers in all species, this would have been a very strange arrangement if getting food was a major threat to survival. Had such people been hard-pressed by hunger, the young would have been drafted into an adult activity, and natural selection would have accelerated their growth to maturity. Obviously food was not a problem. Hunting and gathering liberated the young from the economy and the species for experiments in ways of individual maturing to a degree unknown to other primates.

Experiments by our species in how to live were centered on social learning. Learning, in any animal, puts heavy demands on the central nervous system, which are met by increasing the brain size. If the 170 species of other primates are compared for intelligence and brain size, the two will be found to be consistently related. At a certain size, however—represented by about 500 cubic centimeters of cranial capacity—the progression ceases.

Chimpanzees and gorillas (with brains from 400 to 500 cubic centimeters) seem to be able to learn many things in captivity that they do not learn in the wild. They solve problems, paint, construct edifices, drive vehicles, communicate with hand signals, and do many other things that indicate an intellectual capacity beyond their natural needs. Among them, then, a further increase in brain size and intelligence could serve no function without an entirely different coding device for storing, mixing, and exchanging information. Such an instrument is speech.

The brain size of the larger chimpanzees and that of man's ancestor, *Australopithecus africanus,* are about the same. *Australopithecus* is the transitional figure in prehuman history, between the ancient grain-eating, apelike *Ramapithecus* and the human genus *Homo.* *Australopithecus* took to hunting, using fire, making tools. As *Australopithecus* evolved into *Homo,* the cranium was elongated, increasing the room for brain lobes, where such mental activities as visual association and planning are centered. Later, as *Homo habilis* graded into *Homo erectus,* there was enlargement of the brain width, implying that the lateral lobes, housing speech and memory, were increased to human size.

Psychologists who have reared chimpanzees in their homes, giving them the same care as they do their own children, have confirmed that the chimpanzee's behavior and intelligence are the equivalent or better than that of the children under the age of three or four, when the children master basic language skills.

The complicated patterns of personal interaction, rank, peer group, kin loyalties, clique arrangements, and other aspects of the human social experience are mostly anticipated by and seen in the lives of other primates who do not have true speech. This suggests that the feelings and other emotional and social experiences preceded man in evolutionary time and do not require language. The other primates, however, have relatively little interest in the world apart from their own kind, while man is concerned with the non-human world, which he explores and manipulates. Perhaps language is associated with this extension of intelligence, with the need to label, analyze, store, and retrieve that information which carries relatively little emotional charge and for which there may be no immediate use or significance. If so, it is an adaptation to the enlargement of attention to the non-human environment, and it is not surprising that talk is a poor solution to social problems.

Thus language may be considered an evolutionary experiment, like elephants' trunks and birds' wings. It is not an exception from natural selection. As an instrument of intelligence it allows us to discriminate, differentiate, and remember. These are exceedingly valuable abilities for hunters. An organism with few fixed responses and many choices needs to store information gained from experience. To an insect, for whom choices are few and intelligence a burden, the elaboration of storage, cross-reference, and retrieval would be cumbersome; the stored data must be usable or they are a liability. For large brains storage is not a process like pouring grain into a bin. Classificatory schemes are necessary, which the organism can act upon as though they were ideas, but which are in fact new operations of the nervous system. In man, the ability to store data has been brought together with the necessity of making choices through the instrument of language.

Large size is basic to this evolution. The advantages of bigness are better precision and greater reserve of organs, less vulnerability to predators, more resistance to weather and climate, broader dietary habits—each contributes an increment of further freedom to behavior. These advantages presuppose a world containing a large number of small forms. There is an evolutionary economy of scale that requires an increasing proportion of small creatures for every additional large one.

Large size makes bigger and more differentiated brains possible. Wolves, bears, and chimpanzees have big brains, improved to the point of a wide generalized attention suitable to their respective carnivorousness, omnivorousness, and frugivorousness. By combining the three modes of attention represented by their three types of food habits, a new kind of intelligence is created, with open attention that relates a larger world to the question, "Who am I?" Consciousness becomes a wider, panoramic lens, requiring new perceptual devices for giving meaning to the enormous complexity of the world.

"Who am I?" became an operating principle long before it was ever a histrionic cry of existential alienation. It is not an intellectual question so much as a pattern of organization for a creature with very large brain and body, a combined herbivore-carnivore heritage, a long life full of leisure, and an extended and specialized sequence of immature phases. Harold F. Searles, an American psychiatrist, says: "The human being is engaged throughout his life span in an increasing struggle to differentiate himself increasingly fully, not only from his human but also from his non-human environment, while developing in proportion as he succeeds in this differentiation an increasingly meaningful relatedness to both environment and people."

The two decades of immaturity during which learning begins lead to some beautiful and some unexpected consequences. The human brain does indeed do certain things very well, but the infinite putty theory, which sees no limit to its capacity, is little more than a rite of self-idolatry, which motivates us in the end to kill one another and destroy the natural world. Those who go on too much about the special uniqueness and dignity of man should be made to study the natural history of the brain, to become bird-watchers of the brain, bird-watchers of the mind. Bird-watchers seldom use the phrase "free as a bird." (Birds have something better than random flight.) Mind-bird-watching starts with real bird-watching, by which bird brains come to be known first. An awareness of their beauty of otherness and their sharpened visual sensitivity would help to correct the humaniac influence of the bootstrap-dignity, up-from-the-muck school of evolution.

During these twenty years the answer to the question "Who am I" is subjected to a series of refinements by the young human. His earliest answer is lost to conscious memory, though it is accessible in symbols to the artist, the dreamer, and the psychoanalyst. We will always lack articulate infants to describe their experience as it happens, yet some aspects of those first months of life can be pieced together. Perception and consciousness arise through contact with things. Although in many ways the first two years of life are simply a continuation of embryonic development, it is probably true that the foetus in its uterine environment exists in a subjective unity with the mother, an identity ending at birth, which initiates a series of further separations.

Slowly—the tempo is set by the growth of the nervous system—the individual sorts himself out from the universe. The first phase includes the localizing of the sources of stimuli, recognizing which reality is inside and which outside, becoming familiar with the parts of the body that frequently send signals: the gut, mouth, eyes, hands, the surfaces by which he is held, that are touched by clothing and blankets—patterns mostly of taste and touch. There is no single moment at which the self seems to leap forth, no tiny shout of "Eureka! I am me!" in the virginal mind, but rather a slow realization.

There are objects that glide between the self and not-self, easing the shock of discovery, transitional objects that are both self and other. Perhaps the nipple is the first and most important. The suckling's first view of the not-self beyond the feel of his own weight and the coolness of the air is the mouthful of flesh. In time sucking includes play with the nipple. The breast is perceived as warm and living. The bottle is not. If the nipple is truly at the center of the suckling's being, bottle babies may perceive the universe and themselves as non-living and inert, a psychic wound marring the whole of their search for self and the nature of the not-self. The seen toes, sucked thumb, and held blanket are other transitional objects, joining the self at the mouth with the outside world.

Inside-outside and bodily parts are gradually assembled by experience. The sources of stimuli begin to be localized, as coming from within or without. Parts of the body are localized by touch and kinesthetic sense. The beginnings of true self-consciousness focus about a body surface, or body boundary.

Within is *me*, without is not-me, or other. A face is two eyes and a mouth and elicits a smile of recognition, a genetically determined aid for accepting the non-self. Crying and other muscular movement are necessary in this creation of a personal sensory-motor integrity.

In time, mother is sorted out from the rest of the surroundings and distinguished from other persons, just as true dogs will be distinguished from all quadruped "doggies" and perceived as different from goats and sheep. From recognition come expectation and assumptions. In these first months the tactile-oral, sensory-motor groundwork for all perception is prepared.

Through infancy and childhood a body schema has progressively developed based on inherent perceptual unfolding: awareness of internal and external locations of stimuli, of limb movement and body posture, the realization of the livingness of one's own body in its autonomous functions, feedback such as hearing one's own voice, the sources and control of pain and pleasure—in short, the accumulated experience of an ego, which is a genetically programed part of embryological and infantile experience. In conjunction with this, a second percept more contingent on early good mothering and on the vicissitudes of experience, forms as the juvenile becomes an adolescent. This is the body image, an organization of memory and fantasy, an idiosyncratic, historical outcome of the personal past. Whereas the body schema culminated in acceptance of the discontinuity of reality and the separateness of objects, including one's body, in space and time, the body image is an instrument for the consciousness of self as a person in social space and time. Both stages have ecological dimensions—that is, require certain kinds of non-human objects as well as social feedback.

Discontinuity and Multiplicity

About the age of two true speech is begun. It is added to an infant sound system that will never be entirely replaced—the mood-sound cries, coos and laughter, which indicate conditions and feelings such as location, fear, hunger, discomfort, pleasure, surprise, and curiosity. The adult crooning to the child is a reciprocation.

Sounds of emotion are common among the primates. When these are combined with touch, body postures, and facial expressions they enable a baby primate to signal adequately to its mother. The vocal communications of slightly older primates and adults seem to be extensions of this system. Jane van Lawik-Goodall, in her work on wild chimpanzees, identified over fifty conventional sound and face expressions. Several had different meanings, depending on the specific situation. By combining these, the chimpanzee's repertoire could be significantly increased. In the past such sounds as apes and very young children make were thought to be pre-linguistic; the human supposedly refined the ape system to a more highly organized state, fashioning words from the basic sounds. This may not be so. The two kinds of language are distinct, and people retain the emotive language of primates as a separate language all their lives.

With the first true speech in the small child there are changes in the brain—by this time 60 per cent of its adult size. Speech is a true critical-period behavior—that is, programed by the genes to take place at about twenty months of age. It must be actively undertaken then; if it is delayed too long, linguistic and mental crippling may follow.

The schedule of events is about the same for all humans: from babbling or lallation it goes to object-naming and moves rapidly toward a kind of shorthand expression, a sentence composed of a verb and noun or pronoun, or a verb and adverb. There is little that is arbitrary, accidental, or learned in the sequence of steps by which verbal skill is acquired, though it is clear that meaning is progressively based on the context of the sentence. Of course practice, feedback, and encouragement are essential for the development of speech, and the vocabulary must be given, but speech is far too important to be left only to cultural processes or learning. It is virtually complete as a system by the time the child is four.

The most curious aspect of speech is its relative uselessness in the social context of the small child's life—the vocabulary of some three dozen ape-grunt-and-grimaces would be just as satisfactory. Why did speech evolve? In what way did it improve chances of survival? Why does it surface at so tender an age?

It has sometimes been suggested that, when men began hunting large game, strict coordination was essential and language evolved as a signal system by which the hunters synchronized their activity. But why does a four-year-old boy need a tool he will not use for ten years, and a four-year-old girl a tool she will never use? It seems clear that such a time-critical, preprogramed behavior did not develop primarily as a hunting-communicating skill or even as a tool of cooperation. No primates are more closely integrated than a troop of baboons, and no men hunt more effectively than wolves or lions, yet neither has speech.

With the rapid achievement of primary language, the four-year-old has begun a new phase of the highly subdivided, genetically directed growth of perception. Behind him is the experience of unity with the amniotic pond, which all his life will be the foundation of his security as a living organism. As an infant he has drawn the first rough drafts of body awareness and ego by using his muscles and senses to locate himself relative to and apart from objects. Touch and taste have linked his earliest memory to motion. All later learning will also bear the stamp of this relationship. Directly or indirectly, his later ability to know, think, and feel will depend on that sensory-motor way of enlarging one's powers. From this will come the metaphors of motion and contact—"I was *touched* by your speech, and I *feel* that you are right." Now, in childhood, a new kind of memory will sift experience and hold some available to later recall, but most that passed in the first four years will remain unavailable to conscious imagery.

Adults are likely to think of language as a means to an end, as a tool. For the child it is an organic function whose ends are unknown to him and undirected by him. He is shaped not so much by conditioning or culture as by success in finding signals demanded by his inmost being. The infant spontaneously searches visually for certain patterns, such as the face, lines and edges; the child undertakes a new search for expected figures for which he will also demand names.

The individual emergence of speech is nothing less than the growth of cognition itself—the basic processes of reasoning and knowing. It is an instrument for perceiving, analyzing, and dissecting. Words are signs for things and events; without words these cannot be moved around, associated, recalled, and experience cannot be organized. The verbal naming is the outward act, represented physically in the brain by activity among nerve tracts connecting highly specialized areas.

The large terminology of natural and social forms among tribes of hunter-gatherers is slowly formulated over many centuries. It is stored in the human memory, and to a lesser extent as archives in sacred, symbolic objects, but is mostly transmitted by oral tradition, handed down from generation to generation. In all peoples the maximum number of categories seems to be about three thousand.

Anthony F. C. Wallace, an American psychologist, observed that folk taxonomies tend to have about the same number of kinship terms the world over and that number is about the same as the number of discriminations that an ordinary person can make within the total range of a sensory mode, such as sound or color. Beyond this point, he says, the number of sets, not their taxonomy, increases. Taxonomic hierarchies, however, have a way of pyramiding complexity. His observations led to the conclusion that, "psychologically speaking, it seems likely that the primitive hunter and the urban technician live in cognitive worlds of approximately equal complexity and crowdedness."

Probably there is an optimum number of known and remembered species, places, and anatomical parts intimately connected to the natural selection and evolution of human mental capacity (whose true relationship to the anatomy of the brain is unknown) and that require about ten years or so to learn.

A working language must precede the classificatory scheme, and the stunning performance of language learning in early childhood is one of the most astonishing feats of the human organism. Its beginning coincides with the initiation of the differentiation of a certain area of the cortex of the right cerebral hemisphere from the corresponding area of the left, which is not complete for about eight years. These specialized parts of the parietal-temporal lobe receive nerve tracts from the various association areas near each of the sensory projection areas of the cortex: sight in the rearmost, or occipital, lobe; touch in the parietal lobe; and hearing in the temporal lobe. The degree of this unification is unknown in other animals, even in other primates, whose various sensory association areas are connected to the limbic (emotional tone) system but not to these unique parietal-temporal centers.

In the lateralization process the cerebrum becomes differentiated. In most people the left area, often referred to as "the propositional brain," is associated with naming, language, speech and reading, any kind of sequential linear thought, and especially the combination of simultaneously holding, seeing, and naming an object. It is concerned with the act of analysis, breaking things down into their separate parts. It is connected to motor areas controlling voluntary muscles, to speech memory banks in the nearby temporal lobe, and to a speech center of the frontal lobe, without which there is no forethought and neither idea nor sentence can be finished.

The right side of the cerebrum, the parietal-temporal lobe, is called the "appositional brain." This area stores and mixes information concerning spatial relationships, both internal and external, body image, and whole fields of view. Whereas the left lobe deals with discrete entities and their names, the right perceives wholes. Unconscious activities operate in the right lobe to synthesize and to see patterns, to sing songs, and to move the body in relationship to the total surround. Unlike the language brain, which is associated with analytic and rational thought, with formulating the linear structures of time flow and of speech and writing, the space-and-body brain operates in the realm of artistic and configurational patterns, of intuition and personality.

Even though the child has completed its basic language learning by the age of four, these two areas of the cerebrum continue to develop in their particular ways until the beginning of adolescence. Nerve tracts connecting the two sides, co-ordinating and integrating their functions (the corpus callosum), join the right and left hemispheres.

By means of the word-object ties initiated by speech, differentiation among objects outside the self is made possible, thus enlarging the perception of self and non-self begun in infancy. The identifying process has two main steps. Anyone who has used a taxonomic key knows that it works, first, on the basis of similarities—organisms are classed as alike or grouped —and then by single critical differences that separate two otherwise similar kinds. So are individual plants or animals categorized. Two groups may be similar to one another and very different from a third, so that clusters of groups as well as individuals can be established. In this way all taxonomic systems result in hierarchies and are fundamentally alike.

For the child a classificatory scheme is a tool, based on a series of oppositions, for developing the powers of scrutiny, sorting, and aligning likenesses and differences. Through the linguistic signs for these constitutive units, order is discovered in a world of overwhelming diversity and richness. It is the biological adaptation by which the *umwelt* (a limited set of natural signals to which an organism has fixed responses) was opened up and the means by which the primate capacity for social exploration was extended to the non-human environment. For the adult, language takes on the additional function of providing the foundation for mythical thought and communication—the telling of tales about personified natural things.

The dualism of taxonomic schemes forms a continuum of successive dichotomies. It says in effect: "There are unifying traits within this assemblage that bring its members together, but there are also differences that subdivide the assemblage." A poise or passage is established between the unity of multiplicity and the diversity of a unity. This is not simply a neat set of abstractions or a procedure for classifying but a thought system essential to cognition.

The child is discovering what Bruno Bettelheim, an American psychiatrist, calls "rules of usage which constitute both a grammar of language and a philosophy of the structure of reality." Words are used at first to represent individual objects and then groups—or primitive concepts. In this way the species deals cognitively with its environment, or, in the words of John Donne, "Our creatures are our thoughts."

Classification is the means by which the mind passes from empirical diversity to conceptual simplicity and from there to meaningful synthesis. The diversity is due to the reality of natural species of plants and animals. The act of assigning individuals to a species is the discovery of the unity which underlies diversity and, because of the distinctions between species, the diversity within the unity of life. "The diversity of species," says Claude Lévi-Strauss, the French anthropologist, "furnishes man with the most intuitive picture at his disposal and constitutes the most direct manifestation he can perceive of the ultimate discontinuity of reality. . . . There are probably no human societies which have not made a very extensive inventory of their zoological and botanical environment and described it in specific terms."

It may seem that the young child departs somewhat from the primate strategy of attention and the human mode of intelligence centered on the question "Who am I?" for he seems to be concentrating on birds and flowers, learning kinds of rocks and the names and constellations of stars rather than on understanding himself. This is true only because the most crucial step forward in this process—which is the job of adolescence—cannot be undertaken without the mode of thought and the practical knowledge represented by a long and profound taxonomic experience, undergone intensively by the normal person between his fourth and thirteenth year. This leads to the rather surprising conclusion that the initiation of speech in the child at two years of age, the mastery of primary language at four, and the continued and rapid addition of vocabulary thereafter, are biological adaptations connected with the growth of mental life and have relatively little to do with communication between the child and others.

Whether the kinds of objects provided by the culture truly shape the child's perception or whether they are simply attention-directing may not be very important. In other words, it does not matter much whether one learns twenty-seven kinds of snow conditions or twenty-seven moods of camels; what is important is that the brain matures only by making such distinctions, which it can do only through the operation of language.

The infant, as has been said, is concerned both with localizing the origins of internal sensations and with distinguishing between stimuli originating inside and outside his body. The child completes the basic symmetry of perception by discriminating and naming external objects (species) and by learning a "taxonomy" of the internal structure of external objects. The last is accomplished by the mastery of anatomy.

William S. Laughlin, an American anthropologist, has observed that if the gorilla were to be overtaken by culture he would probably study botany, while the tiger would clearly prefer anatomy. There may be some small primate antecedence for dissection, but the large primates have been opening fruits to get the edible parts for millions of years, and the primate capacity to take things apart implies an awareness of an unseen, internal secret. Men have been butchering medium to large animals for more than a million years. Sometimes, in the late Paleolithic, this was done near kill sites some distance from the home base and the children, but there can be little doubt that dissection was a regular part of education.

In *Man and His Gods,* the American biologist Homer Smith wrote that dissection "has pedagogical possibilities that exceed the more aesthetic study of bees and flowers. The experience can be likened to Alice's adventure down the rabbit hole; it is not one to be shared by everybody, but to be enjoyed only by those who have something of Alice's curiosity as well as her common sense approach to things. One simply cannot explore the insides of a cat and emerge with the same naïve philosophy with which one entered the adventure. The experience shatters certain basic premises frequently encountered in the philosophy of existence, and notably the premise that creation is intrinsically anthropocentric. He who has dissected the warm body of a cat emerges a philosophic rebel prepared, like Alice, to denounce the whole pack of cards including the King and Queen of Hearts."

Every hunter knows what Smith discovered in the comparative anatomy laboratory: there is awe in dissection that seems to spring both from the solemnity of opening the animal's body, making one wish to do it honor, and the arrangement and beauty of its organs. The latter are not lumps of dead matter but a mosaic of entities in functional relationship to one another. They make us aware of our own insides—as though we feel what we see. This is what might be called "function-position thinking," and its consequences go far beyond the bodies of animals. Inded, the interiors of animals are wonderful, uncanny landscapes, new regions as surely as the mountains and valleys beyond the horizon. "As man learned to learn," says Laughlin in the book *Social Life of Early Man,* "he was learning anatomy. The early apprehension of anatomical form and function served to configure ancient man's perception of the world. Anatomical form remains a salient organizing system even in cultural categorizations that have little or no apparent connection with anatomy. . . . The organization of the mammalian body provides a basis for intellectual organization, and anatomical analogies and reasoning are found in all cultures."

Studying the Aleutian islanders, who live largely by hunting large sea mammals, Laughlin has found them to be excellent comparative anatomists, careful dissectors keenly interested in the individual differences they find in spleens, hearts, gonads, stomachs, and lungs. Among them are excellent physicians, even surgeons, and physical culturalists, makers of mummies and performers of autopsies. Their language is full of position analogies that configure space anatomically and organically, based on an expertise derived from their knowledge of the mammalian body, a "salient organizing system" for perceiving themselves and the world.

A surprising consequence of this was observed at the time of the Second World War, when the Allies established large air bases in Alaska and Northern Canada. Eskimos, many of whom had until then lived essentially Paleolithic lives, were employed on these bases. They developed into excellent mechanics: they learned to take apart airplane engines, diagnose and repair them, and reassemble them with astonishing speed. Their hand dexterity was superior to that of farm boys and city men. This ability was due both to their dissecting ability and their hunter-butcher perspective: they saw the machine as an organism, a space-time unity in process, a direction-in-operation, so that they had a feel for it as a whole. Their language indicates place and function in the name of the part.

The child's reaction to anatomy is to ask the names of the parts, but it does great injustice to this activity to think of it as idle curiosity and pedestrian memorization. It is a poetic activity. The poet, says literary historian Elizabeth Sewell, "calls in consciously the whole figure of the human organism of mind and body, fuses it with its own instrument of language, and from this builds up its thoughts in an organic and human frame by which the human being and his universe are to be related and interpreted." She calls this figure "the human metaphor."

This relationship between the details of the external and internal worlds, between species taxonomy and anatomy, is apparent in every individual. Children whose sense of body position is not strongly dependent on external cues (who can hold a vertical posture in a tilted field of vision, for example) also make quite detailed drawings of people and objects that show clearly many separate parts and much diversity. Children whose body position is more dependent on the field of vision and who are less internally aware make global drawings or generalized sketches that show fewer body parts and fewer kinds of things.

Anatomical nomenclature and species recognition are the child's points of reference on a larger series of organization of space and form. In this sense anatomical parts are a society constituting the individual, and they have corresponding equivalents in other individuals and other species. The classificatory mode of perception may lie at the root of human individuality. People are social landmarks. The individual is a member of a clan or band—among hunters the proper name often describes the nature of this membership. Hence he is unique in a more noble way than as a self-directed and self-defined ego associated with self-indulgence, self-expression, and the cult of personality as the epitome of individualization.

Names and Games as the Purpose of Childhood

At this point it may be observed that the young human organism seems to be going a long way around to get at the question "Who am I?" Indeed, the child arrives at a plateau of development in which physical maturation seems to slow down—the "latency period" between four and eleven. There are, of course, physical and personality changes year by year, but ecologically the child's relationship to the natural environment continues almost unaltered. The eventual purpose of his growing internal-external, taxonomic, linguistic form of thinking is beyond his horizon, and he has not the slightest hint of it. While he may use some of that factual knowledge in day-to-day life, its ultimate function is reserved for adolescence. He cannot, however, undertake that adventure until he has more of the raw materials of the poet and religious participant.

Although Christianity may be interpreted as teaching us differently, the fundamental religious activity is not personal conviction, decision, or choice, but behavior as an individual in a cultus—that is, as a member of a religious social group. That membership includes constraints and procedures for all the activities of life, and, equally important, performance and participation in a body of formal activities. Both require a mature capacity for ritual, and this capacity is developed in language and play.

Play is widespread in mammals and particularly in primates. Among them, as well as among humans, play provides exercise necessary for physical development; hence play improves the individual's functional relation to his environment. Motion and vision are profoundly connected, so that it can be said that the whole of the perceptual life of the individual will be affected. "A good motor education diminishes the dangerous emptiness of the heart," remarks biologist F. J. J. Buytendijk. In play, young monkeys work out the basic forms of attention and even the rank order that they will carry into adult society. No doubt young humans also develop and reinforce temperament traits that will influence their status. In man there is solitary play, play with objects, and play with others. There is primate-herbivore play, like that of young gorillas who like to swing, hang, climb, tumble, slide, and wrestle; and there is (a little later usually) carnivore play, more like that of lions or wolves, who stalk, rush, hide, creep, chase, elude, attack, and yield. There is investigative, exploratory play, which carries the young away from mother, and affectionate play, which enhances the bond to her. There is play in collecting and making things, and finally there are games, or ritualized play.

Fortunately for our understanding of the role of ritualized play, ritualized behavior is a widespread activity of higher animals. Ritual is always a signal that condenses (or symbolizes) information about a relationship. It is a posture, sound, or movement that is derived from some familiar activity but in abbreviated or stylized form. It has been widely studied in birds, where, for example, a greeting ritual between two gulls is derived from a drinking posture, which in all birds is accomplished by tilting the bill sharply upward; it signifies a welcome between "betrothed" individuals at a certain stage in the reproductive cycle. Such behavior is innate and species-specific. In man symbolic meanings may be learned and strung together as ceremony, but not until the individual has spent many years at playing games.

Traditional games are, like the human body, bilaterally symmetrical—that is, a balance of two sides. They achieve such an equilibrium that the game is continuously interesting in itself and the outcome is in doubt. The game is always worth playing though no one can guarantee who will win. In makebelieve, where no conventional procedure is set, the children create a new balance by their own rules—that is, by standardized actions. An old pretend game among children is the makebelieve hunt in which one side is predator and the other prey. "Game" animals are those which must be hunted according to the rules of the "game," which protect each side from unfair advantage. In a sense, each side is related to something more enduring through the way it deals with the other side. That more enduring "thing" is the joint human endeavor to interpret and act upon reality in a ritualized way.

In a much deeper sense, then, the outcome of the game is not in doubt. Early games were rituals in which hostile spirits were beaten. It is the destiny of the prey, after all, to be caught, or the ecology—and the hunter and hunted themselves—would be destroyed.

This, of course, is an objective view. The child himself is immersed in the activity of the moment, yet this subjective experience works on the growth of the mind. Later, as the individual remembers his childhood, the natural world continues to be experienced in some highly evocative way, a source of profound continuity with natural processes.

I think this means that ritual play is the preliminary form of an ability that matures later and enables the individual to see the events of daily life in a very large perspective. But in learning to do so, he must remove himself from those events. Play, then, is an alternative to everyday utilitarian activities. To "go out to play" is to go out of the banal envelope of the daily routine of the adults, to leave the system of profane rules, constraints which are inexplicable to the child, which are anchored in a scheme of mundane society where life is too limited and practical. For the child the real world is incomplete. His experience is so fragmental that he cannot possibly understand how and why things happen. In pretending he creates a meaningful whole from these bits and pieces. He and his companions build skeleton dramas of life, or "plays," which have continuity and cause and effect. In this the spatial relations of objects themselves form background or structure, so that the landscape becomes imprinted or internalized in a way that prefigures thought itself. Here the mind's journey begins.

In all mammals the motor patterns of play are basically the same as those of the adult, except that they are always modified. When kittens stalk one another it is the basic cat stalk, subtly altered in rhythm, sequence, or form. The immature organism, in mimicking a future activity, is reaching forward in time to grapple with the unknown. For the young wolf pup in fighting-play, the unknowns to come are the running caribou, whose flying hoofs and hocks will be his moment of truth. The pup seems to be running, attacking, and leg-biting in preparation, and yet it is a game. For young humans the moments of truth will not simply be physical activities. In his everyday experience the child has intimations of things fearful and unknown.

Among the common games of boys is the dramatization of stalking and being stalked, killing and being killed. At about the age of ten the boy's taste for killing and dying is uninhibited and unlimited. In this way the largest and potentially most ominous unknown of his life is taken out of the incomprehensible adult envelope and incorporated as an actuality in his life in a reassuring way—as an event from which he recovers. The drama in which the killing and dying is incorporated formalizes or ritualizes death and diminishes its terror. Adults, especially parents who are ideologically sensitive, generally misunderstand the importance of simulated violence and death in the lives of children who live in cultures where death is not a normal and accepted part of life and is hidden from them. They are also inclined to want to see signs of creativity in their children rather than duplications and imitations.

The repetitiveness in children's play is not accidental. They want familiar stories and game rules. When strange characters, new episodes, or revised sequences are introduced they may object strongly. The rules of games are not kept because of an inherent feeling of fair play—that is an explanation they learn to give—but because of the conservative shape of play itself, because it is intended to stereotype certain sequences of action and experience, to provide practice in standardized utterances and rhetoric. Even the most lively and intelligent children watch television's redundant situation comedies and adventure serials whose patterns are distressingly predictable to adults. The hunger for constant themes is an age-group need and is part of the construction of a coherent and predictable world. To be a critic of its content puts the cart before the horse.

In play, to pretend is to take "as if" as provisionally true: is this an escape from real life, a venture into fantasy, which is more exciting and entertaining than the adult life routine with its incomprehensible comings and goings? The answer is yes, it is more exciting; and no, it is not an escape from life. It is a preamble to a special aspect of real life. Like language-learning, play is programed in the human genes and its developmental expression is age-critical. It is essential for the growth of mental life. Apart from its immediate joyful pleasure, it is preparation for a special adult activity: the "as if" of play is the heart of ritual and, eventually, formal religious activity.

The boundary between as-if and everyday reality is ambiguous, a to-and-fro where one moves between bases as in a game, now remembering that it is really only Joe Smith behind the mask in the ceremony and now suspending that knowledge in transcendental experience. Play and worship are the two human activities removed from commonplace life. One is necessary for the other. Thus the most adult-free, undirected activity of children is a preamble to those most solemn moments of group life. It is a marvelous example of the wisdom of the genes that religion functions and is made possible because of the completely instinctive childhood activity, in spite of all its complex intellectual and aesthetic splendor. The ritualizing activity of play is a biological prerequisite to formal religious experience. It began with ancient hunters' recognition of formal and sacred rules for "playing the game."

The child of ten in the basic society of hunters and gatherers, with the virtual completion of his vocabulary and years of play behind him, has passed a second major stage of sorting out the self and the not-self. He is deeply family- and home-centered and accepts formal relationships. He knows the internal organs of animals and the names of creatures and inanimate things. His muscular and sensory capacities have steadily improved. He is secure within a firm body boundary, evidence of a stable, healthy ego. He is a practical realist in the world of everyday life. He knows all the people around him in their respective roles. He is fond of familiar things. He has learned to estimate dimension and location and to identify causative factors when these change in appearance and position. He has shifted from animism to animals, which has clarified his own being. His fears of the dark, of beasts, of surprise, of being lost have been ritualized in play and have kept him from straying much beyond the friendly terrain of visible environs. He is confident, practical, conversant, and happy. He is a true, loyal being. It is no accident, nor is it the design of any particular culture, that ten is the golden age of childhood. It is at this time that all the child has worked for seems to come to fruition. He is an expert in play, in factual knowledge, and the concrete.

Ten years is that landmark of the lost idyll, the subject of future nostalgia. The ten-year old's euphoria will imprint on his surroundings, drawing him back in adult years to the "scenes of childhood."

Tangled in the web of the juvenile traits are the first auguries of the new direction. At ten, for example, the child has a new interest in memorizing rhymes and songs. He has discovered the place of secrecy in friendship and the excitement of mysterious ceremonies and secret membership. His peaceful, affirmative nature, attachment to family and peer group, and firm hold on his place in the world mark his point of departure into adolescence.

The Initiates

Most children discover the charm of poetry about their twelfth year. I mean poetry in its largest sense, in which words and other signs are felt to have dual relationships and to have new meanings. Riddles and jokes based on puns suddenly become funny. A new period of lallation (sound-meaning experiment) has begun. These seemingly trivial shifts in the use of language foreshadow many changes. Though the integrated personality of the child is swept away and replaced during the next half-decade, the juvenile's linguistic and neuromuscular skills, his progressively improved perception, and the quality of his play prefigure the adult. Beneath the personality changes of adolescence there is a person who is constant.

In most human societies over the past half-million years boys at about the age of twelve have probably been led from the family circle, as they are today among hunting people, into a new training and learning group under the eyes and tutelage of a master. Adolescence is sometimes called a "transition period," even though in some societies it lasts for more than ten years. It is made to sound like an obstacle course between the child and the man. It is rather the most awesome phase of an individual's life.

At this time the adolescent confronts the world pun. Change begins in the image of the family, from which he is spiritually, and often bodily, removed. His new poetic mood, a joy in memorizing, a growing quest for ultimate meanings, and altered social relationships are closely interrelated, for these will lead eventually toward a new image of the cosmic family. This is no simple metaphor, for it is into this figure that the whole weight of his amassed childhood taxonomic knowledge will plunge him like a stone into the sea. While the search for a broader cosmic self goes on his taxonomic task continues, but nature now is to be used in a new way, no longer as subject but as medium. Nouns that had simple meanings to the child take on duality both in themselves and their groupings. The species system, which was a guide to the development of thought, will be a model for an extension of thought, not about the species but about his own kind.

The extent of this basic knowledge has repeatedly astonished scientists working among modern primitive people. One group of Colombian Indians knows two hundred species of a single genus of plants by sight, name, medical, nutritive, ecological, utilitarian, and symbolic use. As many as two thousand plants are recognized by many groups. It is clear, then, that so-called savages are not intellectually impoverished, as Western culture has so long believed. Apparently the absence of writing, of manmade landscapes, and of an elaborate political state has not impaired the development of individual capacity. As Lévi-Strauss has observed, the most primitive people on earth today, the Australian aborigines, are unequaled in their intellectual sophistication, "in their taste for erudition and speculation."

The elaborate constructions of civilization are not necessary in either the biological evolution or the personal development of mental ability; a taxonomy-centered language and the presence of an adequate base of wild forms are. Even in the structure of philosophical thought we see this logic of classification, definition, and meaning. What seems to be a universal desire for practical knowledge may be motivated by personal avarice or by the drive to control and dominate, but a knowledge of hunters does not support this assumption. Indeed, to use the word "motivation" is to replace the biological basis of language with a doctrine of psychological determinism that explains human behavior as competition, avarice, and conditioned reflexes. Language is not a social tactic; it is an activity of the development of cognition.

The cognitive activity of the individual is the basis of social perception and organization. All the forces of self-realization in the young person entering adulthood depend on bringing the language brain of the left hemisphere of the cerebrum together with the artistic function of the right hemisphere in order for him to be initiated into cosmic taxonomy and its social extensions.

The initiate's new family is the clan, which cuts across other kinds of social relationships and yet takes account of them. The classification of plants and animals provides a model for precisely delineating individual, kin, and tribal society. Nature is the model for culture because the mind has been nourished and weaned on it. Applying classificatory thought from the natural to the cultural is totemism. Totemism is not, then, a matter of a simple worship of nature, as Lévi-Strauss has pointed out.

The various plant and animal totems are not simply objects of reverence; they serve as codes for formulating and relating the conceptual systems of nature and of culture. Since the particular habits and other details of animals that men might happen to see and incorporate into such a system are but a small, accidental part of the total possibilities, Lévi-Strauss has emphasized the element of chance mixture, or "bricolage," in the formulation of myths. But I think that in insisting on the odds-and-ends approach to avoid determinism he overlooks the consistent patterns of natural history, whose similarities are real. The knowledge accumulated by observers overlaps. Two distant cultures may incorporate the crow as a figure in a myth about the origin of man but choose very different aspects of the crow's life as significant for themselves. Yet there are consistent traits of crows everywhere, and of ecological relationships between them and other organisms, that define the possibilities and impose parallels wherever related forms appear. Were this not true, successive generations of men in a single clan could not reconfirm the truth of the myth.

In this way, then, animals and plants mediate between culture and nature in the mental life of man. However infinitely diverse the myths of mankind may be, the medium by which myth explains its own internal logic—which is natural history —must be consistent and repeatable. Individuals and generations must be able to repeat the observations demanded by the analogy. Though different details may be observed, there is enough overlapping so that the observers' reports are compatible.

Totemism extends, as I have mentioned, to the functional anatomy of the different parts and systems of the individual animal. It also extends to the terrain. Space itself is a society of named places—not categories such as "river" or "mountain" but proper names, marked in tribal memory and sometimes in myth. Among aborigines the "walkabout" (and perhaps travel among all hunters) is a grand tour of the ancestral past. The sum of these cosmological-anatomical correspondences adds a quality to human experience—a quality now mostly lost or debased (as in naming stalactites in a cave after the monuments, architecture, or furniture of fairy tales). This must surely have been a major factor in the conscious lives of mankind for a long time. Seeing all nature as a society may even have made possible the evolution of intelligence to that acute degree of awareness without which the vast physical universe would be found terrifying, even intolerable.

If there is ever to be a study of the ecology of mind, it must surely take account of the possible place of this organicist totemic mythology as a transitional object. Without this perceptual security blanket there might never have been the capacity to seek and doubt as we know it, and the absence of it, even now, drives men mad.

The basic human pattern in totemic society is to spend some ten years learning how life and non-life are grouped and related before the individual is faced with the formal questions of personal identity. In this way, for hunting-gathering man, his identification as a species comes first and then his identity as a person.

The view of a tolerable world is created anew by each human culture, but it is based on ancient instincts of our species. Such behaviors may even go beyond our kind. Men, like wolves, begin to leave the young pups unattended at about the same time that they are rapidly socialized. Consequently the strongest social bonds are formed with litter-mates rather than with parents. This is the foundation for the organization of the pack. Men everywhere develop in the same pattern, by allegiance to a group of brothers with whom they undergo the forging and testing of their advancing maturity.

Even where this is badly degraded we see it operating. The golden age of American university fraternities and sororities, which ended after the Second World War, existed by exploiting the innate readiness of young men and women to join secret, ritualistic societies. So long as social fraternities were congenial to American society they played a strong if undistinguished role in middle-class life. They were breezily omnipotent, puerile, pervaded by exclusiveness, snobbery, opportunism, competitive striving, and empty rhetoric. These same hypocritical characteristics are seen in many men's clubs; perhaps they are symptoms of mental rickets or malformed psyches in men starved at adolescence for worth-while fellowship that could focus their inherent drive to know, believe, participate, and master.

What the club provides is a small, ritually bonded male group. Club rites are ornamental replicas of adolescent rites of passage on the theme of death and rebirth, in which the individual is programed to lose himself, to regress into a less mature, less differentiated phase. The human organism, as though it were adapted to a drama of mythical resurrection, is invaded by infantile anxieties, fears of being swallowed and of losing the sources of nourishment and comfort. To this state, which is species-normal at about ages thirteen through eighteen, the club—and all initiatory tribunals that ever existed—address themselves.

The function of the intense feelings in the adolescent is to prepare him for a renewed life; an incipient breakdown is necessary in order to become a whole man. Obviously it is a dangerous time, but it does not catch the mature society unprepared. The young man is led into a new life by steps timed to his inner development, coinciding with his abandonment and rejection of childhood, affirming his desire for wisdom and understanding beyond the tangible reality he knows so well, responding to his hero hunger with a personal mentor, and providing, by degrees, a religious panorama worthy of his earnestness and resolution.

In the ascetic company of blood brothers he will learn new skills and secrets, endure pain and trial which connect him through religious ceremony to knowledge of the past and future. As the embodiment of the eternal hunter he must become human by hunting the horse or elephant. Just as natural taxonomy becomes the model for social and individual discriminations among humans, the poetic process allows the ritual reinterpretation of the basic events of life as a model of the timeless cosmos.

Initiation, then, is a series of environmental feedbacks, in which events of a certain shape are called for in sequence by a schedule inherent in every maturing individual. Each of these social occasions must coincide with the appearance of genetically timed innate behavior, and together they culminate in maturity and the young adult's capacity for fidelity. "Fidelity," says the distinguished psychiatrist Erik Erikson, "is that virtue and quality of adolescent ego strength which belongs to man's evolutionary heritage, but which—like all the basic virtues—can arise only in the interplay of a life stage with the individuals and the social forces of a true community."

The adolescent is unaware of many of the psychological aspects of maturing, yet he consciously feels the urgency of his search for persons to whom to be true. Like a spear aimed at the mammoth's heart, his capacity for disciplined devotion must find its target. In the cynegetic society this is not distorted, as it is among modern men, into ideology or the fanatic idolatry of a chief. His fidelity is to the genuineness of his mentors and fellows as persons; to the fairness of the rules by which he is by degrees admitted into full maturity and responsibility; to the veracity of the mythology (or humane natural history) that binds him in timeless community; to the authenticity of the art that is the catalyst to his ritual; to the accuracy of the methods and skills by which tools are made and by which daily life is conducted; and to the sincerity of conviction in the shared cynegetic vision of life.

The formal, ceremonial part of developing the initiate's disciplined devotion is based squarely on his newly felt capacity for poetic dualism. Its elements are dramatized or ritualized experiences of the past, many of them from infancy, and they therefore tap forces from the deepest layers of the unconscious. The infant carries in its genes the capacity to respond to certain signals or sign stimuli, such as the human face, empty space into which it might fall, the nipple in its mouth, wetness on its skin, and so on. It has a readiness for certain other kinds of experience, which are said to imprint its young nervous system —birth, the rhythms of day and night, of sun and moon, of male and female, of waking and sleeping.

The innate responses to the sign stimuli and the imprints of infantile experience provide a body of behavior common to all men and buried deep in their lost memories of childhood. Initiation ceremonies revive these indelible records by repetition in an exaggerated or ritualized style. Such heightened response to a super-normal sign-stimulus is widespread in nature. The classic example, demonstrated by the Dutch ethologist Nicolas Tinbergen, is the preference of the brooding bird for a giant model of its own egg, for which it will abandon its own real eggs and nest. Another is the woolly cloak of hair on the shoulders of the male hamadryas baboon to which young females are strongly attracted. Certain age or sex groups respond to such super-signals with unusual intensity. What animals feel at such moments can only be guessed, but people react with powerful emotions to the exaggerated signals of the infant's face, to erotic anatomy, and to great size and fearful visage.

Art may have begun as a super-signal. The mask, for example, transforms a limited human face (to which the infant innately responded and the child watched for nuances of expression) to a degree of almost intolerable intensity. The mask conceals the most revealing personal traits and eliminates the individual, so that its impact has concentrated, superhuman force. The mask is the transcendent image of the face, calculated to enhance effect and make passion from sensation. Basic expressions imprinted in childhood are exaggerated in the masks of the priest-actors, who, through dramatization, make familiar the unfamiliar god and convert familiarity to rapture. Thus is the face of authority-in-anger, the face of the wind, the face of cunning-coyote transformed into an element of a cosmic drama.

"Take the idea of your birth into a family," says the logic of ceremonial play. "We want you now to think of the birth of the tribe as you know that you yourself were born—just as you might enlarge your awareness of the birth of the bison into that first birth of the herds. We are now going to apply your puny, individual, mortal experience in new ways, to ancestors and gods, in episodes and forms that you will know are true and that will so enlarge your understanding that it will be like being born into a new world."

The infantile experiences being dramatized were not originally embroidered with words, but in initiation rites the polemic and didactic oral traditions of the group complement the ritual homologies. The poetry of the spoken myth is to taxonomy and verbal knowledge what the mask is to the face. To the initiate, the events of childhood, like those of daily life, are all cosmosized. One's childhood relationships to mother and the sounds of the night owl have extended meaning. To those traditional peoples who have been in the mainstream of human experience for a million generations, space and time are inseparable from places and events. Ceremonies that change personal experience of the past are real; it is only in such secular or a-religious cultures as our own, with its arrow of progress, recorded history, and illusions of regulating time and space by measuring them, that the past is beyond reach. But for traditional man ceremonies that simultaneously touch the time stream of the maturing individual in more than one place are the method of mythological discourse.

Tests of endurance and skill are an essential and formal part of initiation. They lead the adolescent to a fuller understanding of himself as an organism and to new states of consciousness. Pain, exhaustion, danger, and isolation are like dangerous drugs —not for children to play with, but in the hands of a wise physician, a doorway to health.

Ritual mutilation, such as adolescent circumcision, gives ceremonies an appropriate agonistic tone. Drugs and inebriants also lift the experience from the mundane to the cosmic. Just as the mask serves to raise the level of perceptual intensity, so pain deepens memory. The candidate is not likely to forget much of what happened. More important, he has learned more about his own ability to endure than childhood taught, and learned that time will require him to suffer. The ordeal binds him to his fellows and reveals new depths in himself.

What has been said of initiation is generally true for boys in both Paleolithic societies of the past (according to educated guesses) and hunting-gathering peoples today. Although girls are also initiated, among many peoples the formalities are fewer and the period briefer. To modern women who are conscious of the exploitative tactics and inferior status imposed on them by agro-industrial cultures, the brevity of female initiation may seem to be an example of unfair sexual discrimination, but that interpretation would not be accurate. Adolescence is different for each sex not only in its cultural but its biological dimension. As American anthropologist Ashley Montagu has pointed out in his excellent book, *The Natural Superiority of Women,* the difference in psychology and maturing schedules in males and females is indicative of their complementary functions in society.

It would be easy to underestimate the female qualities and wisdom selected by evolution based on a division of labor. In gathering, the phenology of plant life is as complex as the behavior of the big-game animals, especially as modified by particular weather and the seasons. Although the woman is oriented to plants, she does not gather as the farmer does—he knows where things are without looking or thinking—for the hunting band is mobile and may use scores of different campsites over the years. That her psychology is profoundly attuned to this activity is supported by studies that show that widespread hoarding instinct is positively related to the female hormone estrogen. That it causes females among rats as well as humans to make little accumulations of food indicates that it was not a consequence of human emergence but a mammalian trait that could be built upon by hunting-gathering people. I am not referring here to stockpiles but to a differential equivalent, say, an Easter egg hunt, where superior performance is rewarded by prestige as well as food, and accumulation precedes and makes possible the opportunity and dignity of being generous.

The women do not hunt; that activity, because of its particular skills and complex symbolic functions, requires a set of mental and physical attributes and training of its own. The gathering activities of women, and their parental, sexual, and social roles are too basic and important to society to trust to the hazards and arbitrariness of learned performance. The woman's outlook is more universal and less preoccupied with clan totems. In the hunting-gathering society the women are no less mobile than men, though the distances involved in gathering are usually shorter; it is only with the coming of agriculture that they have been sentenced to confinement. The young woman's first husband in the cynegetic society is likely to be twenty years her senior, her second more nearly her own age, and her third younger than herself. It is not surprising that she is far more socially sophisticated and insightful, her maturity more advanced than that of males of her own age. Indeed, it seems probable that the absence of a parental Oedipal barrier between daughter and father equivalent to the paternal threat separating mother and son and the presence of widespread father-daughter incest (even today) are indications that natural selection in the evolution of human society has worked toward the imprinting of a dominant male image and the mating and bond of the adolescent girl to the mature man. This might further select for a more rapid advance of maturity in the female without dependence on protracted periods of rite and trial.

The Necessity of Risk and Solitude

The old, infecund members of a species are called "post-repro-ductives" by biologists, and their scarcity in the animal world attests to their relative uselessness to the species. Among small animals old individuals hardly exist. The robin over three years of age is a rarity, and there are probably no menopausal birds or senile mice.

Only where the old play a role in the life of the species are individuals endowed with long survival. In man this function is sapience, the role the preceptor. Old hunters, says Carlton Coon, an American anthropologist, play an increasingly im-portant role with age; they do not "just fade away in a numbing haze of arteriosclerosis, bourbon and television watching."

One of the first, and continuing, modern tragedies has been the replacement of the old man or woman as mentor and guide by written documents. Wisdom, however, does not come simply from living long enough. The individual who flunks adolescence cannot, as an adult, ripen with experience. His continued im-maturity is painful to himself and to society, and he slides into callow senescence, scrabbling to keep his hold on youth because he knows in his heart that some door is opened then or not at all. The effects following the failure of initiation deform the adult and pervert his function as mentor. The child is father of the man. Incapable of carrying out his role properly, perhaps even twisted into rancorous resentment, the adult, in his role as master of initiation, can easily subvert the adminstration of pain and suffering.

For those truly graduated, the segments of life become better defined, enjoyments and responsibilities more precisely linked to particular years. Love and patience mediate the stern realities of the ceremonies. The trials of initiation strengthen not only the ability to endure pain and improve skills but the capacity to endure alone the whole scale of the non-human environment. It is toward this that the biological evolution of longevity in man leads, step by step, no matter how any given society designates the ranks or draws the lines defining the roles of age.

In many hunting-gathering peoples the trial includes a time alone. Wilderness solitude is not a test against the elements, discomfort, and deprivation, for, after all, the young hunter is already an expert in survival. His purpose is more lofty. It is a trial by confrontation. It is to receive the full weight of the cosmos on his head without the shield of society. It is perhaps difficult, in surroundings constructed by men, to imagine such an encounter except as the threat of physical danger, but the personal significance of this experience in a contemporary form is shown in some measure by the Outward Bound program, an international organization that provides three-week wilderness courses. A group of selected adolescents goes into the wilderness with professional climbers, sailors, or simply survival experts. With minimal gear, often under harsh conditions, the group undertakes a series of problems, such as navigation, tracking, climbing, and so on. For a three-day period the participant lives all alone with only a few matches and the clothes he is wearing.

Its many enthusiastic graduates do not say, "It was great—I survived!" They say, "It was great—I got to know myself." The two are related, and the value of cooperative primitive living is not to be overlooked; but although the confidence thus gained may seem extraordinary, actually it is the normal manner of growth in the cynegetic culture and of the human organism.

That trial matures a person is nothing new. It is false, however, to see it as a means to rank by measurement of the young man's qualities, such as stamina, resourcefulness, determination. These internal virtues, which competitive education emphasizes, should be taken for granted as human; indeed, as biological in hunters. Confrontation of the vast, non-human surround makes the difference. Substitutes cannot be manufactured in buildings, machinery, or even social games.

Today the individual is caught in an identity crisis that is worsened by modern solutions. It is just in the second half of the second decade of individual life that *Homo sapiens* is programed to clarify his identity. Everyone who fails will be intellectually, emotionally, and socially retarded the rest of his life. That failure is evident in the epidemic search for self among adults. In part it is a result of seeking maturity by plumbing one's inmost recesses, plowing the inner field of response, feeling, preference, conjuring up the personal profile that will tell one who one is. Psychology, psychoanalysis, the T-group, the encounter group, the sensitivity session, the marathon, the mirror of the novel or film—these are the fashions by which modern man seeks to expose his depths, where it is thought the true self hides. Our loneliness as a species reinforces this neurotic behavior. "Pee-pul . . . who need pee-pul," keened a million-dollar singing star in a song of the early 1960s, and it made her an idol.

This is blind gambling with the minutiae of the personal, the contingent, and the fortuituous. Who we are begins elsewhere. There is no hope of knowing ourselves individually until we know ourselves as a species. The young men and women who return from Outward Bound to report that they have a leg up on knowing themselves are not talking about conversation around the campfire or interpersonal soap operas. Their success is not in analysis at all. They speak of the experience of silence and solitude, of nearly overwhelming immersion in the non-human.

Self-understanding is possible only in relationship to "other." Paleolithic people get the "other" in the proper order: first, the non-self in infancy, then the "other" non-human in childhood, and finally the synthesis of the two in adolescence, which begins in the knowledge of the broader, non-human cosmos. The sometimes painful confrontation of the "other" by the adolescent in traditional initiation is a means of advancing his maturity. Maturity therefore can be said to be measurable on a relatedness scale, not human in its scope but universal.

"The highest order of maturity," says Searles, "is essential to the achievement of relatedness with that which is most unlike oneself." His evidence for this is from the study of schizophrenia. The central problem for the schizophrenic is coping with otherness. He has a profound body-boundary difficulty.

His is the terror of a bad drug trip, the hallucination of inchoate self, a skin that won't hold, the panicky uncertainty about where "I" ends and "other" begins.

The strange and unfamiliar are so terrifying to the acute schizophrenic that he needs an impoverished environment, a bare cell or chemical envelope, to shield him from all that is new and different, including strangers. He is deeply confused about his biological and social identity, and sometimes about whether he is even alive. The world pounds his senses with its frightful barrage, its ominous forms, so that he blocks it out and retires to his dreams in a waking sleep. His recovery is measured precisely by his ability to move again in a diverse and unfamiliar world. In the presence of strangers or the proximity of unusual animals or objects he may bite his lips or pound his head. In this he is but a hair's-breadth from the self undergoing ritually induced pain in initiation. It has taken men half a million years to contrive the circumstances in which such deep unconscious levels can be plumbed for the exaltation that will produce maturity. Needless to say, pain-induction as it relates to the schizophrenic is a last resort for personal survival, while to the initiate it is but a recapitulation of an old mode of endurance, which allows his old child self to die as he enters a realm of cosmic survival.

The relationship of schizophrenia in a society to the failure of adolescent initiation is not clear. Certainly psychosis is in part a result of the genetic predisposition of the victim and in part of circumstances other than the formalities of religious training. No proof of connection between mental breakdown and the quality of pubertal life can be offered. What is seen is the striking similarity between the aims of competent initiation and the achievements of mental growth—or, to put it another way, between the faults of those whom the culture has failed and what psychiatry calls schizophrenia.

Anger is part of a young man's nature, but its occasions and reasons are connected by whim and chance to daily events. To condemn that fine, steady, and somewhat muffled temper forces it outward toward ideological fanaticism or inward where the youth will swallow it for a time and then murder his mother and father.

The idea that conflict between adolescent and parent is due to individual faults and personal attitudes must surely be one of the most dangerous misconceptions of modern man. The repression of this strife, the search for reasons, the entreaties to be good, the pain it causes to the sentimental mind, and the sick ruses by which it is avoided account for a fair share of unnecessary human suffering.

The anger is in part impatience with the childhood routine and parental patter, irritable intolerance of the household round of childhood, readiness to dissolve the bonds of old companionships, all the forms of disquiet that every generation of modern man sees in its young and attributes to some defect in the young themselves or to their own failure as parents. The adolescent is like a swimmer who must cover a certain distance before the tide sweeps him away. In an incompetent society his first signals of desperation are misread. It is hard to know which is more tragic, the adults' tolerant and negative view of sowing some wild oats, with its overtones of privileged irresponsibilty, or the puerile autisms that unguided young people substitute for rites of passage—rites that would have channeled the anger into the demands of the hunt.

The anger of the young man does two things: it turns him away from the past and it thrusts him toward significant encounters ahead. It is the anger of the football team—not meanness so much as aggressive joy. The anger is addressed to an object as big as an elephant. The anger is necessary for a running assault with spears. If elephants could talk, they might say, "We are what that is for."

It is argued whether man is by nature violent or pacific, whether his genes or his society are to blame for his meanness. "If it is by nature, then we are lost because the matter is taken out of our hands," says one side. "If it is by nature, then we are saved," says the other, "because all innate aggression is countered by innate inhibitions." The fact is that the species that has murdered millions of its own kind in the past century alone came into existence—as a species—by virtue of a cunning capacity to kill, but in the cynegetic society the kill is always a singular event; in civilized society predation has been degraded to the slaughterhouse by the machinery of its organized, agro-industrial culture. Large predators rarely kill their own kind. In modern warfare man behaves like a captive animal. Caged creatures show much aberrant behavior, including psychopathic fits of bloody carnage, and many of the same psychotic symptoms as humans in our developed nations.

Elephants, with horses and reindeer, tended and nurtured man's rage for more than a million years. It takes all of the hunter's intensity, effort and strength, wily intelligence, knowledge of natural history, and determined murderous force to stalk and kill an elephant in an open plain with hand weapons. From the elephant's point of view, as from the man's, the activity is beneficial. Who else except men will remove the bad seed? The lion and crocodile glean an infant elephant now and then, but there is no one else to sculpture his species, prune out the weaker of the giant forms, or to hone the elephants' intelligence. How lovingly the two have been at it, treasuring each other, each raising the other to new levels of stratagem and majesty, polishing each other's intellect for a million years.

For the young man the stalk of the elephant is a risk worth taking. Not only as danger surmounted, but because the feeling it gives him is noble, enhancing, enlarging. The search for risk worth taking, tasks worth fidelity, leaders worth following who have ideas worth believing, is the essence of the generation gap, the pith of the youth problem. Thousands of generations of young men have left the parental hearth and the toy spears on which they impaled grasshoppers and taken religious orders that said: "If life is not a risk gladly taken you might as well have the brain of a yam; what you prey on and what you pray are very close; the rage to be is the rage you feel for a ten-foot cave bear, a herd of wild horses, or the terrible mountain of elephant."

Today the adolescent confronts a mountain of surf or a

mountain itself with skis or ropes. He floats down the Colorado River in a kayak, or he shoots a bear or even an elephant. Perhaps the risk seems worth taking simply for the trophies and survival. The task is real and satisfying, but those rewards are only bare bones where a meal is needed. Something is begun that is never concluded. There is today a widespread attempt to define the benefits of wild nature, an attempt which, lacking social and religious dimensions, comes out as a kind of return to fundamental things on the one hand, or as abstractions on the other. Mountains and elephants slip into platonic symbolism from which it is only a step to the perception of the elephant as merely a token of something more real. All hazards and risks are abstracted and interchangeable. Once this relativity is accepted, everything from fighting a war to selling an automobile, closing a merger, or getting elected may be substituted as the worthy trial of a young man. The cynegetic man knows that elephant hunting really means hunting elephants. Hunting and gathering are indeed the prototypes and evolutionary shapers of human behavior, but to see them therefore as symbols is to fall into a semantic trap.

Dream Time as History

Cosmic time is dream time. In the drama of myth the religious man knows that the unity of present time and cosmic time is one of those "as if" situations, which ritual tells him is true, and yet in a corner of his mind he is always aware that Father Cosmic Time is but a mask. Although he acknowledges the mystery of their relation, he knows the difference between being awake and asleep.

In contrast, the schizophrenic (who is used here as the ultimate level of immaturity in everyone) has an organic failure of brain function that interferes with that distinction. He may be said to dream while awake and therefore cannot distinguish between what is dreamed and otherwise experienced. The confu-

sion of the two is part of his impaired ability to separate self and
environment and to recognize the duality of words, to know
metaphor or poetry or myth.

For the schizophrenic, caricature is always sinister and
threatening, and he is chronically fearful of discovering himself
to be non-human. Our normal unconscious fear of phylogenetic
regression (or being an animal) is in the schizophrenic conscious. Considering the strong revulsion against animality in our
cultural tradition and the insistent literary-intellectual assertion
that "man is more than an animal," it would seem that our
society is in this respect immature.

These critical moments of life—initiation, ceremonies of
adolescence—when one must regress in order to move forward
would be impossible were it not that everyone is, in a sense,
a recovered schizophrenic. It is widely recognized among psychiatrists who have studied primitive people that the priest or
shaman is often a recovered schizophrenic, whose sanity and
perceptivity seem more pure. Such men and women have charisma and often a gift for ritualizing connections between dream
time and ordinary time.

Dream time here means two things: cosmic time when the
events of the beginning and of myth occurred, and those events
we experience when asleep. Both sleep and dreaming are general
terms for complex, sequential events in all people. Studies show
how a particular experience is interwoven in the dream fabric;
the basic process is similar throughout humanity and probably
has elements in common with the dreaming of chimpanzees
and other animals.

The evidence is that elaborate cerebrums must dream on a
regular schedule, for restoration (like a tired muscle), or as a
phase in the assimilation of earlier sensory experience, or possibly to mediate between the unconscious and the conscious, as
Freud thought. Brain studies of other large mammals during
their sleep indicate that they dream too. This improves the
chance of eventually understanding the evolutionary significance of dreaming and also confirms the fellowship of higher
animals on earth. As a naturalist I find the dreaming by other

creatures a delightful discovery and a good antidote to the insistence of the singularity of man.

The industrial culture takes less account of dreams than do other societies of men. The dream time of which Australian aborigines speak is for them both past history and the deep present. The idea of past and future, like the capacity to integrate recent experience and dreams, is for the individual a function of the forebrain, one of the last parts of the brain to mature. Although older children may wonder momentarily about life's larger questions, not until adolescence are they deeply concerned about past and future, mortality and eternity. The terror of potential personal dissolution and oblivion is a necessary schizophrenic fear, for it compels an answer in the myths of continuity and eternal life.

It is not prey but carnivores who fear death; in man, not the vegetarian but the meat eater. The prey flees from the predator, but it has no personal experience with death. In its munching of fruit or grass it cannot recognize its meal as a dying organism or part of the cyclic transformation and flow of materials through death. But the carnivore sees death every day. As a sentient being, the human carnivore is forced to have a philosophy about it. His philosophy may be defective. He may pretend he is only an herbivore and live on potatoes, hide his head in pseudo-innocence, and return to the primate patrimony of the flowers. He may imagine that he personally has discovered death and that in some way his anxiety is a personal problem. But it is the carnivore in man that has created sensitivity to death and psychological machinery for a mature perspective of life in death. These cannot be turned off at will or escaped in sleep or in pretending to be a herbivore.

Evolution, not culture, determines what is species behavior and what is personal. Human society has no choice about this, though it creates different cultures. Thus ceremonial initiation based on myth and trial is biological, a specialized activity of all human minds, while the content of any particular ceremony is a cultural matter and varies among different peoples.

The relationship between dreams and wakeful experience is

reciprocal—that is, dreams manifest unconscious thought and are transformed as myths, which are exploited to guide pre-adults into maturity; while ordinary experience is turned into dreams. This can be seen among any group of fifteen-year-old boys in a talk session. Whereas younger boys live out social relations in activity, fourteen- and fifteen-year-olds become raconteurs. Parents of this age group are familiar with a ceremony so common that it is easy to miss—the evening gathering of friends and the anecdotal review of what happened to whom—who wrecked his bicycle, got a new job, won a race, got arrested. The highlights of old events are recounted again and again with much hilarity and sometimes acting out. They are doing exactly what young Bushmen join in doing with older hunters at the end of the hunt. The drama of events is narrated as a fragment of history. Its repetition in time gives it a dreamlike quality. Events are related to landmarks, so that gradually the whole locality becomes the setting of a continuing drama.

Apart from the atmosphere of good-natured teasing, there is a more subtle tone, a guarded gravity, as though something of hidden significance were being affirmed. The events are being linked to a mythology of places, a landscape of events. Modern boys are left with the anecdotes as ends in themselves, but they are hunters at heart and their most solemn and formal group activity is this ritual review. Life is a little history made each day. Some events are winnowed out and in the recounting will become the principal bonds by which friendships will someday be renewed: "Say, do you remember when . . ."

For Paleolithic men this modest history-making continues throughout life. In our time it is cut down by the printed word, the segregation of age groups, and impermanent associations. In Africa the whole clan gathers to hear Bushmen tell, sing, and re-enact episodes from the last hunt. The events are considered at once lightly and solemnly. Places are important—they are the anatomy of space. Events of the distant past are recalled. Things strange and new are turned over carefully. New experiences are woven—primarily through local geography—into an eternal tapestry, continuous with the myths of creation. Only mature individuals who have an oral tradition of storytelling have the wisdom to tie new events to old and real experience to dream time.

For modern boys it is at this point that the whole endeavor —so assiduously recapitulated hundreds of times by every young man—collapses. Like zoo-born lions trying to bury their un-eaten leftovers in the cement floor, young men gather at the end of the day to spin out the eternal from the day's events—except that, once the spinning is done, there is no one else there to do the winding. Autistically, they do the winding themselves. They contrive a rationale from limited and imperfect experience. To-gether they construct a clan mythology that does not fill the need, a sure route to eventual disillusion and cynicism.

No doubt the necessity of planning, of seeing actions in the future, was involved in the organized hunting of large and dangerous game, and recapitulation helped by identifying mis-takes or weaknesses in the organization of the hunt. But if look-ing ahead and looking back were only pragmatic techniques in hunting, myths of creation would not have been involved. Con-cern with the past and future is a way of understanding life.

The life of Paleolithic human hunters must not be im-agined as the race against death that the agro-industrial culture assumes. The hunter spent much of his time in pursuits other than the chase and the kill. Nor was he the defenseless victim cornered in his tree or cave by hungry predators. One should, instead, think of him as lean and muscular, lying on a sunny ridge amid tundra flowers, surveying a distant herd—not hun-grily or apprehensively but in repose, responsive to scent, bird-song, the feel of the earth, relaxed and confident but watching intensely the movements of a herd of fifty horses. He recognizes each individual by sex and age, by its movements, by its role. He sees the drift of the herd in relation to terrain, forage, and predators; rank-order relationships of individuals; subtle signs of sickness and infirmity; the daily round of herd life, feeding, drinking, resting. He compares the pattern of one herd group to that of others. He learns their communications and signals, the nuances of seasonal rhythms in behavior, the effects of stress, aware of these in relation to the season and time of day. He is also listening. His own frequent participation in song has created a constant interiority of orientation—that is, sound is produced from within the instrument or organism and tells about its momentary inner state rather than external condition. For him the human voice is not separate but a model for all sound, and all sound is a voice. On other occasions he will leisurely scrutinize by ear and eye hairy mammoths, wild cattle, cave bears, giant sloths, stags, rhinoceroses, reindeer, bison, and other large mammals.

Even today, watching wild elephants is a deeply satisfying experience. They are an even more beautiful sight than great architecture. One could easily imagine that the whole idea of beauty is derived from watching large mammals.

What emerges from a million years of such study is much more than a practical knowledge for killing—it is a knowledge of the typical life cycle of each species, its details and peculiarities. This is natural history. Natural history is history—the hunter's awareness of the animal in the stream of time. It is doubtful that any chimpanzee or early *Australopithecus* ever regarded wild fruits, nuts, or birds' eggs except as immediate reality.

In the tropics and subtropics little of the omnivore's food comes in herds or flocks. Fruit trees do have a natural history, but year after year, in the same place, at the same time, the tree will bear fruit. For the carnivore preying on herd animals, the same bison can never be eaten twice; to know him is to eat him as an individual; to kill him one must know the species. To know the species means to be able to predict, from a knowledge of its life cycle, its behavior over the seasons and over the decades. Implicit in this concept is that we humans too have a history. The intelligence needed for this has many uses. From good to eat, the elephant has become good to think.

Universal life patterns are obtained by patient observation, culled and winnowed in the telling. The narrations by the poet-historian of pre-literate societies who keeps the secrets of the clan are like tales told by a "hunter" of man who searches out his history and behavior. The oral dramas of creation, dying and returning, of animals and men, of animal-men, of pursuit, travel, search, union, conflict, are aimed at that point in the mind connecting the rich knowledge of the hunter and the wonder at one's own kind.

A large amount of the time is spent by hunting-gathering people with music. Among some Australian aborigines, singing and playing instruments occurs twice daily and involves each person in several hours of music. When to this is added the time spent in ceremonial chant, the narration of myth, and re-counting of personal experience, it is evident how greatly sound predominates in their lives. To be sound-oriented, says Walter J. Ong, an American linguist, is to be at the opposite pole from the modern, print-oriented platonic idealist. The oral, non-abstract, yet poetic mode does not, like writing, create a separate world of its own. Traditionally sound-oriented people are immersed in an event-world that has the vivid yet fleeting ambiance of dreaming. Sound always comes from the inside, molded by hidden surfaces, like the dream from the depths of the psyche. Dream time is the beginning and end, the illumination of sleep by episodes from the interior, where lies hidden the history of the species. The dream and song are ecological factors. As in the development of myth, their basic images have been shaped by the same evolutionary forces that shape the physical traits of species. They are the instrument of social adaptation to nature; they constantly refer to nature and are thus not lost in abstractions. Savage thought, says Lévi-Strauss, is "a consuming symbolic ambition such as humanity has never again seen rivalled, and by scrupulous attention directed entirely towards the concrete."

The Antinomians

The individual awakening of mind is a long and complicated ecological process. Its first phase, in infancy, builds a body articulation. The second develops linguistic cognition. The third is characterized by a deep desire for commitment and poetic and religious readiness for ultimate questions. At each stage a genetically programed development awaits specific releasers for its fulfillment.

For most of human history this stage has been a supreme experience. To see it as such is difficult because the process has broken down. Indeed, the Freudian view of the human life cycle presents the adolescent (rather than society) as sick. This view points to the physiological changes in body function through glandular function, altered metabolic rates, and growth effects associated with puberty. It creates a logic based on inhibited sexuality, instability, genital impulses, libido withdrawal, repressed desires, and so on. Behaviors become allegorical demons or ghosts; id is said to contend with ego, which, backed to the wall, is threatened by dissolution. The Freudians see instincts like wolves surrounding rationality, where the unconscious, previously banished, returns to ambush the youthful conscious. All this, added to boils on the neck and pimples on the face, make the poor in-betweener very unpleasant company, a human battleground where armies of ghosts make war. He is a living cross between Germanic grand opera and Dantean allegory.

The adolescent is viewed by much of modern society as a rather odious bag of symptoms and conflicts, all of which have semi-medical names. No doubt the psychic-restructuring, narcissism, hypochondria, personality and ego regression, psychic volatility, repetition in some strange cryptic form of the anal-oral-genital-phallic-oedipal sequence, childhood locomotor patterns, and renewed anxieties of infancy are all real but are they really normal? It should not be assumed that a nasty id reveals itself as the striving pre-adult climbs laboriously from his basic animality. His infantile behaviors are like the unconscious rerunning of old films and are to be useful again in a totally new light. Much in adolescence is new to the individual, particularly the reversals—the vascillations, altered direction, the maze of doubt and redirections. The adolescent may be engaged in social action; yet he is disengaged, an outsider. He is supremely confi-

dent of himself; he is incomplete and dubious. He is fascinated
with tangible materials and objects; he is abstract. He is raven-
ously hungry and sensuous; he is fasting and ascetic. He is intensely linked to his peers; he is alone, looking at the moon.
He is accused of "ambivalence," indecisiveness, instability, in-
consistency. We assume that he is lost and in trouble, an incomplete person in the throes of change.

A different view of the adolescent, less perplexing to adults
and more nearly true, is to see him moving toward a peak of
discovery and sensitivity that he may never again experience.
His enriched perception of scale, of meaning, of alternatives,
gives him a great swagger of freedom, which is seen by dull and
worried adults as vascillation. The extremes are his measuring
of the range of life. The enormity of what it is possible to be is
opened like a landscape before his eyes, inseparable from what
it is possible to feel and to believe.

Adolescence is not a sickness that is inevitably traumatic
but a highly specialized, profoundly rewarding period of human
life, an evolutionary adaptation that developed during centuries
of high human maturity in small, hunter-gatherer groups. All
its characteristics have an internal logic and purpose.

The young man's irritation with his mother and con-
strained hostility toward his father, his impatience with the
games of children, are part of the built-in, age-specific behavior
of our species. These feelings are reciprocated by the parents—
other people's children may seem more pleasant, courteous,
and cooperative—though parents may not publicly admit it. For
oedipal reasons the young man cannot idolize his father, yet
incipient idolatry is in his blood. The omnipotence which as a
child he saw in his parents is not simply obliterated; it will be
transferred and transformed. Indeed, much of his previous experience, from infancy on, will be unconsciously renewed and
gone through again, under the guidance of a new set of masters
—if the proper masters appear.

The breakdown of the adventure of adolescence results in
a deprivation for the individual clearly visible in his development and character. As in other biological systems, a failure in

environmental feedback leads to self-generated substitutions, spastic vacuum input, or autisms, which are incapable of completing the function of adolescence. The resulting frustration will inflate the normal taciturnity toward parents in undirected, unbridled, and eventually fanatic hostility; the oscillations between violence and withdrawal, cynicism and idealism, will rocket out of normal arc; confidence will gradually shift away from any adult leadership and be redirected toward peers, investing brotherhood with a superficial tutorial role, undermining the neophyte's trust; the normal concern for self-identity will grow into hypochondria and narcissism, herd-following, group exclusiveness, and intolerance. Anxiety about the self interferes with the study of nature; the metaphors making religion possible will slip into arbitrary art forms. Uncompromising asceticism will clash with profligate sensuality and psychedelic masturbation. Hypervigilance will be generated by the schizophrenic fear of depersonalization and produce a hundred forms of deviant behavior—cynical apathy, anarchistic nihilism, violence, and defiance, idiosyncratic behavior such as acting out, learning disorders, lack of purpose, moodiness, procrastination, and negativism.

It may seem strange that the young man finds himself ready to turn from the authority of the family at the same time as he accepts bondage in a peer group. By bondage I mean conformity in manner, fashion of dress, private-group slang, and every other outward indication of subordination and belonging. Adolescence is the ultimate moment of fads and fashions in every aspect of daily life, which becomes a lifelong habit only where maturity never comes. That young intransigents today are spinelessly orthodox or militantly hostile is not due to the adolescent transformation of *Homo sapiens* so much as to the loss of equilibrium in the normal interplay of independence and loyalty, which results in defiance and servitude.

The perverted adolescent has great inner pressure for senseless destruction. His moral absolution is based on felt—"gut"—reactions and the simplistic reduction of complex issues. Repetition, exaggeration, and slogans are taken as validation of assertions, and reasonable arguments are rejected as diversions. All imperfect institutions are condemned by him to destruction and conservatives are persecuted. Revolutionary political activity is the paranoid's haven, where one's delusions are acted out and accepted by others as reality. Normally adolescence should culminate in the individual's taking responsibility for his own behavior rather than, childlike, attributing his actions to his parents or, more intellectually, blaming an uncontrollable or purposeless universe, which the philosopher-child calls an existential absurdity.

Incomplete classification of the self and of the world causes the inept individual to put himself at the center of the universe. An obsession with pure ideal and a readiness for change, combined with a very imperfect world—the unacceptable written history of wars and kings, the myth of the future as endless progress—lead toward a frenzy of reform. He will create a new world with himself at its center, a parody of that initiation which he has been denied.

In suggesting that the collapse of the adolescent karma is the fault of our culture and society, I do not mean to be ideological. It is not something to be corrected by the magic cure-all of right thinking. Derangements of human behavior of this magnitude have their roots in the evolution of human intelligence and nervous systems. The ecology of Paleolithic hunters, particularly the sparse population and stable environment, may have allowed the specialization of human intelligence to a degree that is intolerable in dense populations and an unstable environment.

The limit in brain specialization is probably a point at which failure of the delicately poised processes reaches a frequency that causes social debilitation. The same principle applies to all organs in evolution: natural selection acts to increase size or otherwise modify the structure until it is inhibited by survival costs. In man the peak of cerebral perfection was probably reached more than fifty thousand years ago. The upper limits of mental complexity were higher than today for the reasons I have given and because of a selection for group organization that protected the neurotic from himself and society from him. Because of his highly specialized mental processes, man as a species came to live at the verge of a terrifying realm of madness. Evolution produced a being whose re-employment of the normal substance of infantile behavior, of dreams, and of the adult unconscious was exploited in initiation to achieve maturity. None of this means that the failure of adolescence is the only source of mental sickness and retrograde immaturity or that primitive people are never psychopathic. Substantial amounts of psychopathology in a group have generally been handled in primitive society by ceremonies so excruciating that the survivors were cleansed and their sanity temporarily improved. This was the function of culturally approved forms of torture, mutilation, cannibalism, ostracism, execution, and frenzy. Obviously this kind of shock psychotherapy could spill over into initiation and other religious functions and eventually poison them. To what extent the five thousand years of modern war are a form of such desperate and hopeless purification rite is conjectural, but, to the extent that they are, war cannot be stopped by political decisions.

What is necessary, then, is drastic ecological revampment of our situation and a revival of the lineaments of tribal society. In defiance of mass culture, tribalism constantly resurfaces. Canadian professor Marshall McLuhan's new "tribal man"—immersed in the group, linked by instant media instead of dead print, attuned to ecological rather than static forms—cannot be obliterated. He keeps erupting through the literary, linear, segmented culture like a wild plant that heals the injured soil. But the medium is not enough by itself. The gang or commune operating outside society cannot create from thin air myths embodying real wisdom. No one can live on empty function. There must also be a content, passionately believed in, that relates man to nature, centering all human experience.

If modern myths of creation and the human past are used ineptly in initiation, the new generation denies history. To affirm the group's past requires commitment to that which is beyond control. The adolescent caught short of the true way to maturity desperately reaches for control. He must create the past. The gang is his only hope. To be reborn in that group is a new start. The gang invents its own pseudo-traditions. Fidelity to the gang provides the illusion of its own history and ethic, "clan" terminology and names, and instant pseudo-roles.

An alternative to an acceptable myth of history is to look deep within one's own being for a real past. The normal regression of the adolescent, puting him in touch with his infantile core in order to use it in new ways, carries with it the hazard that his infantile fears of losing his source of comfort and nourishment might drive him backward toward the security of an earlier uterine all-in-oneness instead of forward toward the discontinuities of the natural world. The universe may indeed be such a unity, and there may be human-scale epiphanies—divine manifestations—of that unity which benefit society through the sensitivity of gifted individuals. But if contact with the final nothingness of god-head is the supreme moment, it is also the supreme cop-out from this world.

Primitive man is often said to feel an "identity with nature." This observation stems from an erroneous concept of continuity in nature in which distinctions and boundaries evaporate. Hunting-gathering men are not lost in a fuzzy emotional merger with their surroundings; they are sensitive to delicate nuances that separate and relate. The idea of the mystic trance as the perfect state of consciousness was conceived in agricultural religions, where the idea of nothingness enabled the devotees to escape from an intolerable world. The trance idolizes the subjectivity of the vegetable, the ultimate homogenized life style.

Though mysticism is hardly a way of advancing to a mature life on this earth, it has the redeeming value, if properly used, of allowing those with crippled psyches a new beginning by way of regression to the foetal state. For instance, a subjective return to the earth womb may be helpful for people who have no memory of a good mother or no image of a good Great-Mother goddess and whose lives are therefore seriously deficient. It may help the neurotic whose life has been a succession of hard bottle, hard plow, and hard concrete, who perceives himself and the earth as crusted and inanimate. For those whose culture has taught them that women and earth are vile, psychedelic merger states and mysticism may help to expel the female as demon, the devouring witch of bed and soil.

At the other extreme from this pursuit of nothingness as remedial therapy for a misspent infancy is the obsession with collecting objects and possessions, which is also a gross inversion of a normal process. The necessity of taxonomic knowledge, identified with the development of cognition, focuses the child on things and creatures. This materialistic-mental enterprise operates on a pattern of likeness and unlikeness, of duality and grouping. It could be argued that any collection of furniture, automobiles, or computers can be perceived in the same way. The diversity-in-unity of plant and animal kingdoms, upon which the devlopment of human mentality depends, would seem, then, to have no absolute value. So long as numbers of celebrity photographs, baseball players' autographs, beer cans, or other series of objects with affinities are available, nature would appear obsolete; once launched on his career as creator and collector of his own products, man could make whatever diversity his mind requires.

The fault in this argument is that, in the birth of thought in which discriminations are made among the kinds of plants and animals, another comparison between the self and them is under way. The young human's engagement with the endlessly fascinating game of likeness and difference is more than an abstraction. The "others" are each being matched against the self as living beings like one's self, yet not like one's self, who evoke the mystery of creation and the continuity of a life that is shared. They are the tangible measures of difference. As beings with their own purposes, they are the planet's rebuke to human self-worship. All contain some secrets that can never be known. No coin collection can do this. Human creativity is not infinite; it is species-bound.

The substitution of manmade objects for the species system is a "natural" mistake. Not only is there a parallel logic of diversity, but the adolescent is intent, typically, with his own self-image. The narcissistic trait is the curious dumb hope that one's appearance will, by an inscrutable magic, reveal the true self. In a society with adequate initiation it gives way in time to a more confident and mature attitude. The youths of disabled cultures remain chronically narcissistic. Such was the psychic sickness of classical Greece: a fixation on man and his works as both explanation and goal of society.

The men of Greek and Roman civilizations represent a stage in the struggle toward recovery of that ability to mature which is fully displayed and complete in cynegetic men. The Greeks were unable to cope with the "other," except as it could be represented humanistically. For example, they were capable, technically, of developing machines and incorporating them into the productive economy, but they found machines too uncanny, intolerably humanoid. They could not master the machine as the Eskimo did because they were disabled in youth. In spite of their political and mathematical sophistication, the people of those lands were immature sub-adults whose homocentric bias rotted their ecological relations, who could not face the "other" in the lifelike behavior and autonomy of machines because of their own uncertain identity. They were invalids, deformed by the arrest of maturation, a species-wide syndrome induced by agriculture.

In the modern world, where machines have largely replaced animals, it is perhaps inevitable that they should be treated as totems and seen as models of what we are. The modern lad of eleven is keenly interested in animals and not much in machines; by the time he is thirteen the situation is reversed. He strives to master the machines and to emulate them—to "take on fuel," to "drive ahead." One explanation is that these boys are more mature than their ancient Greek counterparts. Another is that they do not share the Greek sense of the divinity of life and more easily perceive themselves as collections of parts. It is my feeling that both are true, that today's adolescents are much less homogenous and more wide-ranging in their kinds and degrees of maturity as well as failures of development. The true clan model has been preserved, as in the names of athletic teams. There are "wildcats," "panthers," and "falcons," and, as yet, few "bulldozers," "road-graders," or "trucks."

The diversity of modern adolescents is indicative of their drifting state. Without adequate leaders, young people between twelve and twenty seek truth within themselves and guidance from one another. In large, dense populations this autogeny is self-reinforcing. When social or political action is dominated by such groups their members become true antinomians—those against tradition—who put all faith in the force of their own ideas. In the past there have been the Manicheans, the Lollards, the Anabaptists, the Romantics. Each group, focusing its autism on its own passionate heroes, has claimed to have found truth at the heart of being.

In an era of instant communication, antinomians rapidly become politicized. They are fanatically embroiled in causes. Each individual has a social-political idea that makes him feel better, so it must be right. He attaches to some abstraction —socialism, capitalism, fascism, Maoism, liberalism, communism, racism, vegetarianism—and is locked into an uncompromising idealism, exaggerated morality, the repudiation of history, the fear of maturity and adulthood, mass aggression and other violence. The ideologist is the unreconstructed adolescent. He repudiates history, by which is meant any traditional myth of the group past, not simply official history in which the anxiety of the man-nature conflict results in progress.

The ideological antinomian is far more tragic than the urban gang with its ignorance of natural things or the rural commune with its misplaced reverence for the institutions of peasant agriculture. As all ideas become concrete for him and he moves more and more in a world without metaphor, as the abstract crystallizes into "blinding veils of reified ideas," the society he dominates becomes preoccupied with morals and ethics, and everything "other" seems sinister. Whatever his chronological age, he is trapped in adolescence. As the critical period for meeting the developmental demands for maturing tutelage runs out, the individual ages without a bridge to maturity, either drifting without conviction and emotionally incompetent or ideologically fixated. Drugs merely help defer his impotent efforts. Society becomes laced with old adolescents who deeply hate nature and mankind for making them less than human.

The living world now faces a massive failure of interspecies dynamics, signaled by the enormous destruction of life. Its psychological effects are equally devastating. Perhaps its most singular expression is the fear of not being human.

Consciously becoming human is the culmination and end of adolescence. The basic attitude of the mature human being to his non-human environment should be one of relatedness and orientation. Man's genes are programed to raise questions and to demand certain kinds of response from society and experiences in nature. The fear of mortality and individual helplessness are normal motives for questioning. Without answers, we doom ourselves to treat one another, and be treated, as non-human as the only defense against that fear.

6

THE CHOICE: INDUSTRIAL AGRICULTURE OR TECHNO-CYNEGETICS

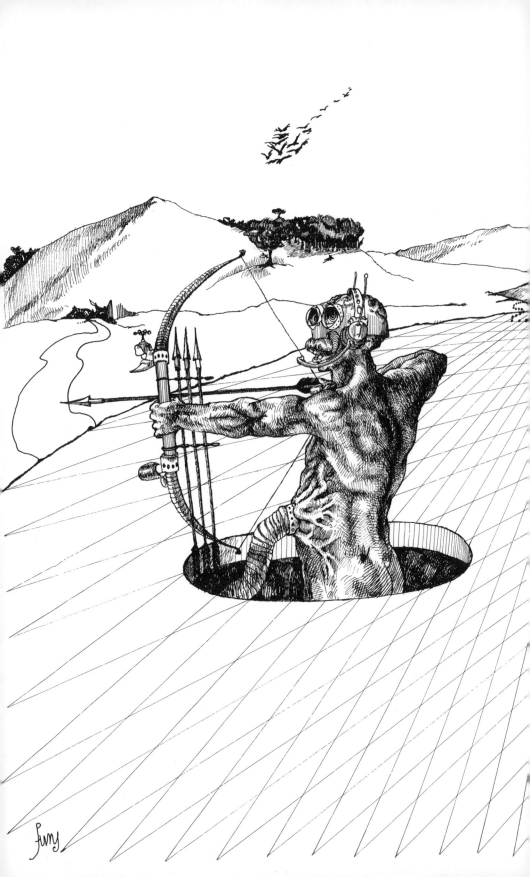

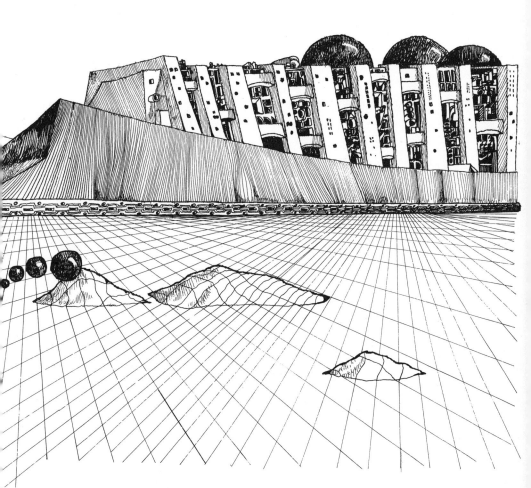

As agriculture replaced hunting and gathering it was accompanied by radical changes in the way men saw and responded to their natural surroundings. Although hundreds of local forms of farming developed, each with its special techniques, they all shared the aim of completely humanizing the earth's surface, replacing wild with domestic, and creating landscapes from habitat. It is not surprising that the world religions have in common a peasant mythology, a "reality" opposing town and country, wild and tame, man and nature. It is frequently said, even by anthropologists today, that man has always attempted to

[237]

maximize his share of the energy and space and that these characteristics are therefore inherent in humanity. But what man is said "always" to have done is part of a mythology of farmers and peasants.

As we question the motives and beliefs of our own time, we are forced to ask questions about the sources of our values and our myths.

It is insufficient to say simply that with agriculture men's attitudes toward the natural world changed, or that the ideas of control and dominance, of choice and self-consciousness, appeared from nowhere, superseding philosophies of participation and dependence.

In *The Savage Mind,* Lévi-Strauss describes the traditional or totemic view of the world as opposed to the caste view, which has succeeded it in most of the world, including industrial society. In the first, social differences among men are analogous to observed species differences. Men are grouped by a system of relations that utilizes a way of thought based on a natural model. Groups of people are differentiated by a terminology defining them as different species.

This idea may repel us at a time of racial and social conflict. To the civilized mind, totemism implies imitation of animals and—far worse than racial discrimination—an illegitimate sanction of the prejudice that holds men to be as irreconcilably different as the fox and crow. However authoritarian the clan and tribal designations may be, they establish a pattern of relationships and the necessary pride in one's own group without subjugating or destroying any other. Totemic men have always known that animal species do not annihilate one another. They see beyond the occasions of predation to the ongoing activity of predator and prey, and names are tokens of that deeper reality of the species. More important, animal behavior is not taken literally as a guide to action. Totemic men do not eat each other, but translate that eating into the far more subtle language of the durable bond based on metaphors of assimilation and nourishment.

The niche differences, which separate species of wild animals, are constantly honed by the evolutionary process of natural selection. The constancy of members of a species is due to mixing and gene-flow within the whole. The same is true of men, except that its social origin is marriage. The rituals that insure the mixing and gene-flow outward from the band or tribe are modeled on the visible analogue of food chains, which are the most universal examples in nature of connections between kinds. Human exogamy, the marriage of women outside the group, is the homologue of predation by which all men keep a genetic continuity and which, in the relatedness between different totemic clans (named for different species), is a ceremonial affirmation of the ecological structure of the world. Exogamy is a way of doing and saying that places its faith in the natural world.

When men cultivate plants and domesticate animals their attention is turned to inbreeding. Diversity and unity are no longer seen as harmonious ends in a single totality. The unity manifested by purity of line is prized at the expense of diversity and protected from intrusion of gene pollution from the outside. The husbandry system, whose forms underlie the foundations of modern thought, excludes wild nature as chaotic, other, and evil. At the root of the modern tragedies of mass homicide and biocide, the substitution of ideology for religion, the disorientation of individual experience, are the ideals of husbandry and the loss of totemic models.

The caste system is the social expression of agricultural ecology. It extends pure-breeding to the human group by its laws of marriage, which are inbreeding and by implication deny the imperative of food-chain relations in nature. Animal behaviors are no longer seen as a language, and their behaviors, rather than their relationships, become models or parallels, so that killing within our kind does indeed seem to reflect a "universal law of the jungle."

All the caste or modern societies contain technological specialists and are therefore subdivided along economic lines. The model of the caste is the farmer's pure strain of livestock or plants, rather than the food chain. It emphasizes discontinuity between castes instead of connectedness. This diversity within the society impairs its outward relationships to other groups of people as well as to other species. All others become remote and alien. The delight of men in natural diversity is perverted to the array of goods, the exchange of which signifies mere object or non-living links between people. In this sense, goods are fatally defective as a language.

Because of this, the structure of the universe is conceived differently. Among hunters there is a homology formally correlating two systems of differences, natural and cultural. Civilized man seeks connectedness in rites of sacrifice, in which a divinity is invoked by the destruction of an intermediary object. Such a hierarchy of beings assumes an irreversible operation for which ecological experience offers no analogy, a historical event as opposed to the past as a timeless present.

For Lévi-Strauss the symmetry of nature and culture differs fundamentally between totem and caste, hunter and farmer. Hunters perceive all species as having roles in a vast society (they "culturize a false nature truly") while farmers perceive human groups as species (or "naturalize a true culture falsely"). This would not be so tragic were it not for the farmer's antagonism to species; he feels that the "other" is a threat to his purity. Lévi-Strauss sees these two approaches as alternatives: a system of social functions modeled on natural species; or a system of pseudo species that corresponds to the diverse niches of creatures in nature. Both are the consequences of an inherent, universal *modus operandi* of the human mind.

Here Lévi-Strauss ends, but it can be seen that one approach is consistent with the ongoing evolution of man as a member of a planetary community, stable societies, and the perpetuation of ecosystems for hundreds of millennia; while the other is associated with worldwide social calamity, war, and environmental deterioration that has already done irreversible damage to the biosphere.

Values and myths also affect the individual behavior of people who believe in them. Certain personality traits assumed to be true of all men are only those of historical men, of men living in time recorded and written. Civilized man's endless waiting and chronic anxiety about productivity, his notion of sacrifice, his stolid submission to drudgery and routine, his idolatry of work and frenzy to escape from work, his competitive pride in family and possessions, his distinctions between himself and all beasts, his self-righteous manipulation of the environment, his political sense of hierarchy and orientation to authority, his willingness to subordinate a remorseless and enduring will to political ends, regimentation, and organized murder—all are characteristic of peasant and city dweller. Each trait can be made to sound virtuous. The sentimentalities in which town people and formal education cloak the realities of rural life and peasant values are among the most cherished and dangerous illusions of modern man.

The farmer as a model of virtue and as a being close to nature is as false an image as that the cultivated and grazed landscape is nature. To the land-user are transferred qualities of social and ecological maturity and sensitivity in fact found only among hunters. This ancient fraud has misled thousands of hopeful and conscientious people into aspiring to go back to the farm in the vain hope of retrieving what the city took. In potato grubbing they will painfully act out their fantasies; in disillusion and puzzlement they will return to the city.

It is true that the pleasures of quiet, space, and fresh air are found in the country. The vacation or escape from the city, first by privileged individuals and then egalitarian masses, has been, since the beginning of civilization, a search for respite and elementary health. But solitude, clean air, and water have not been made by agriculture; they are properties of the natural earth. No doubt many people find relief and have recuperated from disease and the illnesses of stress in the peace, routine, and simple life of the rural environment, and they are grateful for it. Nostalgia is also a factor. Farms are a good place for children. But this is in spite of agriculture: it is not the corn but the wildflowers the children remember. Their play is a special device for compensating for weak spots in the environment. Children are imprinted by place regardless of its features. They are poor judges of that environment in later retrospect. In short, in the bipolar culture of city and country we have created an aesthetic by which people admire the country provided that sooner or later they can leave it—an aesthetic that mistakenly identifies the healthful qualities of all non-urbanized places with peasant life and farming.

The Cultural Basis of Ecological Crisis

Insofar as farmers think of such matters, they are taken in by and gladly exploit the dream of rural virtue. All politicians, hucksters, farm magazines and other media directed to farmers deliberately foster this fantasy. The farmer is assured of his reverence for the soil, his knowledge of nature, his fondness for wild animals, his moral superiority, his political acumen, and so on. But if a farmer is asked what kind of place he likes or why he thinks nature is good, he will not be able to answer unless he is an educated man, a gentleman farmer—that is, a non-farmer who hires "hands."

The reason for this is not hard to find. Peasant existence is the dullest life man ever lived. Since the beginning of the modern world the brighter and more sensitive children have left the dawn-to-dusk toil of the farm to their duller brothers and sisters. Even for those who remain the routine must be leavened or it is intolerable. Rural peoples the world over have scores of holidays and festivals to alleviate their existence. The number of such occasions is proportional to the intensity and specialization of the agriculture. In a relatively diverse domestication there is less need for diversions.

A frontiersman or pioneer is self-sufficient in more than material needs. His subsistence farm is in closer ecological harmony with the natural environment; it might include a vegetable garden, hay and grain fields, fruit trees or bushes, bees, a fish pond, fowl, a variety of hooved animals, pasture, nut trees and other forest, and nearby natural vegetation from which mushrooms and other wild vegetables and wild game are taken.

Farmers in a cash crop, surplus food or fiber production, and monoculture setting, however, require constant social super-charging to remain sane and human. Their pastimes are often shocking and brutal, their religious observances noisy and dramatic. Cock-fighting, bull-fighting, bear-baiting, dog-fighting, men-fights, the debauchery of alcohol and drugs, socially sanctioned remission of standards of morality, public display and civil punishment, and sexual and religious frenzy and indulgence are social attempts to compensate for the nullity.

In the most extreme example of this vacuum, modern industrial irrigation monoculture, rural life is hopeless. The farmer lives in a town, which is socially and architecturally organized to provide a sensory barrage, and, like the peasant of the Old World, he commutes to the fields. This is the climax of ten millennia of separating work from leisure, depriving work of its redeeming, universalizing aspect, reducing leisure to idleness and whim, and separating both from the cultus, the social forms of divine activity. No margin for weeds and wild things is left; there is no recourse to hunting and gathering, no habitat in which man is in scale. It is not surprising that farmers the world over have always been ready to abandon these environments. Their eagerness to leave was implicit from the beginning. That modern farmers are becoming indistinguishable from city men, by place of residence as well as dress and habits, is the culmination of agri-culture with its pseudo-separation of urban and rural.

The depersonalizing and socially destructive forces of the city can be traced to their true origins: the country. If the city as we know it is unhealthy, a breeder of social and racial injustice, the wreck of human community, a sinkhole of crime, a failed complex of educational, religious, sanitary, and transportation facilities, then we have failed to design according to human need. Its rural foundation is no less defective. The country has fed the city with people whose ecological thought has been corrupted with delusions of mastery of nature, who have been trained to be stoic and stolid when the livable city demands sensitivity and creativity. The city has drawn from the hinterland materials and energy, fiber and food, forcing the escalation of monocultures and imposing chemical and industrial methods on agriculture.

There have been dire warnings of future famine due to overpopulation, but famine is not new. Too many people with too little to eat is not a unique tragedy of modern times. It is the ten-, twenty-, or fifty-year cycle of agriculture itself. Ever since the birth-controlling mores of cynegetic societies were broken by the lust for more children and more production, there have been periodic failures in the production of food to keep pace with the production of more babies.

Motherhood, which had a symbolic place in human religion, was monstrously exaggerated in the farmer's preoccupation with fecundity. Women were condemned to the production of children or ostracized for not producing them. The pig and chicken were taken as models for what women should be. Farming put upon human females the job of emulating the barnyard animals, then of becoming baby machines. The mystique and rationale used to enforce and justify this subversion penetrated the center of all peasant religions, where the Great Mother was elevated, not for her essential feminine traits, but as the breeder of men and food. No slaves were ever more cruelly exiled to hopeless toil. The shame and psychological stress of barrenness or the debilitating physiological effect of perpetual pregnancy and lactation were women's share of the life of drudgery.

The subsistence farmer invented security-mindedness. The money farmer outdid him with his seemingly insatiable desire for increasing productivity. That this led into slavery is more than metaphor. According to Daphne Prior, agriculture ceased to be voluntary and became coercive some six thousand years ago, with the emergence of the "autonomous, centralized political unit with the power to collect taxes, draft workers and soldiers and enforce law."

The Perils of the Green Revolution

We stand on the threshold of a new productivity of world agriculture, to be achieved by fertilizer, water control, genetic breeding, and pest control. The Green Revolution is the catch phrase. In effect it says that what we need is simply an intensified land use, which can be done by mobilizing all the modern scientific and industrial tools: improvement of genetic varieties of plants and animals, more efficient operation, capital investment, associated engineering works and industry, better storage, transportation, and distribution. In short, it advocates that the use of most of the earth's land surface (and large parts of its water area) be refashioned after Iowa pig farms or Texas cotton ranches. Until recently its advocates said that it would solve problems of poverty and starvation by increasing the world's food supply as rapidly as the world population grew. Until 1969 this was the official line of the World Food Organization of the United Nations. A tidal wave of scientific refutation and growing public awakening has at last caused some rethinking on the subject, which was as much a fabrication of vested interests and wishful thinking as it was the opinion of agricultural researchers.

It has been replaced by a slightly modified doctrine, that industrial agriculture will alleviate the effects of human density by reducing the magnitude of famine and postponing the crisis. It is argued indignantly that to do less is inhumane.

What, in fact, is the environmental effect of super-agriculture? In the United States land destruction is a matter of record. The erosion of large sections of the Southeast by tobacco and cotton in the seventeenth and eighteenth centuries and the dust bowls of the Great Plains in the twentieth are merely two of the many earlier examples. The combined effects of clearing, plowing, burning, overgrazing, ill-advised irrigation, breaking sods that should never be cultivated, removing timber from slopes that should remain in trees, draining marshes that served as uptakes for underground water supplies—all are documented in a vast literature. Explanations that it was a new continent with unfamiliar climate, that the frontier would always offer a fresh start, that methods were imperfect but would improve with new machines, have been belabored and accepted. A particular farmer in his time and place is not to be regarded as a greedy monster but only as a cog in the wheel of society.

The total damage to the continental environment has probably been underestimated. Much of it has been hidden by the buffering effect of long-accumulated reserves and the continued productivity of lands that are nevertheless losing their reserves of soil capital. The huge literature of lamentation and guilt has been countered by "practical" observations that, as long as productivity is high, losses are unimportant. It has been said that the rape of the continent was necessary to make us powerful and rich, that by being rich we are better able to solve problems caused by exploitation while at the same time living well. It can be convincingly shown that forest conservation will be practiced by forest industries and soil conservation by farmers as these become economically imperative; that the decline in natural resources will gradually be leveled by rising economic incentive.

Such arguments can be so neatly woven by professionals in the "resource field" that one is struck with awe and admiration at their beautiful simplicity. The way in which self-correcting means are built in, the aura of destiny and inevitability, the justification of past and present that relieves us of responsibility are more than seductive; they are ravishing.

For trapping the modern farmer and his wife within this dialectic we can thank academia—the land-grant universities and their affiliated state agricultural colleges. Wasteful and expensive even by modern American standards, most agricultural institutions cannot find applicants for all their fellowships, their proliferated courses are underenrolled, and their large faculties overpaid. The agriculture schools are carefully protected and fed by an industry grossing about fifty billion dollars a year in farm products alone (and some hundred billion in the making of agricultural supplies and equipment) and by the

minions of that industry in government. Walk on the campus
of any agricultural school. Look in the classrooms. Sit in on
classes. Look in the libraries. Stroll through the model dairies.
Count the students. You will see the most elaborate educational
machinery for the education of the smallest group of professionals in academia. Compare what you see to the educational
plant for biology or physics, or for history or literature.

Their bulk, duplication, and cost are not the worst. Home
economics and agricultural training have from their inception
been inimical to the creative wholeness of the family subsistence
farm, in which those virtues of rural life which survive can be
found. Among these are first-hand knowledge of weather, organisms, terrain, the development of manual skills in fashioning
the crafts of rural life, knowledge of materials and textures in
the making of things and of foods to be used.

Home economics, by its relentless advocacy of mechanization and consumerism, has sold the farm woman short. She no
longer sews, churns, knits, bakes, preserves, works a garden, or
participates in the care of animals. She is linked to the stores
and to the society of the town. What is more, she will assure you
that she likes it that way—though she may have simply escaped
from the drudgery of the farm to a new set of equally pernicious
stresses. I have no intention of arguing differently; as I have
said, there is no reason, sentimental or rational, for perpetuating
the hand toil of peasant life. Beyond her experience is the total
price of continuing the farm at all, the cost to the land, to the
biosphere, and to society as a whole (including the additional
cost of urbanizing the farm family). The farm woman has been
sold short because her instinctive concern for the organic and
her womanly generosity and feeling for wholeness have been
diverted into new social activities or de-fused by litter cam-
paigns and beautification projects. She has been removed from
the immediate scene of the farm. She is no longer a witness or
participant. Her potential human and feminine reactions to the
banality and monotonous horror of the new industrial farm are
no longer a threat to its continuation. This is the Women's
Auxiliary of the Green Revolution.

The Green Revolution is moving to complete the industrialization of the earth's land and sea surfaces. Its thrust will take two main directions, accompanied by chemical warfare on a scale precedented by the massive use of herbicides in the Vietnam war. The first is the genetic development of new superstrains of crop plants. The second is the irrigation and cultivation of the world's deserts. Neither can solve the world's food problems because of the exponential form of human population growth. Both are prescriptions for ecological disaster. They are the logical and final development of the poor ecology of agriculture that first ruined small areas and good soils, then extensive areas where the more vulnerable communities of natural life had less intrinsic stability. The principle is the same everywhere: the intensity of technique is commensurate with the rapidity and magnitude of potential calamity. By impoverishing an already fragile habitat with uniform crop plants and destroying its native life, the Green Revolution, in the name of a holy crusade, will create balances that cannot be kept, crops that cannot be protected, landscapes so foreign to the desert climate that their precarious existence will require ever-increasing inputs of chemical and mechanical control. When greenhouse projects the size of the Sahara desert topple, as they surely will, the consequences will make past famines in India look like minor incidents.

When the environmental crisis became a national preoccupation in 1970 attention was centered on pollution. The old conservation movement, with its gentlemanly voice of alarm over land, soil, and water, seemed almost obsolete. Neither the new radical youth element nor the establishment environmentalists had much good to say for it. Their dismissal of old-fashioned conservation of land and water as of no importance was shortsighted not only historically but ecologically as well. Pollution is only the debris resulting from mispractices and mispolicies relating people to the land.

Of course air pollution and water pollution have been the conspicuous aspects of the environmental situation, and to these the public could easily respond. More devastating, however, has been the destruction of soils and forests, which has been ignored —for an insidious reason: the harvest has been increasing. American economists and geographers, among others, have long boasted that American agriculture has been the most efficient on earth. When Premier Khrushchev of the Soviet Union visited the United States in 1956 it was an Iowa farm that he wanted to see and was pridefully shown. In the dust-bowl days of the 1930s, when farms were buried under suffocating layers of silt and abandoned, the lesson had seemed clear: land misuse led to economic failure. Since then, in Iowa as in other deep-soil Midwest states, land misuse has produced affluence. There are full barns, great rows of gleaming farm machinery, children in college, high land prices, and gross incomes for many farmers of more than a hundred thousand dollars per year. The lesson has been forgotten for the sake of economic gain.

To say that the most productive Iowa farms are among the most mismanaged lands in the world produces furious counterclaims. Nevertheless it is true. The Midwest cornfields, the cottonlands of Texas, the timberlands of the Northwest, the interior valleys of California—the most productive and "efficient" agriculture on the continent—are the homes of havoc. There the devastation, though invisible, sets the style for the Green Revolution.

The tools that keep the crops greening in Iowa, as elsewhere, are chemicals. In the past the one practice that has redeemed agriculture ecologically throughout the whole of its history has been the spreading of manure. Whenever this practice has been abandoned, cities, regions, even empires have obediently followed their soils into extinction. Everywhere that agriculture has endured, a suitable ratio of animals to cultivated land is found, and the deliberate and careful husbanding of human waste and other organic matter for fertilizer.

Organic matter does for a soil what no pure chemical elements can do. In addition to nutrients, it is a source of humus, essential for soil structure. Soils with adequate humus hold reserves of water and nutrient elements and therefore have the physical, chemical, thermic, and textural qualities that favor rich microbial life and the growth of plant roots, and produce nutritional balance in the harvest. If they are not impacted by the weight of heavy machines such soils withstand drought and storm, the plow and harrow, good years and bad. They remain intact and productive indefinitely if crops are properly rotated and occasionally rested.

Beginning with the mid-twentieth century, combinations of chemical nitrogen, potassium, and phosphorus have been increasingly used and sold as a "complete" fertilizer. Most farmers have used these together with calcium as a fertilizer program. Here and there, where other nutrient elements were lacking in particular soils, these too have been added. Coupled with chemical pesticides, herbicides, and the heavy planting of new strains of crop plants, crop yield has gone up. Meantime the soil has gone steadily down in structure and holding capacity. The massive doses of fertilizer have leached through, poisoning underground water and polluting by enrichment city reservoirs and lakes. One consequence of such pollution is heavy algal growth, which suffocates other life in lakes and is generally combated by another round of expensive chemical treatment.

The combination of crop strains that have been produced for characteristics other than nutritional value (uniformity, appearance, bulk, storing qualities, disease-resistance) and chemical fertilizing that omits organic matter and the two dozen other chemicals necessary to life has ruined the nutritional quality of soil and harvest. The complexity of a natural soil makes it comparable to a quasi-living being, an organism, or a kind of organ of the biosphere. It is also part of a larger ecosystem. The agronomists train the industrial farmer to sacrifice everything for crop productivity: fencerows, natural soil, trees, wildflowers, small mammals, insects, birds, natural brooks, and a truly quality product. As experts who also advise the powerful chemical companies, they permeate academia and dominate the theory if not the practice of commercial farming.

The travesty of chemical farming that engulfs the young farmer continues to enmesh him with its propaganda throughout his life. Mediated by the county agent, technicians of government agricultural agencies, the bureaucrats of subsidy and marketing programs, the industry-dominated farm media, and all the "agri-businesmen" together create rural Disneyland, a self-contained, self-explanatory, and self-judging sham.

No single farmer, no matter how educated his perception, or what his intuition with respect to the preservation of the soil and the natural community, can escape it. Surrounded by neighbors who compensate for the compacting of soil by their heavy machinery and for its functional failure by increasing the dosage of pure chemicals, he cannot reduce his harvest and still get the loans he needs; he cannot get sufficient manpower or animal power, reduce his field and farm size. He cannot survive economically if he allows space for wild creatures, or gives some of the harvest to pests, or uses varieties of crop plants with lower yield but higher food value. Indeed, he would be ostracized formally and informally. The system would crush him.

The successes and failures of chemical pesticides are well known. Their celebrated "control" of insect and fungal pests is conveyed in detail in advertising, textbooks, and "history" books. In time all target organisms become resistant by genetic selection, beneficial forms are harmed, and the biosphere is poisoned. The genetic response of pests is a fact that the industry is happy to admit in order to divert attention from the more serious effects of chemical pesticides and to justify the continued issuance of new compounds.

The replacement of one chemical pesticide with another, then another, and so on, not only works but is consumerism at its best. It is not only commercial but can be measured for success and progress. Ecologically, the swath of death cuts through the environment without reference to enemies or friends. Like using a cannon for surgery, it simply removes good and bad alike. In some places delicate species of insects and other invertebrates, in no way harmful to man, have been extinguished. As ecologists have pointed out for many years, some of these are parasites or predators on the pest organism.

Some pesticides, such as DDT, remain in the soil, air, and

water for many years, poisoning and repoisoning as they pass through food-chain systems in nature. They are stored in the fatty tissues of meat-eaters. The labor and expense it has taken to limit the use of DDT have been enormous. Yet how pathetic that effort seems when hundreds of substitutes are possible, many already in use, some better, some worse, all of which control by general destruction—the environmental equivalent of giving whole-body x-irradiation to control cancer.

Fortunately for man, his evolution toward carnivorousness over the past four million years progressed only to a point of eating around 30 per cent meat. Were he a true carnivore he would now be suffering far more DDT accumulation in his system. His tragedy would parallel that of peregrine falcons, brown pelicans, sea lions, and hundreds of other birds and mammals that live wholly on meat. As it is, every bite of meat from whatever source now carries its portion of DDT into the body, where part of it will be stored. Young adults have been accumulating DDT for more than twenty years, and will continue to accumulate it throughout their lives even if the use of DDT is eliminated. What this will mean to the health of the people now in their twenties as they approach their sixties cannot be foreseen, but the result will not be good. Nor is there any escape, since much DDT was applied by air and, instead of falling at once to the ground, entered the world's atmosphere and is falling slowly around the planet, a poisoned dew.

To expect contrition from agri-industry for the DDT episode would perhaps be too much. To expect intelligent reappraisal of the role of chemical pesticides is not too much. Nonetheless the chemical industries are fighting government regulation of DDT. Their answer to the problem is more research and more careful testing of substitute products. There is no evidence of redirection, only escalation of a chemical approach that will lead to catastrophe.

When the use of herbicides, hormones, and antibiotics in animal husbandry and seed and fruit treatment, and the use of disinfectants, preservatives, color and taste enhancers in food

are objectively examined, the evidence is that we are poisoning
and defrauding ourselves. To suppose that the damage done by
each is an isolated instance or is caused by a transitory weakness
in detail in the technology is delusion. Chemical agriculture
fails because agriculture is an imperfect union of wild and tame.

The fate of domestic plants and animals now hangs in the
balance. In peasant agriculture the selection for seed size or
fruit color, for wool or milk production, was counteracted by
hardiness or physical fitness, use qualities, and taste. Now industrial agriculture seeks mutations for extreme milk or beef
production in cattle and ear size or position in corn, on the assumption that the weaknesses and unfitness that accompany
them can always be countered by chemical disinfection, addi-
tives, and other substances that violate the organism and the
environment.

Directly and indirectly these chemical poisons are passed on
to us, either through our consumption of the farm product or
through the environment. The modern creation of "animal
machines" also changes the animals' tissues. The physiology and
biochemistry of animals kept throughout their lives in cages are
altered, adversely affecting the nutritive quality of such products
as eggs and milk as well as the flesh itself.

The psychological effects, or life experience, of such captives must not be overlooked, not only for reasons of humane
concern but because of their influence on body chemistry. Pigs
that have been harshly treated in advance of slaughter undergo
stress changes in their alimentary systems releasing a highly
poisonous bacterium, *Salmonella,* into the gut from pouches
along its wall. At butchering, *Salmonella* may then contaminate
the meat. The toxins produced kill more people than any other
kind of food poisoning. Recently new strains have been identified that are not susceptible to any known antibiotic treatment.

There is some evidence that the more industrialized agriculture becomes the less nutritious and delectable is its produce.
Vegetables grown under irrigation or hydroponically (that is,
in nutrient liquid) are notoriously tasteless. Where fowl are

kept in highly artificial and confined pens, egg quality is down —by the industry's own standards, which are poor enough from the consumer's point of view.

There is no doubt that modern agriculture is moving into a new phase of animal husbandry that will fully justify the term "industrial." No animal will have a life as it is ordinarily thought of in the image of the barnyard community of the subsistence farm. The animals will be contained and manipulated only for their usefulness. Insofar as they are able to feel, perceive, and respond, their experience will be limited to slings or scaffolds in closed chambers, punctuated by the drone of machines that castrate, inseminate, vaccinate, medicate, remove excrement, extract by-products, and sluice a total-food-soup into them, ending with the needle, gas jet, or knife.

This has been foreshadowed by the industrial slaughterhouse, a logical and necessary adjunct of scientific farming. Every person in a developed nation should be required to tour a slaughterhouse, and he should do so after learning any one of the hundreds of ceremonies of apology, prayer, and symbolic commitment to the prey that attend the hunt by cynegetic men. As more is learned about the responses of plants and animals, either the killing must increasingly be hidden from sight and consciousness or it must be done in religious affirmation. By "must" I do not mean courses of action to be taken. I mean that we will be forced into one of two directions by the future. Chemical agriculture, like chemical warfare, is slaughter at a distance—death poorly directed and unseen battles won in a war that will be lost—that is lost in the winning.

None of the fairy tales by which the war against nature is described is more fanciful than that told by modern economics. That one man with his machines can produce enough food and fiber for one hundred people for a year from two hundred acres is a typical example. It has been assumed that costs outside capital investment and operational expenses, such as soil and environmental deterioration, would show up eventually in his accounting books. To a limited extent they do, as he piles more and more chemicals onto the land and into his stock to compensate for what the soil no longer provides, as he builds dams and drills deeper wells for water the soil no longer holds, and as he enlarges and intensifies his operation in the face of an increasingly unstable ecosystem. These costs are measured in dollars, but the time lag is so great that many of the biological expenses have not yet materialized as cash losses.

The dollar calculations still look good in the farmer's own book, but his book includes public money in the debit column, which he has not earned. Some of this is clearly shown as subsidy in the form of government conservation payments; other items, like farm price supports, are not so marked because they are less direct—but no less real. The gross dollar value of farm crops in the United States in 1970 was about fifty billion dollars per year, expenses about thirty-five billion. Of the fifteen-billion-dollar profit, five billion came directly from government price and payment subsidies. If agricultural colleges with their scholarships, county, state and federal free services to the farmer, incentives, industrial handouts and favors to the farmer written off as tax-exempt expenses, adjusted land taxes, income-tax angles whose loopholes are second to none could all be taken into account, the ten-billion-dollar net would vanish like a dream. It is only fair to add that different types of farming vary in these respects. Some kinds feed less at the public trough than others. The point is that the total has never, to my knowledge, been calculated, but would probably run to a huge deficit. It has been called "the largest disguised income-transfer program in history."

In addition, agriculture is costly far beyond the boundaries of the farm. The pollution to the environment from the industries serving agriculture (and many other industries and services) begins with mining and smelting to get the ores to make farm machinery and strip mining for coal, and runs through the manufacturing processes, which are especially destructive and noxious among petro-chemical industries, to the final transporting of them to the farm. The boast that each acre of a modern farm can feed twenty or thirty times the number of men on it looks good when compared to peasant farming, but the calories of food energy produced per acre are fewer than the fuel energy put into the manufacture, transportation, and operation of the machinery.

Subsistence agriculture is directly based on photosynthesis. Solar energy is channeled to the consumer directly through the farm crops. Even the muscle energy from man and animal working the farm is derived from the crops themselves. When the energy from fossil fuels is added by mechanization the crop production is raised at an unseen expense to the whole biosphere. The input of fossil fuel raises the photosynthetic output slightly, but this is like running a huge generator in order to turn on a few more electric lights. The resulting pollution is not the only hidden cost. Petroleum is one of the richest potential sources of new food products on earth; the day may come when people will virtually weep to realize how much of it was squandered by burning. To argue that by then man will be able to replace it is fallacious because energy will be required to make the substitute for petroleum. It is like the argument that, having squandered rich soils, agricultural technology will make it possible to farm poor ones; the fallacy is that to do so will require an increased energy and materials input from the outside.

At the forefront of the Green Revolution is the genetic development of new crop varieties with higher yields. That some of these are less nourishing, and most poorer tasting, may be dismissed as the necessary price of more carbohydrates and fats for a growing population. Each new miracle plant does not simply replace a less efficient form; it replaces hundreds and hundreds of varieties. Originally domestication was a local affair. Plants adapted to the particular soils and climate were cultivated in each area. Hybrids of the domestic plant and its wild relatives sprang up along field boundaries, a rich reserve of genetic variability. Close to their wild origins, the native varieties were less productive than the new strains but more stable and resistant to local diseases.

In 1930, 80 per cent of the wheat grown in Greece was composed of scores of local varieties. By 1966, less than 10 per cent were native strains. The rest was a single imported super-plant. The biology of evolution, the principles of ecology, and the history of agriculture guarantee that sooner or later a disease will devastate that alien. Where previously diseases were local and food shortages in any year equally restricted, super-crops and massive famine are natural partners.

Though it was destructive enough in its own way, subsistence agriculture was broadly based, not only in diversity of crops, but in the closer-to-wild-type genetics of each. The inverted pyramid of super-strains must be propped up as each becomes weaker in vitality. Every year increased chemical and mechanical supports, infusions of capital and energy, must be added from the outside. The input to keep them alive increases until it surpasses the energy contained in the crop. The crop's vulnerability to disease increases with its increasing purity. The long-range virulence of the disease organism increases as it evolves by mutation and selection to counter the protective measures of the farmer. For every breed and variety a debacle is inevitable.

Agriculture works best where it is least perfect. Where the farmer still hunts and gathers and keeps many kinds of plants and animals; where he produces little surplus or cash crop, has wild lands and bushy fencerows on his farm, uses no chemical pesticides, fertilizers, or treatments, is minimally dependent on distant industries, and grows crops that are adapted to local conditions and correspond in structure to the wild types of the area (cereals in grasslands, orchards in forest lands), the enterprise will be more ecologically fit and durable.

This is the agriculture that the Third World seeks to escape. Though it is benign environmentally and efficient in its ecological accounting, it cannot support large populations, which already exist. It cannot support science, art, urban life, all the institutions that require leisure, education, and freedom to experiment. Man cannot go back to peasant mixed agriculture any more than he can turn time's arrow.

Nor can man continue to perfect industrial agriculture,

to maintain the idea of the farm at all. Life on the planet simply cannot afford more genetic narrowing. The moral and nutritional administration of domestic animals is failing. Forcing the soil with machines that pollute and that waste fossil fuels is catastrophic.

Progress in the efficiency of desalination of ocean water is rapidly bringing all the world's arid lands within reach of vast irrigation schemes. Unless our course is altered, the years from 1970 until the end of the century will see the construction of huge pipelines running thousands of miles into the interior of all the continents. Besides being irrigated by reactor-operated desalination processes, soils will be heated and fumigated. The night sky will be illuminated; gigantic electric-generating plants will empower fertilizer factories so that several multi-crops will be grown per year. On the surface this seems to be the epitome of progress and human betterment. However, a factory mono-culture—the dream of engineers and politicians—is a dependent enterprise, requiring heavy indutsrial support for sifting the planet for minerals and energy. As the Gobi, Sahara, Mohave, and Australian deserts are invaded, the natural buffers that have so far helped protect the planet will collapse. The dream of progress will become a nightmare.

The economic and social superiority of modern farming as a way of life is a fiction; as technology it is destructive; as a Green Revolution hopeless.

The New Cynegetics

The modern environmental crisis is a result of a state of con-sciousness as much as it is the outcome of bad technology. It may be infinitely more difficult to transform human sensibility than to pass laws and build new cities. Reordering our view of time, welcoming the dead as part of us, affirming a planetary ecology centered on food chains, extending the scope of history to the personal and to the cosmic—these are the essentials of the trans-formation. Just to put them on paper reveals how foreign to our thought these are. Ferreting out and treating the existential disease that isolates us from the past, and therefore from the future, is the most important step in recovering a livable world.

Corrective action in modern life is associated with the forces of political organization, the alignment of parties and generation of policies and programs, with new legislation and decision, with ideology aimed at altering the beliefs and convictions of others, as well as controlling their behavior. To ideologize is to accept or give a set of ideas, as if this were new clothing to take off or put on. It is just this activity which is inconsistent with cynegetic man.

To look upon the cynegetic qualities of our pre-history, even as presented here, is to shop for ideas that one may sift, sort, use, and cast off. The impasse this contradiction reveals seems absolute. If the very act of trying on ideas is incompatible with the acceptance of those ideas as living principles, we seem to come to a dead end.

However, that is only because we have forgotten time. Though it may, indeed, be impossible for anyone already old enough to read to achieve the experience of a cynegetic and religious perception of the world in the sense described here, he can make it possible for his children in some small ways, and they can make it possible for their children in larger ways. The strategies for the authentic life are blueprinted in the genes. In those crucial experiences of childhood play and exploration, in the impulse to name and classify and anatomize, in the yearning for skill tests, heroes, and the "other," in ceremonial revelation of workable myth—in all these and more to be discovered and understood—are the moments when the perception of nature is fixed and the heart of the hunter-gatherer comes to the surface.

For most of us today, the only possibility is to press forward with externalities, modifying the physical and political surroundings as best we can, hoping that more mature beings than ourselves, who know how and why they belong to the past, will occupy the planet after us.

Recorded history has altered man's environment and his world but not himself. Whether there will ultimately be a future depends on the synthesis of human nature and human ecology, as manifested in hunting and gathering peoples, with a sophisticated technology to rid the earth of agriculture, its industrial extensions, and mental correlates.

Most people seem to agree that we cannot and do not want to go back to the past, but the reason given is often wrong: that time has moved on and what was can never be again. The truth is that we cannot go back to what we never left. Our home is the earth, our time the Pleistocene Ice Ages. The past is the formula for our being. Cynegetic man is us. The attempt to revive our humanity and recover values and behavior does not mean giving up science, art, medicine, law, machines, music, or anything else.

Food Technology

If the earth is to remain a good place for a sane life, attention will have to be paid more to the middle ground: to the terrain of human scale and its space, the distance a man can walk or see, to the reality of flowers, houses, trees, streams—all the things in the unfashionable middle-size range, remote from molecules and planets alike.

It is in this middle range that we live as conscious, moving beings; it is land form and vegetation. However primitive or complex the future world technology may be, a certain scale must be preserved. It is the lived-in space and the experience of the terrain that industrial agriculture, open mining, and city anti-architecture are destroying. This is not a sentimental allusion to scenery: it is the liberation of the earth's surface from gargantuan forces that are altering it and making it uninhabitable. The need is as basic as the need for food and water. Heterogeneous, textured environments—woodlands, streams, and rocky outcrops—a familiar nature imaged by the mind's screening and perception, diversity and choice in natural environment, as well as domesticated land and urban places, are essential for the life of the body, mind, and spirit.

The future depends on the right combination of chemical

and ecological projects—not on gigantic industrialized land or water projects—and on the separation of most technology from land use and its perfection in the production of food and fiber in factories. With the abandonment of agriculture an even more sophisticated chemical industry will come into existence. What we eat and use will come largely from factories, but not factories grafted onto nature: no eggs from drugged chickens in cages attended by conveyor belts. Theoretically it is feasible to synthesize proteins and other complex organic molecules, but that is a tedious, expensive process. The enzyme systems, which already exist in living cells, can be used to make proteins at three levels: by cultivating the domestic plant or animal, tissue culture, and the culture of one-celled organisms—the microbes. The first has failed. The second is not technically feasible because growth-control processes soon deteriorate when only part of an organism is cultured. The microbes, however, can do anything that higher organisms can do and more. They can be grown without harm physically (and probably spiritually) in "farms" of room size. Vast numbers and varieties of bacteria, yeasts, protozoans, and algae are found over the earth, many poorly known. They can make all the amino acids known to be essential to human health and most of the vitamins. Photosynthetic forms carry out basic sugar synthesis as efficiently as any conventional crop plant. Others live directly on feces or other organic wastes.

The aerobic thermophilic bacterium, *Hydrogenomonas eutropha,* lives on human sewage in a liquid medium and can be made into a high-quality food, rich in lysine, one of the essential amino acids; it is 93 per cent digestible after sonic treatment or cooking, which is higher than the digestibility of many foods now eaten.

Types of yeast are known to produce one ton of pure protein from each two tons of the petroleum on which they can be grown. At this rate the petroleum now used as fuel each year would feed fifty-four billion people—sixteen times the present world population. Thus the oil burned to operate the machines of the present industrial farms would feed more people when channeled through yeasts than the farms now feed, and free the earth's skin from us as parasites. Synthetic fats or margarines indistinguishable from butter can also be made from petroleum.

The production of non-food materials accounts for about one-fourth of the product of world agriculture. The science of synthetic fibers is ahead of that of microbial food production. Wool, rubber, cotton, leather, and many other materials are already being replaced. The chemical wastes produced must be kept from the environment, but many of these, as well as most of the sewage of cities, can be neutralized by microbial action in treatment plants set up for this purpose. This, in turn, would yield useful by-products.

The thought of microbial food may be repulsive, partly because of culturally conditioned food habits, partly because medical science is as drug-centered as agriculture. Following the discovery of the microbial basis of infection and communicable disease, a near-hysterical prejudice against germs has developed. The study of ecology is not required in the education of physicians, and their professional isolation from healthy people and their continued orientation to the use of drugs, fostered by the drug industries, has created a bias that infects society. Our puritanical antipathy to germs is more bizarre than any race prejudice in light of the fact that the world is bathed in microbial life. All higher forms of life on earth would die within weeks if the microbes were destroyed. They are a necessary part, internally and externally, of every individual plant and animal, including people. Without them the great wheels of revolving nutrients in the soil and water would cease to turn.

For the consumer, food technology based on microbial life is not a shelf of bad-tasting medicines or of pills or food bars. It means a wide range and choice of foods, some of which might resemble familiar fruits or vegetables, many of which would be new. These are not artificial foods, not substitutes for something lost, but new sources that already exist in nature. The techniques for extracting protein from almost any kind of green leaf have been available since the 1940s and have proved that the amount of available leaf protein is twice that of wheat—and leaves can be grown in three-dimensional spaces far removed from and unlike field agriculture.

The present drift toward worldwide super-plants might be repeated by microbial food technology if care were not taken to avoid it. Such foods lend themselves to pre-cooking and vending, so that a wide distribution of dispensing machines would contribute to the blenderizing of daily life. By obliterating cultural differences in foods and preparation, as well as eating patterns, the food-factory might make mankind more culturally homogeneous than it now is. If local customs and differences are valuable, the new system would have to be modified so as to maintain or increase regional specialities and food habits, and the social and artistic aspects of preparation and consumption. The new techniques would make it possible to rescue the companionship, variety, skill, and ceremony of eating, which have been eroded by specialized agriculture and mass packaging and distribution. Perhaps in the future there will be a sharper distinction between those meals taken for convenience, for which a food bar might suffice, and real meals carrying their full share of the psychological and philosophical benefit. Final preparation of microbal foods would be done in a kitchen, and they would be fully modifiable as ethnic or esoteric cooking.

This is therefore not a retreat from technology—nor to it— but rather a realization that culture and nature need to be separated in the human economic sphere. At the research level this can be done by reversing the trend of the life sciences over the past half-century. The separation of the ecological and the molecular in the scientific laboratory has been reflected by their destructive competition in actual land use. By lifting the burden of that conflict from the land, biochemistry and microbial biology make possible the recovery of a livable planet, complementing ecology rather than opposing it.

The transition to non-land-based subsistence might take half a century. A few kinds of crops, such as special medicinal or nutritional plants, might never become factory products, but perhaps three-quarters of the earth could be freed from its present destructive use. As much as 10 per cent could be released immediately—the technology is available. Such a project is in direct opposition to the Green Revolution, which is poised to increase the amount of land cultivated and to intensify agriculture.

Objections may be made on the grounds that the earth already has a large amount of empty space. Such observations are still common but ecologically naïve. Empty space is an illusion: in a planet having diverse climatic patterns, soils, and plant and animal communities, space must be dedicated to the preservation of that diversity.

Twenty per cent of the earth's surface is more than enough to hold all human structures, residences, and industries and still allow for small private gardens to produce familiar fresh fruits and vegetables. Gardens might be limited in size by law, and their produce made illegal to sell. This is horticulture—not agriculture—and its direction would be away from the use of chemicals and toward organic fertilizers and compost. There would be a symbiotic interspersion of protective and usable plants in an aesthetic layout and a regimen that connected the owner with the seasons and other rhythms of life in his leisure, enlarging, not anesthetizing, his sensibilities.

On Freeing Animals

Domestic animals would no longer be kept, while private gardens with their domestic plants could be retained. Though this may seem contradictory at first sight, these two kingdoms of life have very different perceptual and psychological relationships to man. Gardening is a health-giving form of human activity. Keeping domestic animals and pets is not. Plants are seldom seen as surrogate people, and there is little danger of the kind of projection and transference to them that are so familiar in psychiatric medicine. The essential otherness of plants is readily perceived and respected, however much they may be altered by domestication.

Because of man's background as a hunter and the psychological and religious role of animals in his evolution, he should not keep animals—not as pets, domestics, stuffed skins, pictures, or any other representation. The exceptions to this would be for psychotherapeutic or religious reasons. The deeply entrenched fictions of farm-city culture include the notion that pets encourage such virtues as care-giving, discipline, companionship, and so on. This sentimental, romantic-humanitarian concept presumes, therefore, that children particularly benefit from keeping dogs, cats, and birds. More nonsense has been written about the dog's relationships to men, including hunters and early farmers, than about any other animal, encouraged by the dog's popularity as a pet. Being a carnivore—and thus both scarce and in competition with man for food—the dog, I suspect, is relatively unimportant in civilization compared, say, to the goat or camel. We are inclined to put great store on him as a companion, but that is because of our modern personal isolation and our sick ecology. There are still many societies in the world that demonstrate what more fully mature men think of such a companionship (or neurotic zoophilia) by eating the dog whenever they can. Basic lessons on the relationship of man to man are better learned among men. Understanding of the relationship of man to animal is of major importance, but what man creates in animal breeding has no counterpart in nature and will mislead the child.

When children or adult neurotics make substitute people out of their animals they put demands on them that far exceed the animals' capabilities. The human authoritarian control exercised over pets creates an illusion of social adjustment. The animals are unconsciously expected to fulfill human roles; they are not thought of as species with their own purposes, different from men and deserving honor for their difference. Instead, they are pseudo-totemic fathers, mates, slaves, children, brothers, scapegoats, doormats, and sexual objects.

Zoos are similarly destructive. They do not enhance curiosity so much as, by a kind of saturation and antisepsis, neutralize it. Visiting the zoo is like offering bread and water to men whose mental health requires a diet of rich, diverse, wild, non-human life. Animals isolated from their natural habitat are ecologically dead. Physical death stalks zoos daily. Captives die at epidemic rates and are steadily replaced through an elaborate, international machinery of capture and distribution, which, hidden from the public, allows the zoo the image of an ongoing community of happy, protected animals.

Zoos, pets, and domestic animals give us personal satisfaction only because of the ecological poverty of our lives. The unpleasant reality is that they are perversions. Abolishment may seem unnecessarily harsh, as each of us remembers with pleasure some animal he has known. A form of totemism, however, would be more satisfying and fulfilling to the human spirit, and remove the burden of our pathology from those broken beings in the zoo and yard.

Animal movies, pets, zoos, and toys serve as crude substitutes for an inborn need. Because we have them we are less concerned for the survival of wild animals. Wild forms are allowed to slip into extinction a little more easily.

It is impossible to overestimate the ecological crime of species extinction, which is the only irreparable environmental damage by man. Extinction is caused by alteration of the habitat. The measures necessary to avoid it are the same that preserve the biosphere as a whole. The prevention of extinction should be the criterion for a plan or policy or environmental activity of any kind. If there were human associations devoted to each species of animal, as there are to different breeds of dogs, each creature on earth would have a political constituency —which, in this age, may be its only ticket to survival. Each club would be an amateur admiration society following the best traditions of natural history. Activities would include correlation of information, monitoring status, study and participation in related research, and the political work necessary for the protection of each club's particular totem species. If all land and water use were required to face review by survival committees representing each organism that would be affected, no other environmental safety system would be necessary. The social-psychological needs of the human individual to know and to participate, to be linked in some way to the "other," to the reality of true wild species, would be served.

Education

The basic questions asked by children are "What is it?" "What does it do?" I believe that every child under ten has three ecological needs: architecturally complex play space shared with companions; a cumulative and increasingly diverse experience of non-human forms, animate and inanimate, whose taxonomic names and generic relationships he must learn; and occasional and progressively more strenuous excursions into the wild world where he may, in a limited way, confront the non-human.

The study of play environment is in its crudest beginnings. As more is learned about the relationship of physical and mental development, play as ritual, the roles of mobility and space in cognition and mental imagery, and the nature of exploratory behavior in development, the different requirements for each age group will emerge. Nothing is known about how play in the dark—or at night—differs from play in the light; how play in water, in climbing, in tunneling (as in hay) relates to the usual play on the ground. For the most part children have been allowed simply to play in the environs of the household, street, or fields. The design of playgrounds has been capricious, regarded as a time-spender or exercise machine.

The proper design of play space—and since people will live in cities this must be designed and cannot be left to chance—must take into consideration the relationship between the child's development and his habitat. The cynegetic habitat is essentially open country with accessible cover—not very specific at first glance, but terrain is seldom smooth and vegetation seldom uniform. Opportunity for novelty and the unexpected is important. I remember the exact place and the intensity of excitement when, at age five, I found my first box turtle as it crawled along in a light spring rain; and I remember that the fascinating and somewhat daring aspect of selling magazines was that it took me, at seven, beyond the familiar neighborhood limits.

The collection and study of plants and animals is more important than any other learning activity. It is not simply a matter of knowing the names of many kinds of rocks or flowers, but of knowing where to find them, which traits are unique and which are shared with other members of the same species or with other species. This is more than a matter of learning to see or to examine, or an exercise in "wonder." Taxonomic training establishes a framework into which the accumulated encounters with the non-human can be fitted in an orderly way, making possible mature confrontations with the new and unknown.

The internal structure of plants and animals must also be seen. Squeamishness about taking creatures apart, so often encountered among today's youth, is a measure of the extent to which parents and society try to isolate themselves and their children from life. Those who cannot stand the sight of intestines, blood, or death have been cruelly removed from reality. The claim that they are sensitive or that they are passionately devoted to the living whole animal is a self-deception masking fear. The idea that only exteriors or whole animals are suitable for study is nonsense. When approached with an appropriate sense of wonder and discovery, of gratitude to and respect for the dead creature, dissection of hunted game is an excursion into new terrain—and therefore into new realms of the mind. It is appropriate, moreover, that the organism be eaten (if edible) after dissection. Assimilation is a suitable expression of love.

Children between the ages of six and twelve should, then, be more or less continuously engaged in an accumulative taxonomy and in the study of anatomy and physiology. Other kinds of life science should be included, especially natural history. No aspect of science that involves invisible entities or abstract symbols should be learned at this time. The great middle ground of the sensual—the visible, audible, tangible—is the landscape of mental growth of the child. To teach him mathematics is to create a world of abstractions; he will forever be unable to see the distinctions among things themselves. He should learn to read but his reading should be circumscribed and limited, so that he does not confuse words and symbols with the things for which they stand—and to save his eyesight, which suffers permanently from too much artificial light, flat surface, close-up use. Instead, as a schoolchild he should meet and explore biology, geology, languages, geography, astronomy, oceanography, soils, and perhaps certain social sciences. He should know nothing of chemistry, mathematics, or physics until he is finishing his second decade of life, except what he picks up informally. The study of documentary history should be delayed until his third decade.

Every child should become as expert as his nature allows in the use of his hands—in gathering and preparation of materials, and in making useful objects from wood, stone, clay, leather, paper, bone, metal, and other materials with hand tools. He should spend time cooking and caring for younger brothers and sisters.

The child's relationship to art is a difficult matter. The child should be protected from cultural relativism and culture-bug adults. Before twelve he should draw, dance, make music, weave, sew, mimic, sculpt, and make pots, but he should be insulated from art history and works of great artists and never go to museums.

In the cynegetic society he would be introduced gradually to the great wilderness, which, as I propose later, would occupy the centers of islands and continents, unmodified by human action. All travel in three-quarters of the earth's land surface would therefore be on foot. The earliest excursions of the young child might be as an infant with his mother and other women and children on a gathering expedition. Later he will come with a small class and its master to make his first identifications, and, in time, his first collections. As he approaches the end of childhood he might make the first excursions without adults, to gather, to test his skill in hunting small game, to explore, or simply to encounter briefly the full non-human character of the universe.

In the sequence described, the child in the new cynegetic society lays the solid groundwork of perception. He builds a practical knowledge of self and the diversity of the "other" on concrete reality. His body and senses mature together with a powerful conviction of physical certainty, a sense of reality—of the presence of nature. The shocks of adult life will not jar his foundations. Perhaps more important, he begins his mental life right-side-to, from the tangible to the intangible, from concrete to abstract, physical to mental.

From the ages of eleven to thirteen some important changes in the content and format of the lives of children would take place. These would be timed to each individual's maturational age as well as his calendar age, though only special exceptions would be more than two years out of phase. There will be new peers, new living arrangements, new subjects in education. Bodily skills will take on a more adult aspect. Abstract subjects of all kinds will be approached, and the juvenile's built-in release of interest in religious, moral, and ethical ideas will guide the new learning, largely via poetry.

In a series of steps he will move into new social configurations. Literally and figuratively, his relations with his family become looser and at the same time more formal. Etiquette allows him to become separated but not alienated from his family. He will undertake increasingly severe physical training in the company of the fraternal group with whom he lives and works. While his academic work will be directed increasingly to the unique and particular potential of the individual, the study of literature and art, discussions of values and philosophy, and tests of skill and daring will be shared with the basic group—the initiatory class.

His tasks will gradually include more and more of the activities and problems of society as a whole. By the time he is seventeen his altruism will be absorbed in social and ecological field projects. This period of public service will outlast most other phases of his initiation, even beyond his twenty-fifth year. Not until after that will he begin a professional career.

If mythology is taken to mean a coherent sequence of images

and metaphors by which the society conceptualizes and communicates its position on ultimate questions, then the main function of adolescence is to build a personal identity that is securely yoked to the rest of mankind, to life as a whole, and to an orderly cosmos. From the poetry to which he is introduced in his twelfth year, the performing arts in his thirteenth and fourteenth, and the visual arts thereafter, he learns the things of the mind and spirit. All art in such a society is functional at the heart of the religious participation. None is collected for qualities or emotions that are abstract ends and nothing more, or because of the excellence of the artist. I am not speaking of art in the service of the state, in which content and style are dictated. I do mean allowing the specially gifted to perform the most important tasks of society: the ceremonial communication of what is central. This does mean the end of the romantic, pseudo-cultural cult of genius, patronage, museum collections, the catechism of art history, and ostracism of the artist from the mainstream of society.

Cynegetic man by definition is a hunter and gatherer. For him these activities would be the central myth and central reality. From the age of thirteen the adolescent youth would move into a series of increasingly extended and arduous expeditions for which childhood and juvenile skills and his knowledge of natural history had prepared him. All hunting would be done by groups of men, preceded and followed by ceremonial affirmation of the symbolic aspects of the hunt, centering on the gift of life and the interrelationship of living and non-living through food chains as the fundamental connotation of interdependence, the relation of the living to the non-living.

All hunting will be done only with hand weapons. There will be no machines, no guns carried even for emergencies, no ambulances, cameras, or meat trucks, no lackeys to set up camp, no dogs or other domestic animals. It will be truly hazardous. The young man, hunting in a group of about six, including experienced leaders, will undertake more difficult roles in the hunting of more dangerous game as time passes. For two or three years he will be in the wilderness for months at a time, alternating hunting with instruction in the more difficult intellectual and devotional matters which can be as easily taught in the open as in the classroom.

Meat not consumed in the field will be carried back to the city, sometimes with the help of women and older childen, who also should participate in the cutting up of the game and the reverence felt for the dead animal. Game so returned will be used by the family and kin of the hunter or given by him to neighbors and friends.

As the young man approaches his twentieth year, he may decide to continue to hunt for some years and to be the mentor of younger groups in the field. Most, however, will spend increasing time at activities of their choice: academic, artistic, skilled, or professional. At the age of twenty he will be engaged at different times of the year in three basic activities: field expeditions, study in his chosen area, and social service.

By the middle of his third decade of life the formal portion of his public service and longer expeditions will have been completed (unless he continues them occupationally), and he will be engaged in increasingly sophisticated professional study. At different times in his life he will be expected to renew his wilderness skills and to devote service to society. As many as 20 per cent might continue field study through scientific ecological research as a main vocation.

Even in a true cynegetic technocracy there is no reason not to develop and use complex and sensitive instruments for monitoring and analyzing the environment, or computers for storing, sifting, and retrieving information. There is no valid reason for not using whatever tools can be contrived. In many laboratory aspects of modern biology these are needed; in many field studies plants and animals themselves monitor and record the effects of many environmental changes. Lichens are precisely attuned to air chemistry, and aquatic plants to water. It is as though, in the laboratory, men need extensions of themselves to see at molecular levels, while in the texture of the natural community they are molecule-sized.

The education of females will be different in more respects

from that of males in the cynegetic society than it is in present industrial societies. Girls will not participate in the hunting of large mammals, but they will spend as much time in the great wilderness as the boys. So long as human populations are overly large the woman's normal role of gatherer and provider cannot be fulfilled. Nonetheless, she will begin participating in gathering expeditions as a child and continue them throughout her life. She will have a more dominant role in the life systems than she now has, particularly in the architectural design of living and teaching spaces. As the center of all primate social organization, women will probably occupy most social-political offices and direct care-giving services, such as medicine and education. They will move into positions of responsibility at a younger age than males, and the phases of their initiation will be shorter.

Older members of society may generally be expected to spend most of their time in administrative roles in the city and its environs, though a surprising number may shift to periods in the wilderness after their family duties are completed. The natural history learned in childhood, the intricacies of religious and quasi-religious celebrations that parallel the growth of the hunter, many of the artistic skills, will not be written down in books but carried in memory. These and the protocol of initiation will be in the hands of old men and women, the ripest, wisest minds.

On the Use of Space

By the twenty-first century, modern man might be able to recover some of the principles followed by early cynegetic man —among them, low human density and large natural spaces. Constantinos A. Doxiadis, the Greek architect-planner, is widely known for his designs of human settlements, which are wisely rooted in such basic principles as the maximum contact of man with the non-human species and an urban pattern in which human mobility determines distances and optimum scale and size. He proposes a maximum city size of about fifty thousand people, in which no one is more than a ten-minute walk from the center.

If eight billion people (an estimate of world population for the year 2020) were to live in some 160,000 cities of this size, and these cities were uniformly distributed over the earth's fifty million square miles of land, only some three hundred square miles of land would surround each city (allowing two square miles for the city itself). Cities would then be only about seventeen miles apart, and no true wilderness would be possible. If, instead of being dispersed in the interiors of continents, they were constructed in a broken line on the perimeters of the continents, the whole of the interior could be freed for ecological and evolutionary systems on a scale essential to their own requirements and to human cynegetic culture.

Perhaps cities like those designed by Paolo Soleri, an Italian architect-planner, with their machinery beneath ground, strung in a narrow ribbon, would provide maximum surface-volume relationship between men and nature. One side of the ribbon might be separated from the sea by a thousand-yard band of gardens and parks; the other would overlook more gardens and the beginning of true wilderness short of the horizon. Inter- and inner-city transportation would be greatly simplified by the linear structure.

Except where estuaries and marshes require protection, the continents and islands of the world would have a five-mile-wide ribbon of human settlement. Within the settlement there would be land transport, and air and sea transport could link centers —though none of the air travel should move over land. Nature would be separated from the works but not the lives of men, for men would live in both worlds. The confusion that has plagued mankind for ten millennia between what is made by him and what is not made by him would be ended.

As mankind moves into the new cynegetic mode there will be changes in the architecture of the city. If much of the man-made part was built high into the air and far below ground, the residential, office, business, and industrial components could easily be built within a square mile. Residences, located at the periphery, would be immediately adjacent to family gardens and spacious parks, with the wilderness no more than five miles distant.

Within an average city of fifty thousand, architectural design would separate people into groups of about five hundred, and, within them, into family combinations of no more than about thirty, whose formal social relationships would be centered on preparing food and eating together—even if the main portion of their diet would come from centralized kitchens and the food taken together would only be the symbolic wild-meat course. Each sub-unit of five hundred, with its own uniquenesses and specialties, would be a self-contained social entity, even though much of the municipal housekeeping and advanced technology would have to be centralized. It is less a matter of economic and spatial independence, more a matter of separation of governing, teaching, working, and living units. A full human experience requires truly belonging to a tribal unit—a level of organization that would become more important and feasible as world population declines.

With creative urban design and the abandonment of suburbs, which the world can no longer afford, most families in a world population of eight billion (probably the lowest leveling point now possible) could have a garden, but family cooking may have to be limited because of both fuel limitations and polluting effects on the atmosphere. In order to enjoy private gardens and public parks within walking distance, people will live in compact quarters in very large buildings. Eating and recreation would be carried out in clan-sized (twenty-five) groups of families. Properly designed, such an arrangement would seem less crowded than present city life. Architecture will take into account our mammalian and primate nature as well as our human values and customs.

This recognition of the functional unit size of tribe and clan seems to me to be a modest and simple guideline by which the design of urban space may be linked to demographic and social principles. It should not be taken as an expression of the yearning to retribalize on the naïve expectation that human problems will be magically solved. Most of the modern talk of retribalizing is romantic—the delusional aesthetic of nineteenth-century industrial society.

The disenchanted and leaderless young people of the 1970s dreamed of returning to primitive ways and experimented with living in communes. Hundreds of young men and women went to live in remote villages all over the world. Many of them discovered that freedom "to do your thing" and tribal life were not compatible. Personal freedom, in fact, is greater in an industrial bourgeois society than it is in tribal society, where in all important matters (except personal adornment) innovation is anathema.

Forward to Tribal Society

Lack of opportunity is not the reason tribal society does not change; it is because change is intolerable. To the extent that the new society is tribalized, therefore, it will resist change. This need not mean that invention and experimentation will be halted; only that its application to human life will be limited, a resistance sorely needed to minimize the exploitative forces of the market. Worth measured in money and the blind circle of work and reward of the consumer society, with its immature goals and herd-following of fashion, would be eliminated. The conception of both society and the future would be returned to the hands of elders—of adults—where it belongs.

The sensory experience made possible by the municipal cynegetic tribal unit would remedy the one-sided hypervisualism brought on by books, films, pictures, walls, and human faces. The visual and abstract perception of the world has usurped other sensory modes and forms of communication. The metaphors for cognition are all spatial and visual, reducing things to surfaces and abstractions.

Sound is concerned with interiority, because the interior of the musical instrument, like the human lung, is the source. Touch is the final recognition and affirmation of external reality, of self and not-self. Smell is the interpenetration of self and environment at a molecular level far more encompassing and eventful than eating and being eaten. These are the modes —along with the visual—of the traditional hunting culture. Because of sound the universe is a dynamic, event-filled place, never static, never wholly storable. The icon, the fixed idea, motionless objects, objects as nature, are all replaced by active being, the noun-verb oneness of events.

Our readiness today to re-examine the validity of traditional society with its dynamic and polemic qualities, to listen to the poet as historian, to back off from the idea that truth is only a semantic tangle of relativity, to reconsider the way in which subjective and objective could be related, to listen and touch, to reduce our numbers, and to take less possession of the earth—all are signs that cynegetic man deep within us is stirring.

The main thrust of modern studies of man leads us by degrees toward recognition of the universal dimensions of problems of violence, of personal alienation, and of environmental disorder. We move now with increasing speed toward a day when the futility of ideological answers and industrial techniques will be obvious. Then it will be necessary to recover prehistory, to make a new start by the affirmation of the pre-men in us.

There are many striking parallels between post-industrial men and hunter-gathering men. They are both highly mobile, non-territorial, non-soil-working, nature-interested, much-leisured, function-oriented, small-familied, and altruistic. The most modern urban men are ready to abandon, if they only knew how, civilization based on war and competition and on an industry so heavy that the human personality as well as the surface of the earth is stamped with its obscenity. Most important of all, the urban man today is less deformed, in spite of his lack of nature contact, than the peasants, farmers, and their small-town collaborators who have predominated in the agricultural era. The modern city man was not born on a farm, and his world was not perverted by the spectacles of the barnyard. New shifts in social thought bring urban man and hunting man closer in their mutual belief in traditional as opposed to existential behavior, in permanence instead of progress, in small-group democracy rather than mass society.

What has been sketched here is not a utopia. No enlistment posters are up. Through understanding ourselves the future can be shaped without revolution. It is time to confront the division between man and the rest of nature, between ourselves as animals and as humans, not by the destruction of nature or by a return to some dream of the past, but by creating a new civilization. As such, a cynegetic world is not a vision of a lost paradise; it is inevitable, a necessity if we are to survive at all.

Appendix

Bibliography

Index

Appendix

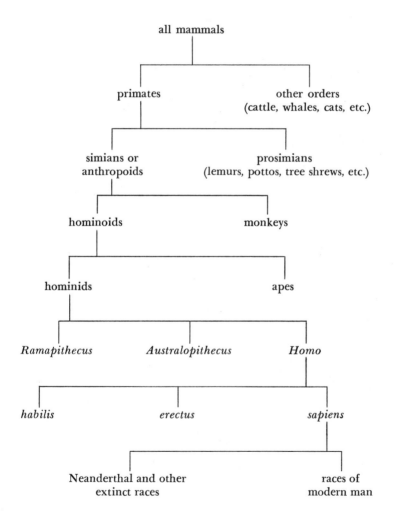

TIME AND EVENTS IN HUMAN EVOLUTION

This table is a composite from many sources. In some cases the dates represent an averaging of various experts' estimates of times and durations. The terminology is deliberately selective and incomplete, in the hope of providing reference points for the reader.

The table refers primarily to Africa and southern Europe; technology and taxonomy are dated according to the earliest records. In looking at such a table, it is important to remember that events and species appeared in and disappeared from different places at different times. Fossil hominid bones were for many years given different names from place to place, even though some were closely related, with a resulting maze of names that baffles the inexpert. There are recent indications that such provincialism is diminishing and the naming of man's ancestors becoming reconciled with general zoological principles.

YEARS AGO	GEOLOGIC PERIOD	CULTURE	TECHNOLOGY	TAXONOMY	POPULATION
14,000,000	Late Miocene		occasional tool use, like chimpanzee today	*Ramapithecus*, a grain-eating omnivore	
4,000,000	Late Pliocene desiccation			early *Australopithecus*, a loping, scavenging, carrying hominid of 450–650 cc brain capacity	
3,000,000	Early Pleistocene	Paleolithic	pebble tools; osteo-donto-keratic materials with traditional techniques		
1,500,000		Oldowan at Olduvai Bed I		*Australopithecus africanus*; forethought and sustained attention	
1,000,000	1st glaciation		biface tools, fire for protection and warmth, cave habitation	*Homo habilis*: first true man, hunting moderate-sized animals, 650–800 cc brain capacity	125,000

Years	Climate	Tool tradition	Technology	Hominid	Population
800,000	warming	Olduvai Bed II Abbevillian	several score kinds of tools making and keeping of fire; language	*Homo erectus:* specialized large-game hunting; gathering with specialized tool use and sexual dimorphism; 800–1100 cc brain capacity	
700,000					
500,000	2nd glaciation warming	Achuelian	built dwellings; wooden bowls	*Homo sapiens:* insight, reasoning, abstraction; religious traditions; 1200–1600 cc brain capacity	
400,000	3rd glaciation warming				
300,000					
200,000					
100,000	4th glaciation part I	Mousterian	73 kinds of tools: blade and flake tools; ceremonial burial; digging sticks	Neanderthal people	1 million
70,000	part II				
40,000	part III	Aurignacian	240 kinds of tools; increased use of fire in cooking; hafted tools; cave art; bow and arrow; tool and art simplification; sickle blades	Cro-Magnon people (modern man)	3.3 million
20,000		Solutréan			
12,000	part IV				5.3 million
10,000	Recent; warming many extinctions	Neolithic	domesticated sheep, goats, cereals		
6,000	catastrophic ecology		irrigation, pottery, metal, war, states wheel, trade, ideology, writing		86 million

Bibliography

Adler, Nathan. "The Antinomian Personality: the Hippie Character Type," *Psychiatry*, 31:4 (1968).

Allen, William. *The African Husbandman*. London: Olive and Boyd, 1967.

Andrew, R. J. "Evolution of Facial Expressions," *Science*, 142:1034 (1972).

Ardrey, Robert. *African Genesis, a Personal Investigation into the Animal Origins and Nature of Man*. New York: Atheneum, 1961.

——. "Four-Dimensional Man," *Encounter*, 38:2 (1972).

——. *The Social Contract, a Personal Inquiry into the Evolutionary Sources of Order and Disorder*. New York: Atheneum, 1970.

——. *The Territorial Imperative, a Personal Inquiry into the Animal Origins of Property and Nations*. New York: Atheneum, 1966.

Bachelard, Gaston. *The Psychoanalysis of Fire*. Boston: Beacon Press, 1964.

Bardaz, Jacques. *Tools of the Old and New Stone Age*. New York: Natural History Press, 1959.

Bartholomew, G. A., and Birdwell, J. B. "Ecology and the Protohominids," *American Anthropologist*, 55:481 (1953).

Benchley, Bell. *My Friends, the Apes*. Boston: Little Brown, 1942.

Benedict, Ruth. *Patterns of Culture*. Boston: Houghton-Mifflin, 1961.

Bettelheim, Bruno. *Obsolete Youth*. San Francisco: San Francisco Press, 1969.

Bicchieri, M. G. (ed.). *Hunters and Gatherers Today*. New York: Holt, Rinehart and Winston, 1972.

Billingham, R., and Silvers, W. *Immunobiology of Transplantation*. Englewood Cliffs, N. J.: Prentice-Hall, 1971.

Binford, Sally R., and Binford, Lewis R. "The Predatory Revolution, a Consideration of the Evidence for a New Subsistence Level," *American Anthropologist*, 68:508 (1966).

——. "Stone Tools and Human Behavior," *Scientific American*, 220:4 (1969).

Birdsell, Joseph H. *Human Evolution*. Chicago: Rand-McNally, 1972.

——. "On the Population Structure in Generalized Hunting and Collecting Populations," *Evolution*, 12:189 (1958).

Bishop, Walter W., and Clark, J. Desmond. *Background to Evolution in Africa*. Chicago: University of Chicago Press, 1967.

Blos, Peter. "The Child Analyst Looks at the Young Adolescent," *Daedalus*, 100:4 (1971).

——. "The Second Individuation Process of Adolescence," *The Psychological Study of the Child*, XXII:162 (1967).

[285]

Bly, Robert. *The Light Around the Body.* New York: Harper and Row, 1967.

Braidwood, Robert J., and Wiley, Gordon R. *Courses toward Urban Life.* Chicago: Aldine, 1962.

Bronson, Gordon W. "The Development of Fear in Man and Other Animals," *Child Development,* 39:2 (1968).

Bordes, François. "Mousterian Cultures in France," *Science,* 134:803 (1961).

Bower, Gordon H. "Analysis of a Mnemonic Device," *American Scientist,* 58:5 (1970).

Brace, C. Loring, *et al.* "Whatever Happened to Hairy Man?" *Science* (Letters), 153:362 (1966).

Brain, C. K. "Adaptations to Forest and Savannah: Some Aspects of the Social Behavior of Cercopithecus Monkeys in Southern Africa," *Wenner-Gren Symposium 31: Primate Social Behavior.* Chicago: Aldine, 1965.

Bresler, Jack (ed.). *Human Ecology.* Philadelphia: Addison-Wesley, 1966.

Bronowski, J., and Bellugi, Ursulla. "Language, Name and Concept," *Science,* 168:669 (1970).

Buettner-Janusch, John. *Evolutionary and Genetic Biology of Primates.* New York: Academic Press, 1963.

———. *The Origins of Man.* New York: John Wiley, 1966.

Burkill, I. H. "Habits of Man and the Origin of the Cultivated Plants of the Old World," *Proc. Linnean Society.* London: 164:12 (1953).

Butzer, Karl W. *Environmental Archeology.* Chicago: Aldine, 1964.

Calder, Nigel. *Eden Was No Garden, an Inquiry into the Environment of Man.* New York: Holt, 1967.

Cambel, Halet, and Braidwood, Robert J. "An Early Farming Village in Turkey," *Scientific American,* 222:3 (1970).

Campbell, Joseph. *The Masks of God.* Vol. I: *Primitive Mythology.* New York: Viking, 1959.

Carneiro, Robert L. "A Theory of the Origin of the State," *Science,* 169:733 (1970).

Carthy, J. D., and Ebling, F. J. (eds.). *The Natural History of Aggression,* New York: Academic Press, 1965.

Caspari, Ernest. "Selective Forces in the Evolution of Man," *American Naturalist,* XCVII:5 (1963).

Chance, M. R. A. "Attention Structure as the Basis of Primate Rank Order," *Man,* 2:4 (1967).

———. "The Sociability of Monkeys," *Man,* 55:176, (1955).

———, and Mead, A. P. "Social Behavior and Primate Evolution," *Symposium of the Society for Experimental Biology,* 7:395 (1953).

Chedd, Graham. "Hidden Peril of the Green Revolution," *New Scientist,* October 22, 1970.

Childe, V. Gordon. *Man Makes Himself.* New York: New American Library, 1956.

Chomsky, Noam. *Language and Mind.* New York: Harcourt Brace and World, 1968.

Clark, Graham. *From Savagery to Civilisation.* New York: Henry Schuman, 1953.

———. *The Stone Age Hunters*. New York: McGraw-Hill, 1967.

Clark, J. Desmond. "The Evolution of Culture in Africa," *American Naturalist,* 97:15 (1963).

———. "Human Ecology During the Pleistocene and Later Times in Africa South of the Sahara," *Current Anthropology,* 1:4 (1960).

———. *The Prehistory of South Africa*. London: Pelican, 1959.

Clarke, C. H. D. "Autumn Thoughts of a Hunter," *Journal of Wildlife Management,* 22:4 (1958).

Cloudsley-Thompson, J. L. (ed.). *The Biology of Deserts*. London: Pergamon Press, 1954.

Cobb, Edith. "The Ecology of Imagination in Childhood," *Daedalus,* 88:3 (1959).

Collins, Desmond. "Culture Traditions and the Environment of Early Man," *Current Anthropology,* 10:4 (1969).

Comfort, Alex. *Sexual Behavior in Society*. London: Duckworth, 1950.

Coon, Carleton. *The Hunting Peoples*. Boston: Little-Brown, 1971.

———. *The Story of Man*. New York: Knopf, 1962.

Corner, E. J. H. *The Life of Plants*. Cleveland: New American Library, 1968.

Crile, George. *Intelligence, Power and Personality*. New York: McGraw-Hill, 1941.

Crook, John Hurrell. "Cooperation in Primates," *Eugenics Review,* 58:2 (1966).

———. "Evolutionary Changes in Primate Society," *Science Journal,* 3:6 (1967).

———, and Aldriche-Blake, P. "Ecological and Behavioral Contrasts Between Sympatric Ground-Dwelling Primates in Ethiopia," *Folia Primatologia,* 8:192 (1968).

———, and Gartlan, J. S. "Evolution of Primate Societies," *Nature,* 210:1200 (1966).

Dahlberg, Albert A. "Dental Evolution and Culture," *Human Biology,* 35:237 (1963).

De Lumley, Henry. "A Paleolithic Camp at Nice," *Scientific American,* 220:5 (1969).

DeValois, Russell L., and Jacob, Gerald H. "Primate Color Vision," *Science,* 162:443 (1968).

Devereaux, George. "Childhood Traditions in Two American Indian Tribes," *Psychological Study of the Child,* I:319 (1945).

———. "Mohave Ethnopsychiatry and Suicide: the Psychiatric Knowledge and the Psychiatric Disturbances of an Indian Tribe," *United States Bureau of American Ethnology,* Bulletin 175 (1961).

Dobzhansky, Theodosius. *Mankind Evolving*. New Haven: Yale University Press, 1962.

———, et al. *Evolutionary Biology*. Vol. IV. New York: Appleton-Century, 1970.

Doob, Leonard W. *Becoming More Civilized*. New Haven: Yale University Press, 1960.

Doxiadis, Constantinos A. "Eikistics, the Science of Human Settlements," *Science,* 170:393 (1970).

Driver, Harold E., and Massey, William C. "Comparative Studies of North American Indians," *Transactions of the American Philosophical Society* (n. s.), 47, Part 2 (1957).

Dubos, René. "Environmental Determinants of Human Life," in David C. Glass (ed.), *Environmental Influences*. New York: Rockefeller University Press, 1968.

———. *Man Adapting*. New Haven: Yale University Press, 1965.

DuBrul, Lloyd. "The General Phenomenon of Bipedalism," *American Zoologist*, 2:205 (1962).

Eiseley, Loren. *The Immense Journey*. New York: Random House, 1946.

———. "On Extinction," *American Scientist*, March, 1963.

Eisenberg, J. F., et al. "The Relation Between Ecology and Social Structure in Primates," *Science*, 176:863 (1972).

Elkin, A. P. "Elements of Australian Aboriginal Philosophy," *Oceania*, 40:2 (1969).

Endleman, Robert. "Reflections on the Human Revolution," *Psychoanalytic Review*, 53:169 (1966).

Erikson, Erik H. "Childhood Traditions in Two American Indian Tribes," *Psychological Study of the Child*, I:319 (1945).

———. *Identity and the Life Cycle*. New York: International Universities Press, 1959.

———. *Identity, Youth and Crisis*. New York: Norton, 1968.

Eskimo: Edmund Carpenter, Frederick Varley, Robert Flaherty among the Avilik. Toronto, 1959.

Estes, Richard B. "Predators and Scavengers," *Natural History*, 76:2 & 3 (1967).

Etkin, William (ed.). *Social Behavior from Fish to Man*. Chicago: University of Chicago Press, 1967.

Fernandez, James. "Persuasions and Performances: Of the Beast in Every Body and the Metaphors of Everyman," *Daedalus*, 101:1 (1972).

———. "From the Primate Patrimony to the Fellowship of the Flowers," *Dartmouth Alumnae Magazine*, February, 1970.

Fischer, Seymour, and Cleveland, Sidney E. *Body Image and Personality*. New York: Van Nostrand, 1958.

Fossey, Dian. "Making Friends with Mountain Gorillas," *National Geographic*, 137:1 (1970).

———. "More Years with Mountain Gorillas," *National Geographic*, 140:4 (1971).

Fox, Robin. "The Cultural Animal," in J. F. Eisenberg and William S. Dillon (eds.), *Man and Beast: Comparative Social Behavior*, Washington, D. C. Smithsonian Institution, 1969.

———. "In the Beginning: Aspects of Hominid Behavioral Evolution," *Man*, 2:3 (1967).

Frankel, Sir Otto H. "Genetic Dangers in the Green Revolution," *World Agriculture*, 19:3 (1970).

Freeman, Derek. "Thunder, Blood, and the Nicknaming of God's Creatures," *Psychoanalytic Quarterly*, 37:3 (1968).

Frunkes, George. "Impairment of the Sense of Reality as Manifested in Psychoneurosis and Everyday Life," *International Journal of Psychoanalysis*, 34:123 (1962).

Gabel, Creighton (ed.). *The Achievements of Paleolithic Man.* Englewood Cliffs, N. J.: Prentice-Hall, 1964.

Galle, Omer R., *et al.* "Population Density and Pathology: What are the Relations for Man?" *Science*, 176:23 (1972).

Galston, Arthur. "Crops Without Chemicals," *New Scientist*, June 3, 1971.

Gartlan, J. S. "Structure and Function in Primate Society," *Folia Primatologia*, 8:2 (1968).

Gerschwind, Norman. "The Organization of Language and the Brain," *Science*, 170:940 (1970).

Gesell, Arnold. *The First Five Years of Life.* London: Methuen, 1940.

———. *Youth, the Years from Ten to Sixteen.* New York: Harper and Row, 1956.

Ginsberg, Benson E., and Laughlin, William S., "The Multiple Basis of Human Adaptability and Achievement: A Species Point of View," *Eugenics Quarterly*, 13:3 (1966).

Glass, David C. *Environmental Influences.* New York: Rockefeller University Press, 1968.

Goodman, Morris, *et al.* "Immunology and Systematics of the Primates, I, The Catarrhini," *Systematic Zoology*, 20:1 (1971).

Greene, David. "Environmental Influences on Pleistocene Hominid Dental Evolution," *BioScience*, 20:3 (1970).

Gulick, Addison. "A Biological Prologue for Human Values," *BioScience*, 18:12 (1968).

Hafez, E. S. E. (ed.). *Behavior of Domestic Animals.* Baltimore: Williams and Wilkins, 1962.

Hall, G. Stanley. *Adolescence, Its Psychological Development.* New York: D. Appleton, 1905.

Hardin, Garrett. *Exploring New Ethics for Survival: The Voyage of the Spaceship* Beagle. New York: Viking, 1972.

———. "The Tragedy of the Commons," *Science*, 162:1243 (1968).

Harlan, Jack R. "Agricultural Origins: Centers and Noncenters," *Science*, 174:468 (1971).

Harms, Ernest. "Adolescence: Not Only a Beginning and an End, but a Total Human Experience," *Adolescence*, 1:2 (1966).

Harrison, Ruth. *Animal Machines.* New York: Ballantine Books, 1964.

Hawkes, Jacquetta. "Paleolithic Art," *History Today*, VIII (1958).

Hayes, K. J. "The Virilizing Effect of Wheel Running in Male Rats," *Hormones and Behavior*, 1:3 (1971).

Hemmer, Helmet. "A New View of the Evolution of Man," *Current Anthropology*, 10:2 & 3 (1969).

Hewes, G. W. "Food Transport and the Origin of Hominid Bipedalism," *American Anthropologist*, 63:687 (1961).

Hockett, Charles F., and Ascher, Robert. "The Human Revolution," *Current Anthropology*, 5:3 (1964).

Hole, Frank. "Investigations of the Origins of Mesopotamian Civilization," *Science,* 153:605 (1966).

Holloway, Ralph L., Jr. "Tools and Teeth: Some Speculations Regarding Canine Reduction," *American Anthropologist,* 69:63 (1967).

Howard, John. "New Proteins: Animal, Vegetable, Mineral," *New Scientist,* February 25, 1971.

Howell, F. Clark. "Recent Advances in Human Evolutionary Studies," *Quarterly Review of Biology,* 42:4 (1967).

———. *Early Man.* New York: Time-Life, 1965.

———. "European Northwest African Middle Pleistocene Hominids," *Current Anthropology,* 1:3 (1960).

———, and Boulière, François. *African Ecology and Human Evolution.* Chicago: Aldine, 1963.

Howells, William. *Mankind in the Making.* New York: Doubleday, 1967.

Hutchinson, G. Evelyn. "The Naturalist as Art Critic," *Proceedings, Academy of Natural Science of Philadelphia,* 116:5 (1963).

Huxley, Julian, *et al. Evolution as a Process.* London: Allen and Unwin, 1954.

Hvarfner, H. (ed.). *Hunting and Fishing.* Lulea, Sweden: Norbottens Museum, 1965.

Hyams, Edward. *Soil and Civilization.* London: Thames and Hudson, 1952.

Jacobson, Edith. *The Self and the Object World.* New York: International Universities Press, 1964.

Jarrard, Leonard E. *Cognitive Processes of Non-Human Primates.* New York: Academic Press, 1971.

Jerison, Harry J. "Brain Evolution: New Light on Old Principles," *Science,* 170:1224 (1970).

Jewell, P. A. (ed.). *Play, Exploration and Territory in Mammals.* New York: Academic Press, 1966.

Jolly, Alison. "Lemur Social Behavior and Primate Intelligence," *Science,* 153:501 (1966).

Jolly, Clifford J. "The Seed-Eaters: a New Model of Hominid Differentiation Based on a Baboon Analogy," *Man,* 5:1 (1970).

Kanzer, Mark. "The Communicative Function of the Dream," *International Journal of Psychoanalysis,* 36:260 (1955).

Kellogg, Winthrop C. "Communication and Language in the Home-Raised Chimpanzee," *Science,* 172:808 (1971).

Kestenberg, Judith S., M. D. "The Role of Movement Patterns in Development, III, The Control of Shape," *Psychiatric Quarterly,* 26:3 (1967).

Kiell, N. *The Universal Experience of Adolescence.* New York: International Universities Press, 1964.

Kochetkova, V. I. "On Brain Size and Behavior in Early Man," *Current Anthropology,* 11:2 (1970).

Kortlandt, Adrian. "How Do Chimpanzees Use Weapons When Fighting Leopards?" *Yearbook, American Philosophical Society.* 327, New York: 1965.

Krantz, Grover S. "Brain Size and Hunting Ability in Earliest Man," *Current Anthropology,* 9:5 (1968).

Krauss, Robert M. "Language as a Symbolic Process in Communication," *American Scientist,* 56:3 (1968).

Kumer, Hans. "Comparative Biology of Primate Groups," *American Journal of Physical Anthropology,* 27:357 (1967).

La Barre, Weston. *The Ghost Dance, Origins of Religion.* Garden City, N. Y.: Doubleday, 1970.

Lancaster, Jane B. "On the Evolution of Tool-Using Behavior," *American Anthropologist,* 70:56 (1968).

Laughlin, William S. "Adaptability and Human Genetics," *Proceedings of the National Academy of Science,* 60:1 (1968).

Lee, Richard B. "The Population Ecology of Man in the Early Upper Pleistocene of South Africa," *Prehistorical Society Proceedings* (n. s.), 29:235 (1963).

———, and DeVore, Irven (eds.). *Man the Hunter.* Chicago: Aldine, 1968.

Lenneberg, Eric H. *The Biological Foundations of Language.* New York: John Wiley, 1967.

Leopold, Aldo. *A Sand County Almanac.* New York: Oxford University Press, 1949.

Leppik, Elmar E. *Evolutionary Correlation Between Plants, Insects, Animals and Soils.* Journal Paper j-4234. Ames: Iowa Agriculture and Home Economics Experiment Station, 1963.

Leroi-Gourhan, André. "The Evolution of Paleolithic Art," *Scientific American,* 218:2 (1968).

———. *Treasures of Prehistoric Art.* New York: Abrams, 1967.

Lévi-Strauss, Claude. *The Savage Mind.* Chicago: University of Chicago Press, 1968.

———. *Totemism.* New York: Beacon Press, 1962.

Lewin, Bertram D. *The Image and the Past.* New York: International Universities Press, 1968.

Leyhausen, Paul. "Communal Organization of Solitary Mammals," *Symposium of the Zoological Society of London,* Vol. 14 (1966).

Linn, Louis. "Some Developmental Aspects of the Body Image," *International Journal of Psychoanalysis,* 36:36 (1955).

Lommel, Andreas. *Shamanism: the Art of the Early Hunter.* New York: McGraw-Hill, 1967.

Lopreato, Joseph. "How Would You Like to be a Peasant?" *Human Organization,* 24:4 (1965).

Lorenz, Konrad. *On Aggression.* New York: Harcourt, Brace, 1966.

———. *Studies in Animal and Human Behavior,* trans. Robert Martin, Vol. II. Cambridge, Mass.: Harvard University Press, 1971.

Lovejoy, C. Owen, *et al.* "Primate Phylogeny and Immunological Distance," *Science,* 176:803 (1972).

Lowdermilk, W. C. "Conquest of the Land Through 7,000 Years," *United States Department of Agriculture Information Bulletin 99,* 1953.

Luria, A. R. *The Mind of a Mnemonist.* New York: Basic Books, 1968.

Lystad, Robert A. *The African World.* London: Praeger, 1965.

Marshack, Alexander. "Upper Paleolithic Notation and Symbol," *Science,* 178:817 (1972).

Martin, P. S., and Wright, H. E., Jr. *Pleistocene Extinctions, the Search for a Cause*. New Haven: Yale University Press, 1967.

Mateles, Richard I., and Tannenbaum, Steven R. (eds.). *Single Cell Protein*. Boston: The M. I. T. Press, 1968.

May, Rollo. *Love and Will*. New York: Norton, 1969.

Mayr, Ernst. *Animal Species and Evolution*. Cambridge: Harvard University Press, 1963.

McKeown, T. "Early Environmental Influences on the Development of Intelligence," *British Medical Bulletin*, 27:48 (1971).

Modell, Arnold H. *Object Love and Reality*. New York: International Universities Press, 1968.

———. "The Transitional Object and the Creative Act," *Psychoanalytic Quarterly*, 39:2 (1970).

Money-Kryle, R. E. *Man's Picture of His World*. London: Gerald Duckworth, 1961.

Montague, Ashley. *The Natural Superiority of Women*. New York: Macmillan, 1953.

Morris, Desmond. *The Human Zoo*. New York: McGraw-Hill, 1969.

———. *Men and Apes*. London: Methuen, 1966.

———. *The Naked Ape*. New York: McGraw-Hill, 1967.

——— (ed.). *Primate Ecology*. Chicago: Aldine, 1969.

Mountford, Charles P. (ed.). *Records of the American-Australian Scientific Expedition to Arnheim Land*. Melbourne: Melbourne University Press, 1960.

Muuss, Rolf E. *Theories of Adolescence*. New York: Random House, 1966.

Napier, John. "Evolutionary Aspects of Primate Locomotion," *American Journal of Physical Anthropology*, 27:333 (1967).

———. *The Roots of Mankind*. Washington, D. C.: Smithsonian Institution, 1970.

Neel, James V. "Lessons from a 'Primitive People,'" *Science*, 170:815 (1970).

Nelson, Richard K. *Hunters of the Northern Ice*. Chicago: University of Chicago Press, 1972.

Newton, Grant, and Levine, Seymour. *Early Experience and Behavior, a Psychobiology of Development*. Springfield: Charles C. Thomas, 1968.

Noback, Charles R., and Montague, William (eds.). *The Primate Brain*. New York: Appleton-Century-Crofts, 1970.

Olson, Charles. *Pleistocene Man, a Curriculum for the Study of the Soul*. Buffalo, N. Y.: The Institute of Further Studies, 1968.

Ong, Walter, J. "World View and World as Event," *American Anthropologist*, 71:4 (1969).

Ortega y Gasset, José. *Meditations on Hunting*. Trans. Howard Wescott. New York: Charles Scribner's Sons, 1972.

Philbeam, D. R., and Simons, E. L. "Man's Earliest Ancestors," *Science Journal*, 3:2 (1967).

———. "Some Problems of Hominid Classification," *American Scientist*, 53:237 (1965).

Pike, Magnus. *Synthetic Food.* London: John Murray, 1971.

Pirie, N. W. "Leaf Protein as a Human Food," *Science,* 152:1701 (1966).

Polyak, Stephan. *The Vertebrate Visual System.* Chicago: University of Chicago Press, 1957.

Porter, Ian. *Heredity and Disease.* New York: McGraw-Hill, 1968.

Premack, David. "Language in Chimpanzees?" *Science,* 172:808 (1971).

Prior, Daphne. "State of Surrender," *The Sciences,* 11:1 (1971).

Protsch, R., and Berger, R. "Earliest Radiocarbon Dates for Domesticated Animals," *Science,* 179:235 (1973).

Rank, Otto, and Sachs, Hans. "The Unconscious and Its Forms of Expression," *American Imago,* 21:1, 2 (1964).

Read, Herbert. *Icon and Idea: the Functions of Art in the Development of Human Consciousness.* New York: Schocken Books, 1955.

Redfield, Robert. "The Peasant's View of the Good Life," *Peasant Society and Culture, an Anthropological Approach to Civilization,* Chicago: University of Chicago Press, 1956.

Reik, Theodore. *Myth and Guilt, the Crime and Punishment of Mankind.* New York: G. Braziller, 1957.

Reynolds, Vernon. "Kinship and the Family in Monkeys, Apes and Man," *Man,* 3:2 (1967).

———. "Open Groups in Hominid Evolution," *Man,* 1:4 (1966).

Robinson, J. T. "Australopithecines and the Origin of Man," *Smithsonian Report,* 1961.

Roheim, Geza. *The Gates of the Dream.* New York: International Universities Press, 1952.

Rule, Colter. "A Theory of Human Behavior Based on Studies of Non-Human Primates," *Perspectives in Biology and Medicine,* 10:2 (1967).

Russell, Claire, and Russell, W. M. S. *Human Behavior, a New Approach to Human Ethology.* Boston: Little, Brown, 1961.

———. "The Sardine Syndrome," *The Ecologist,* 1:2 (1970).

Sachs, Hans. "The Delay of the Machine Age," *Psychoanalytic Quarterly,* 2:404 (1933).

Sahlins, Marshall. *Stone Age Economics.* Chicago: Aldine, 1972.

Sarich, Vincent N., and Wilson, Allan L. "Immunological Time Scale For Hominid Evolution," *Science,* 158:1200 (1967).

Sauer, Carl. *Agricultural Origins and Dispersals.* New York: American Geographical Society, 1952.

Schaffner, Bertram (ed.). *Group Processes, Transactions of the Second Conference.* New York: Joshua Macy Foundation, 1956.

Schaller, George. *The Mountain Gorilla: Ecology and Behavior.* Chicago: University of Chicago Press, 1963.

———. "The Relevance of Carnivore Behavior to the Study of Early Hominids," *Southwestern Journal of Anthropology,* 25:307 (1969).

Schiefelbusch, Richard L. (ed.). *Language and Mental Retardation.* New York: Holt, 1970.

Schilder, Paul. *The Image and Appearance of the Human Body.* New York: International Universities Press, 1958.

Schultz, Adolph H. *The Life of Primates.* London: Universe, 1969.

Scott, Paul. "Social Behavior in Dogs," *American Zoologist*, 4:161 (1964).

Searles, Herbert. *The Non-Human Environment in Normal Development and in Schizophrenia*. New York: International Universities Press, 1960.

Sears, Paul B. *The Ecology of Man*. Eugene: University of Oregon Press, 1957.

Service, Elman R. *The Hunters*. Englewood Cliffs, N. J.: Prentice-Hall, 1966.

Sewell, Elizabeth. *The Human Metaphor*. South Bend: University of Notre Dame Press, 1964.

———. *The Orphic Voice*. New Haven: Yale University Press, 1958.

Shengold, Leonard. "The Metaphor of the Journey in 'The Interpretation of Dreams,' " *American Imago*, 23:4 (1966).

Shepard, Paul. "A Theory of the Value of Hunting," *Transactions, 24th North American Wildlife Conference*, Washington, D. C., 1959.

Simmons, Leo W. *The Role of the Aged in Primitive Society*. New Haven: Yale University Press, 1945.

Simons, Elwyn. "The Early Relations of Man," *Scientific American*, 210:1 (1964).

Simopoulos, V. "On Form and Symmetry in Mental Functioning," *Psychoanalytic Review*, 56:3 (1969).

Singer, Charles, *et al*. *A History of Technology*. Vol. I. New York: Oxford University Press, 1954.

Singer, Jerome. "Looking into the Mind's Eye," *Transactions, New York Academy of Science*, series II, 33:694 (1971).

Singh, Sheo Dan. "Urban Monkeys," *Scientific American*, 221:1 (1969).

Slobodkin, Lawrence B. "How to be a Predator," *American Zoologist*, 8:43 (1968).

Smith, F. A., and Miller, G. A. *The Genesis of Language*. Cambridge: The M. I. T. Press, 1966.

Smith, Phillip E. A. "The Solutrean Culture," *Scientific American*, 211:2 (1964).

Snyder, Richard. "Adaptive Value of Bipedalism," *American Journal of Physical Anthropology*, 26:2 (1967).

Solecki, Ralph S. "Prehistory in Shanidar Valley, Northern Iraq," *Science*, 153:605 (1966).

Soleri, Paolo. *Arcology: the City in the Image of Man*. Cambridge: The M. I. T. Press, 1969.

Spurway, H. "The Causes of Domestication: an Attempt to Integrate Some Ideas of Konrad Lorenz with Evolution Theory," *Journal of Genetics*, 53:325 (1955).

Struhsaker, Thomas T. "Behavior of Vervet Monkeys and Other Cercopithecines," *Science*, 156:1197 (1967).

Tanner, J. M. *Growth at Adolescence*. New York: Oxford University Press, 1962.

Tejera, Victorino. *Art and Human Intelligence*. New York: Appleton-Century-Crofts, 1965.

Theoday, J. M. (ed.). *Genetic and Environmental Influences on Behavior, 4th Eugenics Society Symposium*. New York: Plenum, 1968.

Thomas, Elizabeth Marshall. *Warrior Herdsmen.* New York: Knopf, 1965.

Thomas, William L. (ed.). *Man's Role in Changing the Face of the Earth.* Chicago: University of Chicago Press, 1956.

Thorpe, W. H. *Learning and Instinct in Animals.* Cambridge: Harvard University Press, 1963.

Tiger, Lionel. *Men in Groups.* New York: Random House, 1969.

———, and Robin Fox. *The Imperial Animal.* New York: Holt, 1971.

Tinbergen, N. *The Study of Instinct.* New York: Oxford University Press, 1952.

Tinker, Jon. "One Flower in Ten Faces Extinction," *New Scientist,* May 13, 1971.

Turnbull, Colin. *The Forest People.* New York: Simon and Schuster, 1961.

Tuttle, Russell H. "Knuckle-Walking and the Problem of Human Origins," *Science,* 166:953 (1969).

Ucko, P. J., and Dimbleby, G. W. *The Domestication and Exploitation of Plants and Animals.* Chicago: Aldine, 1969.

van der Post, Laurens. *Heart of the Hunter.* New York: Apollo, 1961.

Van Hooff, J. A. R. "Facial Expression in Higher Primates," *Symposium of the Ecological Society of London,* 8:97 (1962).

Van Gennup, Arnold. *Rites of Passage.* Chicago: University of Chicago Press, 1960.

Vetter, Harold J. *Language, Behavior and Psychopathology.* New York: Rand-McNally, 1969.

Virgo, H. B., and Waterhouse, M. V. "The Emergence of Attention Structure Amongst Rhesus Macaques," *Man,* 4:1 (1969).

Wallace, Anthony F. C. "On Being Just Complicated Enough," *Proceedings of the National Academy of Science,* 47:4 (1961).

Waller, Robert. "Out of the Garden of Eden," *New Scientist,* September 2, 1971.

———. "Modern Husbandry and Soil Deterioration," *New Scientist,* February 5, 1970.

Washburn, S. L. "Behavior and the Origin of Man," *Proceedings of the Royal Anthropological Institute of Great Britain and Ireland,* 1967.

——— (ed.). *Classification and Human Evolution.* Chicago: Aldine, 1963.

——— (ed.). *The Social Life of Early Man.* Chicago: Aldine, 1961.

———. "Tools and Human Evolution," *Scientific American,* 203:3 (1960).

———, and Jay, Phyllis. "More on Tool-Using Among Primates," *Current Anthropology,* 8:3 (1967).

———, and Jay, Phyllis. *Perspectives on Human Evolution, 1.* New York: Holt, 1968.

———, Jay, Phyllis C., and Lancaster, Jane B. "Field Studies of Old World Monkeys and Apes," *Science,* 150:3703 (1965).

Waterbolk, H. T. "Food Production in Prehistoric Europe," *Science,* 162:1093 (1968).

Weiner, J. S. "Pattern and Process in the Evolution of Man," *Proceedings of the Royal Anthropological Institute of Great Britain and Ireland,* 1965.

Werner, Seymour, *et al. The Body Percept.* New York: Random House, 1965.

Weyl, Nathaniel, and Possony, Stefan T. *The Geography of Intellect.* Chicago: Regnery, 1963.

Wheeler, Reuben. *Man, Nature and Art.* New York: Pergamon Press, 1968.

White, Burton L. *Human Infants: Experience and Psychological Development.* Englewood Cliffs, N. J.: Prentice-Hall, 1971.

Wilbur, George B., and Muensterberger, Warner (eds.). *Psychoanalysis and Culture.* New York: International Universities Press, 1951.

Winder, Alvin E. *Adolescence: Contemporary Studies.* New York: American Book, 1968.

Winnicott, D. W. *Playing and Reality.* New York: Basic Books, 1971.

———. "Transitional Objects and Transitional Phenomena," *International Journal of Psychoanalysis,* 34:89 (1953).

Wolberg, Donald L. "The Hypothesized Osterodontokeratic Culture of the Australopithecenes," *Current Anthropology,* 11:1 (1970).

Wolf, Eric. *Peasants.* Englewood Cliffs, N. J.: Prentice-Hall, 1966.

Wright, H. E., Jr. "Environmental Changes and the Origins of Agriculture in the Near East," *BioScience,* 20:4 (1970).

———. "Natural Environment of Early Food Production North of Mesopotamia," *Science,* 161:334 (1968).

Wynne-Edwards, V. C. *Animal Dispersion in Relation to Social Behavior.* London: Hafner, 1962.

Yazmajian, Richard. "Biological Aspects of Infantile Sexuality and the Latent Period," *Psychoanalytic Quarterly,* 36:2 (1967).

Index

Paul Shepard received his A.B. from the University of Missouri in 1949, his M.S. from Yale University in 1952, and his Ph.D., also from Yale, in 1954. He spent 1961 in Wellington, New Zealand, as a Fulbright Research Scholar and received a Guggenheim Fellowship in 1970. Dr. Shepard has taught at at the University of California and at Knox, Smith, and Pitzer colleges and is currently Visiting Professor of Environmental Perception at Dartmouth College. He is the author of *Man in the Landscape,* joint editor of *The Subversive Science,* and a contributor of occasional articles to such magazines and newspapers as *Saturday Review, Natural History,* and *The New York Times.*